WHEN IS SEPARATE UNEQUAL?

This book does not start from the premise that separate is inherently unequal. Writing from an "anti-subordination perspective," Ruth Colker provides a framework for the courts and society to consider what programs or policies are most likely to lead to substantive equality for individuals with disabilities. In some contexts, she argues for more tolerance of disability-specific programs, and, in other contexts, she argues for more disability-integrated programs. Her highly practical investigation includes the topics of K–12 education, higher education, employment, voting, and provision of health care. At the end of the book, she applies this perspective to the racial arena, arguing that school districts should be given latitude to implement *more* use of racial criteria to attain integrated schools because such environments are most likely to help attain substantive equality from an anti-subordination perspective. The book measures the attainment of equality not on the basis of worn-out mantras but instead on the basis of substantive gains.

Ruth Colker is one of the leading scholars in the United States in the areas of constitutional law and disability discrimination. She is the author of eight books, two of which have won prizes. She has also published more than 50 articles in law journals such as the *Harvard Law Review*, *Yale Law Journal*, *Columbia Law Journal*, *Pennsylvania Law Review*, *University of Virginia Law Review*, and *University of Michigan Law Review*. She has been a frequent guest on National Public Radio to comment on disability and constitutional law topics.

Colker is the Heck Faust Memorial Chair in Constitutional Law in the Michael E. Moritz School of Law at The Ohio State University. Before joining the faculty at Ohio State, she taught at Tulane University, the University of Toronto, the University of Pittsburgh, and in the women's studies graduate program at George Washington University. She also spent four years working as a trial attorney in the Civil Rights Division of the United States Department of Justice, where she received two awards for outstanding performance.

Professor Colker was a recipient of Ohio State University's Distinguished Lecturer Award in 2001, the University's Distinguished Diversity Enhancement Award in 2002, and the University Distinguished Scholar Award in 2003. She is a 1978 graduate of Harvard University and a 1981 graduate of Harvard Law School.

Disability, Law and Policy

The **Disability, Law and Policy** series examines these topics in interdisciplinary and comparative terms. The books in the series reflect the diversity of definitions, causes, and consequences of discrimination against persons with disabilities, while illuminating fundamental themes that unite countries in their pursuit of human rights laws and policies to improve the social and economic status of persons with disabilities. The series contains historical, contemporary, and comparative scholarship crucial to identifying individual, organizational, cultural, attitudinal, and legal themes necessary for the advancement of disability law and policy.

The book topics covered in the series also are reflective of the new moral and political commitment by countries throughout the world toward equal opportunity for persons with disabilities in such areas as employment, housing, transportation, rehabilitation, and individual human rights. The series will thus play a significant role in informing policy makers, researchers, and citizens of issues central to disability rights and disability antidiscrimination policies. The series grounds the future of disability law and policy as a vehicle for ensuring that those living with disabilities participate as equal citizens of the world.

WHEN IS SEPARATE UNEQUAL?

A Disability Perspective

Ruth Colker
The Ohio State University

CAMBRIDGE
UNIVERSITY PRESS

CAMBRIDGE UNIVERSITY PRESS
Cambridge, New York, Melbourne, Madrid, Cape Town, Singapore, São Paulo, Delhi

Cambridge University Press
32 Avenue of the Americas, New York, NY 10013-2473, USA

www.cambridge.org
Information on this title: www.cambridge.org/9780521713818

First published 2009

Printed in the United States of America

A catalog record for this publication is available from the British Library.

Library of Congress Cataloging in Publication Data

Colker, Ruth.
When is separate unequal? : a disability perspective / Ruth Colker.
    p. cm.
Includes bibliographical references and index.
ISBN   978-0-521-88618-5 (hardback) – ISBN   978-0-521-71381-8 (pbk.)
1. People with disabilities – Legal status, laws, etc. – United States.
I. Title.
KF480.C658 2009
342.7308′7–dc22   2008028631

ISBN   978-0-521-88618-5 hardback
ISBN   978-0-521-71381-8 paperback

To my mother, Janice Seiner Colker, for her love, compassion, and wisdom

Contents

Preface

It's hard to pinpoint when I began writing this book. When I authored the article entitled "Anti-Subordination Above All: Sex, Race, and Equal Protection" in the *New York University Law Review* in 1986, I was not yet thinking seriously about disability issues on a theoretical level. As I began to do volunteer legal work for individuals with HIV in New Orleans, Louisiana, in 1986, I began to learn a great deal about how society mistreats many individuals with disabilities. And I began to see the challenges faced by the political and judicial systems in fashioning effective remedies when such discrimination has taken place.

I joined the faculty at the University of Pittsburgh School of Law in 1993, and I began to think more systematically about disability issues as I began teaching in this area of the law and writing one of the first casebooks for students to use to study the Americans with Disabilities Act (ADA). For the next decade, my work on disability was mostly of a practical nature. I conducted empirical research on the effectiveness of the ADA, wrote extensively about its legislative history, and analyzed whether the decisions under this statute were consistent with Congress's intent. During those many years of devoting myself to legal issues involving disability, I did not seek to develop a theory to explain my various views on this topic.

When Martha Nussbaum invited me to participate in a legal theory workshop at the University of Chicago in the fall of 2006, I decided that it was time to apply my anti-subordination perspective to disability. I sought to find coherence to my disability work in the areas of employment, education, and voting. This book is an outgrowth of those reflections.

Acknowledgments

This book has been made possible by generous assistance from the Michael E. Moritz College of Law at The Ohio State University, and feedback from many individuals over the years. I received excellent bibliographical and research assistance from former Moritz librarian Sara Sampson, as well as current Moritz librarian Katherine Hall. Many Moritz students have provided research assistance that is reflected in this book, including Pamela Bridgeport, John Billington, Christopher Geidner, Lana Knox, Megan Ledger, Liza Luebke, Chad Eggspuehler, and Catherine Woltering. I was able to hire these students due to a Distinguished Scholar research grant from The Ohio State University.

I would also like to thank Martha Nussbaum for her invitation to speak about disability theory at the University of Chicago Law & Philosophy Workshop in fall 2006; that invitation sparked the development of many ideas underlying this book. Faculty at the Moritz College of Law provided useful and constructive feedback at a summer workshop in July 2006. Faculty at the University of Cincinnati Law School also provided useful feedback at the workshop held in November 2006; I particularly thank Suja Thomas for making that invitation possible. This book has also benefited from a symposium held at Emory Law School and the Thornburgh Family Lecture at the University of Pittsburgh School of Law in fall 2007. Finally, this book has benefited from discussions with James Brudney, Martha Chamallas, Sarah Cole,

Acknowledgments

Daniel Tokaji, Elizabeth Emens, Roanne Flom, Scott Lissner, Amanda Lueck, Deborah Merritt, Heather Sawyer, and Marc Spindelman. Of course, the views expressed are my own.

A special word of thanks is necessary for Chapter 6. That chapter is excerpted from an article that I jointly authored with my colleague Daniel P. Tokaji, which was published in the *McGeorge Law Review* as part of an ABA-sponsored voting rights symposium. I have included this chapter with permission from Professor Dan Tokaji but note that much of this chapter reflects his important work on this topic.

And, of course, this book would not be possible without the support of my family. My children generously shared the household computer so that I could refine many of these arguments. And my son teaches me on a daily basis how individuals with disabilities make choices to enhance their lives. I hope this book can help expand those choices.

1

Introduction

As CATHARINE MACKINNON HAS OBSERVED, "IT IS common to say that something is good in theory but not in practice. I always want to say, then it is not such a good theory, is it?"[1] This book aspires to build a disability theory that works in practice.

On the basis of my review of the empirical literature, my reading of the relevant statutes and case law, and my experience as a parent raising a child with a disability, I believe that we should measure equality from an anti-subordination perspective. We should adopt practices based on our conviction that they will help individuals with disabilities overcome a history of subordination in our society. Empirical analysis can be an important tool in helping us determine what types of practices are most likely to attain substantive equality. Although integration can be an important tool in our attempts to attain substantive equality, we should not assume that integration is presumptively more effective than tools that have some separate or segregating elements.

I offer those opening remarks with the knowledge that some people will immediately misunderstand me. They will accuse me of being against integration. They will accuse me of not sufficiently valuing individuals with disabilities, and the contributions they offer to society.

---

[1] Catharine A. MacKinnon, *From Practice to Theory, Or What Is a White Woman Anyway?*, 4 Yale J. L. & Feminism 13 (1981).

But nothing could be further from the truth. I fully embrace integration when we have reason to believe that it is an effective tool to attaining meaningful, substantive equality. I simply do not presume that integration is the same as equality; I insist on proof in concrete situations that integration serves the goal of equality.

On the basis of my review of the relevant literature, I support more segregated tools in some settings and more integrated tools in other settings. For example, children with autism in the public schools should be placed in the regular classroom (with appropriate support) when we believe that educational environment is most likely to serve their educational needs. But that educational environment should not be considered presumptively better than a more segregated educational environment where they can receive one-on-one behavioral therapy. The appropriate educational environment should be chosen on the basis of likely results supported by the empirical literature rather than presumptions. Similarly, students in higher education with learning disabilities should be provided testing practices that are most likely to demonstrate what they have learned in a course. Segregated or special testing practices should not be preferred to more integrated solutions when more integrated solutions are likely to improve testing practices for both students with disabilities and other students. In both contexts, the issue is which practices are likely to be effective, not which practices are integrated rather than segregated.

I have been writing from an "anti-subordination" perspective since I authored an article in the *New York University Law Review* in 1986 entitled "Anti-Subordination Above All: Sex, Race, and Equal Protection."[2] Under this perspective, I argue that we should adopt social and legal policies that help groups, such as women, gay men, lesbians, and racial minorities, overcome a history of subordination. We should not concern ourselves with individual claims of different treatment by

---

[2] Ruth Colker, *Anti-Subordination Above All: Sex, Race, and Equal Protection*, 61 N.Y.U. L. Rev. 1003 (1986).

dominant groups such as white, heterosexual men because "difference" is not the same as "subordination."

An anti-subordination perspective differs from "formal equality" because it encompasses approval of race- or gender-specific policies that help achieve substantive equality. In the gender context, under this perspective, single-sex schools for women as well as leave policies for the benefit of pregnant women are appropriate, because they can help women overcome historical barriers in education or at the workplace. Formal equality theorists, by contrast, disapprove of gender-specific policies and argue that we should only offer assistance to all parents or people with medical needs rather than single out pregnant women for assistance.[3] Similarly, formal equality theorists would oppose all state-supported single-sex education irrespective of whether the intended beneficiaries are men or women.[4] In the race context, under an anti-subordination perspective, race-conscious affirmative action and Afrocentric schools can be important tools to help overcome a history of racial subordination in our society. Formal equality theorists would oppose both those remedies.[5] An anti-subordination perspective does not accept the premise that "separate is inherently unequal" because it recognizes an important role for gender-specific and race-specific policies in our society as a means of helping create substantive equality.

---

[3] The Family Medical Leave Act reflects a formal equality perspective. Professor Wendy Williams argued that it was important that this statute not single out pregnant women as being entitled to leaves that would not be available to nonpregnant persons. See Wendy Williams, *Equality's Riddle: Pregnancy and the Equal Treatment/Special Treatment Debate*, 13 N.Y.U. Rev. L. & Soc. Change 325 (1984–85).

[4] See, e.g., *United States v. Virginia*, 518 U.S. 515 (1996) (invalidating state-supported single-sex university).

[5] On May 20, 2008, a three-judge panel of the D.C. Circuit ruled that the United States Treasury violated federal law by not making the currency accessible to those with visual impairments. It is too soon to know how, if at all, this decision will be implemented. See *American Council of the Blind v. Paulson*, 525 F.3d 1256 (D.C. Cir. 2008).

I began to think about how to apply an anti-subordination perspective to the field of disability discrimination in the late 1980s as I became immersed in litigation on behalf of individuals with disabilities who faced employment discrimination. My primary entry into the field of disability discrimination was the AIDS crisis as I witnessed society overreacting to the risk of HIV transmission by seeking to criminalize consensual sexual behavior and discharging individuals from employment who were perceived as being HIV-positive. I had the opportunity to work on both a legislative and a litigation level to try to protect individuals from discrimination. This work taught me about some of society's deep-seated fears and hatred of some individuals with disabilities.

In 1990, I read Martha Minow's book *Making All the Difference*[6] and began to think how my "anti-subordination" perspective on race and gender might also apply to disability discrimination. Professor Minow's compelling rendition of the story of Amy Rowley and the Supreme Court's failure to insist that she have a sign language interpreter in her grade school classroom helped me see how principles of formal equality would not be adequate to theorizing about this area of the law. Under the Court's formal equality approach, Amy had little entitlement to extra resources to allow her to participate effectively in the classroom under principles of substantive equality.

In the 1990s, my work in the field of disability discrimination moved beyond my initial work on behalf of individuals who were HIV-positive to include a broad spectrum of disability-related issues in the arenas of employment, housing, transportation, and accessibility. I began to ask: What would it mean to apply an anti-subordination perspective to disability equality theory? How does integration work as the preferred remedy in this area? In Chapter 2, I seek to define an anti-subordination perspective as applied to the disability context. Chapter 3 will seek to

---

[6] Martha Minow, *Making All the Difference: Inclusion, Exclusion, and American Law* (1990).

identify who are individuals with disabilities from an anti-subordination perspective. Chapter 4 will begin a discussion of remedies and the role of integration as a remedy in the educational context.

It has been easy for me to conclude that an anti-subordination perspective makes sense in the disability context because of the history of subordination faced by individuals with disabilities in our society and the inability of a formal equality model to justify important principles such as "reasonable accommodation" that are essential to substantive equality for some individuals with disabilities. I will make that argument more fully in Chapter 2. The harder question has been the role of integration as a remedy in the disability context.

My perspective on integration has been influenced by my personal experience in raising a child with a disability.[7] As I became immersed in disability rights work, I gave birth to my second child, who was diagnosed as having significant impairments when he was about three years old. As do most parents, I want my child to succeed in the mainstream world and worry about whether he will ever be able to live independently and support himself financially. I hope that he will live as an adult under conditions of substantive equality, and I recognize that an integrated environment is likely to be an aspect of the equality that he seeks as an adult. Nonetheless, I do *not* assume that integration is always the correct *tool* for helping him attain substantive equality as a child or as an adult. Segregated, special education tools may be an important vehicle in an effort to provide him and other children with the skills and abilities to live independently as adults. Similarly, adults with mental illness or drug addictions who live on our city streets may experience an "integrated" existence, but it is not one of substantive equality. It is important not to confuse integration with equality. Integration is not a

---

[7] I hesitate to use the word *disability* in describing my son because it is such an ambiguous term. I use it here to connote that he qualifies for special assistance under the Individuals with Disabilities Education Act as a child with an impairment who needs such assistance to succeed in school.

desirable end, in itself, absent substantive equality. Segregation may be an appropriate tool in the path toward substantive equality.

I have brought my integration skepticism developed in the race and gender context to the table as I help make choices for my child's development (and observe choices that he makes for himself). As a preschooler, for example, he was placed in a classroom for part of the day to receive early intervention services. He was already spending about five hours a day in a traditional preschool, child care classroom but was given the opportunity to spend about three hours per day in a special classroom (in the same building) for children who had been diagnosed as disabled. Most of the children who had disabilities had little or no language development and were very awkward both physically and socially. It was an absolutely wonderful room with as many as three teachers for eight students and my son flourished in that setting for several years before starting elementary school. But there were some odd elements to the class that, with hindsight, I suspect were created to be in compliance with federal law's emphasis on integration. The teachers had to bring in "typical role models" for part of each class to comply with federal law, even though my son and many of the other students were spending the rest of their day in a regular preschool classroom with typically developing children. When I observed the classroom, I saw that the typical role models, with their much greater language development, dominated the class and made the teachers' jobs more difficult. Later, I did empirical research that supported the conclusion that the integration model is not appropriate for all children in all settings. I discuss that literature in Chapter 3. As my son has grown older, I have also seen him sometimes seek more segregated settings as a way to avoid the noise and distraction of a regular classroom. Although he does not have the language to discuss segregation versus integration, he intuitively makes some decisions in favor of segregation to further his educational outcomes.

Despite my observations and research, I am wary of criticizing the integration presumption that is so prevalent in disability theory.

I understand that I might be criticized as an "outsider"[8] who is reinforcing the negative elements of segregation as they have been forced upon individuals with disabilities. Moreover, I worry that my perspective would be viewed as too "paternalistic" since it does evolve, in part, from my experience as a parent. I also know that my critique of integration can easily be misunderstood as opposition to integration. In truth, I simply want to make sure that we keep our focus on substantive equality and do not allow unthinking adherence to integration as a strategy to prevent us from obtaining substantive equality for individuals with disabilities. I maintain my aspirations for my son that he will live an independent existence as an adult under conditions of substantive equality while I also skeptically observe whether integrated settings are the best way to help him achieve those goals.

I also realize that a critique of integration should not be based on merely the example of K–12 public education. I have therefore sought to understand how that critique might be useful in other areas of the law. Chapter 6 extends that critique to the voting rights area, asking how we might better serve the interests of voters with disabilities if we do not single-mindedly seek integrated remedies. While recognizing that it is important to make public polling places as accessible as possible for those who desire to vote in integrated environments, I conclude that we need to do more to make it possible for people to vote from the privacy of their homes. While federal law has made enormous strides in making public voting more accessible, the integration focus has deterred us from thinking about those who do not desire to vote in public polling places.

In this book, I only have space to consider a few examples in depth of the results that might be attained under an anti-subordination perspective that is agnostic about the remedy of integration. I invite the

---

[8] By most conventional definitions of disability, I am what is called the "temporarily able bodied." I have strabismus and monocular vision but, aside from my tennis game and a few scratches on my car, those visual impairments have little impact on my life.

reader to consider how this perspective might be applied to other areas. For example, the federal courts have recently become involved in the legal issue of whether the United States Treasury is violating federal disability law by using a currency that is not readily distinguishable to individuals with visual impairments.[9] This lawsuit was brought by the American Council of the Blind (ACB), which emphasizes the importance of this issue to the independent functioning of individuals with visual impairments in our society. The National Federation of the Blind (NFB), however, considers this lawsuit to be a waste of time, arguing that it distracts the public from the real issue, which is that "the blind need jobs and real opportunities to earn money, not feel-good gimmicks that misinform the public about our capabilities."[10] From an anti-subordination perspective, is it important to change the currency so that blind people can lead more independent lives, or is this problem really a nonissue, as claimed by NFB, because blind people learn gimmicks such as folding paper money to distinguish between denominations? What tools are most likely to improve the economic independence of individuals with visual impairments – a goal shared by both ACB and NFB? I do not know the answer to that question but suggest that it can best be answered from an anti-subordination perspective that is agnostic about integrated versus segregated remedies and seeks to make decisions based on sound empirical research.

Chapter 7 concludes this book with reflections on racial integration. My investigation of disability equality from an anti-subordination perspective has heightened my thinking about some of the difficult issues facing society in the racial context, particularly K–12 education. In the final chapter, I closely examine the available empirical data on effective educational environments and argue that formal equality has impeded the courts from recognizing that we need *more*, not less, attention to race-conscious remedies in the public education context. Ironically,

---

[9] *American Council of the Blind v. Paulson*, 463 F. Supp.2d 51 (D. D.C. 2006).
[10] http://www.nfb.org/nfb/NewsBot.asp?MODE=VIEW&ID=102&SnID=111849590.

the law of race discrimination has made it virtually impossible for school districts to create the kind of race-conscious educational plans that are likely to be the most effective in attaining substantive equality.

In sum, formal equality has outlived its usefulness. By focusing, instead, on how to achieve positive outcomes for all our citizens, we may be able to attain more substantive equality. An anti-subordination perspective needs to dictate our future in the race, sexual orientation, gender, and disability contexts with a close and balanced consideration of empirical data. The remedy of integration has a role in that process, but it should not be the only remedy we pursue in our search for substantive equality. Data rather than unsupported presumptions should guide our policies.

2

Anti-Subordination Above All: A Disability Perspective

HE FIELD OF DISABILITY DISCRIMINATION IS undertheorized; it conflates "separate" and "unequal." Theories of justice typically do not consider the example of disability or, if they do, proceed from a pure "integrationist" perspective. Although an integrationist perspective played an important historical and structural role in helping to close some horrendous disability-only institutions, it fails to recognize that the government may need to retain some disability-only services and institutions for those who need or want them while protecting others from coercively being required to accept such services or being placed in such institutions. An absolutist integrationist perspective disserves the disability community by supporting an inappropriately high threshold for the development and retention of disability-only services and institutions. An anti-subordination perspective should replace it.

Well-known equality theorists have incompletely considered the example of disability discrimination. John Rawls's theory of justice, for example, presumes that society consists of "free and equal persons ... who can play the role of fully cooperating members."[1] Douglas Rae mentions individuals with disabilities in passing as part of his "need-based person-regarding" equality, but his discussion of disability is degrading with passages such as "Perhaps, *no* services

---

[1] John Rawls, *Justice as Fairness: A Restatement* 24 (Erwin Kelly ed. 2001).

could make a crippled child as happy as her healthy friends, but her special needs may nonetheless require special services equal to and different from those of her playmates."[2] Martha Nussbaum's work is an important exception to this pattern,[3] but her "capabilities approach" is flawed because her focus on ten functional abilities as a prerequisite to being truly human "excludes some individuals with intellectual disabilities, and only indirectly assists others."[4] Similarly, Martha Minow did some early and important work on difference that recognized the existence of disability,[5] but her work was on such a general level that it failed to grapple with the special nuances presented by disability issues.

There are undoubtedly many reasons for the exclusion of disability from theories of equality. The disability rights movement arguably developed later than the race or gender civil rights movements. Whereas Congress enacted major race-based and gender-based civil rights legislation in the 1960s, it did not begin to enact disability-based civil rights legislation until the 1970s. It was not until 1990 that legislation comparable to the 1964 Civil Rights Act was enacted in the disability context.

Possibly, theorists avoided discussions of disability equality because the theoretical issues raised by this type of equality are different. One can argue that differences based on race or gender should not affect one's position in society, but disability differences are arguably more relevant to one's position in society. Disability equality poses the difficult task of talking about something akin to "reasonable accommodations." Given the challenge posed by defending "affirmative action" in the race and gender contexts, one can imagine a desire to avoid this thorny aspect of

---

[2] Douglas Rae, *Equalities* 99 (1981).
[3] See, e.g., Martha Nussbaum, *Frontiers of Justice* 111 (2006) (criticizing Rawls's exclusion of disability from his theory).
[4] Michael Ashley Stein, *Disability Human Rights*, 95 Calif. L. Rev. 75, 77 (2007).
[5] Martha Minow, *Making All the Difference: Inclusion, Exclusion, and American Law* 81–86 (1990) (discussing education for children with disabilities).

equality theory. Nonetheless, I will try to extend an anti-subordination perspective to include consideration of disability equality issues.

My use of the anti-subordination model is based on Catharine MacKinnon's path-breaking work in feminist theory. MacKinnon argues that we should understand sex discrimination as a problem of dominance and submission rather than as a problem of different treatment.[6] "In this approach, inequality is not a matter of sameness and difference, but of dominance and subordination. Inequality is about power, its definition, and its maldistribution. Inequality at root is grasped as a question of hierarchy, which – as power succeeds in constructing social perception and social reality – derivatively becomes categorical distinctions, differences."[7] Because disability discrimination is about society's treatment of a certain kind of perceived difference, it fits well into this framework.

Admittedly, the application of an anti-subordination perspective to disability theory is not met by widespread acceptance among disability theorists. Gareth Williams offers one of the most nuanced discussions of this approach.[8] He agrees that "the oppressive quality of everyday life for many disabled people is indubitable, and the origins of much of this oppression lies in the hostile environments and disabling barriers that society (politicians, architects, social workers, doctors, and others) erects."[9] But he argues that this model does not work well for three reasons: (1) that most disabilities arise from chronic illness that emerges over time, (2) that nondisability is only a temporary category, and (3) that the body, not just society, plays a role in disability.[10]

---

[6] Catharine A. MacKinnon, *Toward a Feminist Theory of the State* 241 (1989).

[7] Id. at 242. Owen Fiss also discussed the concept of group-based discrimination in his important work on equality. See Owen M. Fiss, *Groups and the Equal Protection Clause*, 5 Phil. & Pub. Aff. 107, 154–55 (1976).

[8] Gareth Williams, Theorizing Disability, in *Handbook of Disability Studies* 123 (Gary L. Albrecht, Katherine D. Seelman & Michael Bury, eds., 2001).

[9] Id. at 135.

[10] Id. at 135.

He then argues that it is "curiously solipsistic" to "say that disability is social oppression and that the body has nothing to do with it."[11] Despite these misgivings, he acknowledges that "the social model or minority group perspective is a powerful story, supporting a theoretical perspective that needs to be argued and justified."[12]

Unfortunately, Williams overlooks the fact that those who have chronic illnesses, such as HIV, have not been protected from society's stereotypical and subordinating views about disability. And the fact that everyone will inevitably become disabled does not seem to have made much impact on our treatment of disability within society. Finally, the approach suggested in this book does not try to take "impairment" out of disability theorizing. The legal definitions of disability, which will be discussed extensively in this book, include an "impairment" requirement in defining who is disabled and deserving of legal protection. Hence, the anti-subordination model is a good fit in the disability context despite the differences between disability and other categories included in this model.

One of the key advantages of an anti-subordination model is that it places the focus of the inequality paradigm on groups that have historically faced mistreatment. Hence, discrimination against African Americans is understood as being worse than discrimination against whites. Discrimination against women is considered worse than discrimination against men. And, for my purposes, discrimination against individuals with disabilities is considered worse than discrimination against those without disabilities.

A lack of power rather than different treatment, in itself, is the root problem of inequality. I call this approach an "anti-subordination" approach to move it beyond the context of sexual dominance and submission which were the focus of MacKinnon's work. Although MacKinnon did not discuss the concept of disability, her work on

---

[11] Id. at 135.
[12] Id. at 136.

dominance theory provides a good model for theorizing about this concept.

Other theorists have supported the concept of anti-subordination through different terminology. Kenneth Karst supports such a perspective through what he calls "equal citizenship."[13] Cass Sunstein builds on MacKinnon's work in developing what he calls the "anticaste principle."[14] Samuel Bagenstos applies an anti-subordination perspective to disability and describes an anti-subordination perspective as recognizing that "socially salient groups (defined by race, sex, disability, or other characteristics) are systematically excluded from important opportunities in society."[15]

The anti-subordination approach[16] has two key, interrelated advantages over the formal equality approach. First, it allows one to discuss inequality in a context like disability where a sameness/difference approach is not likely to yield satisfactory results. Because "dis"ability is, by definition, concerned with ways that people differ from each other, it does not make sense to limit the concept of inequality to situations in which similarly situated people are treated differently. Second, it allows one to talk about "different treatment" such as affirmative action or reasonable accommodations as a remedy to inequality without being accused of having created inappropriate discrimination through remedies. Under an anti-subordination perspective, different treatment is only problematic when grounded in a context of lack of power or subordination. Thus, the "reverse discrimination" problems that have pervaded current legal doctrine, which is grounded in formal

---

[13] Kennth L. Karst, *Foreword: Equal Citizenship under the Fourteenth Amendment*, 91 Harv. L. Rev. 1 (1977).

[14] Cass R. Sunstein, *The Anticaste Principle*, 92 Mich. L. Rev. 2410 (1994).

[15] Samuel Bagenstos, *"Rational Discrimination," Accommodation, and the Politics of (Disability) Civil Rights*, 89 Virginia L. Rev. 825, 840 (2003).

[16] Building on my work, Samuel Bagenstos has also used an anti-subordination approach in discussing disability inequality. See Samuel R. Bagenstos, *Subordination, Stigma, and "Disability,"* 86 Virginia L. Rev. 3997 (2000). Bagenstos, however, does not share my skepticism of integration as a remedy.

equality theory, are largely absent from an anti-subordination approach.

An examination of the development of equality theory within the legal system in Part I of this chapter can help demonstrate how the tension between formal equality and anti-subordination developed. Part II will then argue that disability equality theory must embrace an anti-subordination perspective in order to attain meaningful equality for individuals with disabilities. It will use examples from efforts to attain an adequate education for children with disabilities and the health care deinstitutionalization movement to make this argument.

I. FORMAL EQUALITY VERSUS ANTI-SUBORDINATION

Both a formal equality and an anti-subordination perspective can be useful tools to understanding the problem of inequality. And, in many contexts, both perspectives yield the same result because subordinating practices also often violate principles of formal equality. An examination of some of the history of the development of equality doctrine can show where an anti-subordination perspective and a formal equality perspective yield the same results, and where they differ.

Although one could start a discussion about legal equality at nearly any point in United States legal history, a good starting point is *Plessy v. Ferguson*.[17] In that test case, Homer Plessy challenged the constitutionality of Louisiana's classifying him on the basis of race and insisting that he sit in a "blacks only" railroad car. The Supreme Court upheld the state statute, finding that any "badge of inferiority" was one that private individuals chose to impose on the situation. The state was not considered responsible for the link between formal inequality and societal subordination. In his famous dissent, Justice Harlan disagreed, arguing that "our Constitution is color-blind, and neither knows nor

[17] 163 U.S. 537 (1890).

tolerates classes among citizens."[18] Harlan's dissent tied together the problems of formal inequality and subordination by recognizing that the Louisiana classification helped perpetuate class differences among citizens. Those class differences can be understood in terms of social hierarchy, thereby perpetuating subordination.

By contrast, the majority decision in *Plessy* did not recognize the problems of formal inequality *or* subordination. The Court refused to hold the state responsible for the ways in which formal inequality created conditions of subordination in society. Beginning in the 1940s, the National Association for the Advancement of Colored People (NAACP) Legal Defense Fund (LDF), under the leadership of Thurgood Marshall, tried to educate the Court about the connection between formal inequality and subordination to overturn *Plessy*. LDF knew that it could not overturn the holding in *Plessy* in one stroke. So it used an incremental approach to draw to the Court's attention how state-supported separate institutions contributed to the subordination of African Americans in society.

In these early cases, LDF was not choosing a formal equality approach over an anti-subordination approach, or vice versa, because these cases challenged *both* formal inequality and subordination. They involved state policies that explicitly differentiated on the basis of race *and* subordinated blacks. Many of these cases involved public education. These cases did not raise any issues of affirmative action. They presented the simple question of whether states should be able to offer a segregated and inferior education to African Americans.

One of the first cases to reach the Supreme Court was brought by Ada Lois Sipuel. She had applied to the University of Oklahoma Law School, the only law school in the state. She was rejected because Oklahoma law prohibited education of both races in the same facility.[19] Oklahoma had established a program wherein it financed out-of-state

---

[18] Id. at 559.
[19] *Sipuel v. Board of Regents*, 199 Okla. 36, 40, 45, 180 P.2d 135, 139, 144 (1947).

legal education for blacks rather than desegregate the all-white law school. The Oklahoma Supreme Court held that it was not unconstitutional to defer the installation of a law school for blacks until the need for one was made clear.[20] The United States Supreme Court handed down a unanimous, per curiam opinion obligating Oklahoma to provide the plaintiff with a legal education in conformity with the equal protection clause "as soon as it does for any other group."[21] The Oklahoma court then ordered the defendants to comply with the Supreme Court,[22] and the Oklahoma Board of Regents created a separate law school for blacks. The plaintiff sought a writ of mandamus in the Supreme Court to challenge that remedy, but the Court denied the motion, making a narrow finding that, on remand, the state trial court had complied with the Court's mandate by barring the state from raising as a defense the plaintiff's failure to demand a separate but equal legal education.[23] Hence, the Court allowed the state to resolve the problem of inequality by creating a separate law school for African Americans. This solution, however, created neither formal equality nor substantive equality.

Other states responded to the *Sipuel* litigation by opening institutions of higher education for blacks to avoid desegregating white institutions. LDF challenged that response because of the message of inferiority it sent to society about blacks' intellectual capabilities. It brought the case of *Sweatt v. Painter*[24] to argue more strongly than it had in *Sipuel* that the Supreme Court should rule that state-mandated segregation has no place in education.

The Court's opinion in *Sweatt* acknowledged the link between separate education and subordination. For the first time, the Court recognized the subjective factors that caused the black institution to be

---

[20] Id. at 40–41, 180 P.2d at 139–140.
[21] *Sipuel v. Board of Regents*, 332 U.S. 631, 633 (1948).
[22] *Sipuel*, 199 Okla. at 588, 190 P.2d at 438.
[23] *Fisher v. Hurst*, 333 U.S. 147, 150 (1948).
[24] 339 U.S. 629 (1950).

inferior to the white institution and ordered that a black student be admitted to a school previously restricted to whites.[25] However, the Court refrained from overruling *Plessy v. Ferguson*, leaving plaintiffs to argue in individual cases that particular schools for blacks were unequal to their corresponding white schools.

Faced with the prospect of arguing cases one by one for the next half-century in an attempt to attain better education for African Americans, LDF pushed for a stronger statement from the Court about the harm to African Americans caused by segregation. In formal equality terms, it asked the Court to declare that race-specific policies had no place in public education. Finally, in 1954, the Supreme Court held in *Brown v. Board of Education*[26] that racially separate education cannot be equal education.

A superficial examination of *Brown* suggests that the Court emphasized formal equality over the principle of anti-subordination in its famous statement that "separate . . . [is] inherently unequal."[27] However, closer examination shows that the Court also adopted an anti-subordination analysis in condemning the education offered to African Americans. Under a pure formal equality model, race-segregated schools would have been equally detrimental to whites and blacks. Everyone would suffer from state-sanctioned segregation. The Court, however, considered the harm to be visited on what it called the "colored children" because it gave them a "sense of inferiority."[28] Thus, the decision embraced both anti-subordination and formal equality.

The Court did not have to choose between a formal equality and an anti-subordination perspective until it was asked to consider the issue of whether *whites* could make a claim of race discrimination and whether *men* could make a claim of gender discrimination. In those cases, the dominant group in society was making a claim of

---

[25] *Sweatt*, 339 U.S. at 635.
[26] 347 U.S. 483 (1954)
[27] Id. at 495.
[28] Id. at 494.

discrimination based on formal equality, not anti-subordination principles. By allowing whites and men to bring equal protection cases, the Court began to elevate principles of formal equality over the principle of anti-subordination.[29]

The affirmative action cases gave the Court its most difficult challenge in choosing between formal equality and anti-subordination theory. Under formal equality principles, one would argue that race-conscious standards are problematic even if their purpose is to help African Americans overcome a history of subordination. Under anti-subordination principles, however, such policies would be tolerated so long as they did not have an invidious purpose or effect on a racial minority.

The first major affirmative action case heard by the Court was *Regents of University of California v. Bakke*,[30] in which a white male applicant to the university's medical school claimed that he was a victim of "race" discrimination through operation of the university's race-conscious admissions plan. The university defended its program as a necessary step to promote diversity in the medical profession and argued that such a benign goal should not be judged by the Court's "strict scrutiny" framework that normally applied to racial distinctions. Justice Powell wrote the opinion that served as the judgment of the Court and that is usually considered the pivotal decision in that splintered decision. He stated that "racial and ethnic distinctions of any sort are inherently suspect and thus call for the most exacting judicial examination."[31] Only five members of the Court reached the constitutional issue in that case; four members of the Court concluded that the

---

[29] In *McDonald v. Santa Fe Trail Transportation Co.*, 427 U.S. 273, 278–296 (1976), the Court interpreted the Civil Rights Act to apply to white plaintiffs, and in *Kahn v. Shevin*, 416 U.S. 351 (1974) and *Craig v. Boren*, 429 U.S. 190 (1976), the Court permitted men to make a claim of sex discrimination under the Fourteenth Amendment.

[30] 438 U.S. 265 (1978).

[31] Id. at 291.

university program was unlawful under Title VI of the Civil Rights Act of 1964. Recognizing the split on the Court between anti-subordination and formal equality, Justice Brennan authored an opinion that was joined by three other members of the Court, which argued that the Court should not "let color blindness become myopia which makes the reality that many 'created equal' have been treated within our lifetimes as inferior both by the law and by their fellow citizens."[32] Instead, the Brennan opinion concluded that race-conscious programs that seek to serve benign purposes should be upheld as constitutional so long as they do not "stigmatize any group or single out those least well represented in the political process to bear the brunt of a benign program."[33] The Brennan opinion therefore chose anti-subordination over formal equality.

While the Brennan opinion clearly permitted race-conscious programs that were fashioned to overcome a history of subordination, the Powell opinion was less clear on that point. The state had made four arguments to defend its race-conscious admissions program: "(i) reducing the historic deficit of traditionally disfavored minorities in medical schools and in the medical profession ... (ii) countering the effects of societal discrimination ... (iii) increasing the number of physicians who will practice in communities currently underserved; and (iv) obtaining the educational benefits that flow from an ethnically diverse student body."[34] Powell rejected the first justification, accepted the second justification but only when there is concrete evidence of prior constitutional or statutory violations by the state, accepted the third justification but only where it is clear that the admissions program serves that goal, and accepted the fourth justification. Under Powell's approach, a broad argument that a race-conscious admissions program sought to overcome societal discrimination would not suffice; the state would have to acknowledge its own prior discriminatory conduct in order to meet his standard. Nonetheless, Justice Powell, along

[32] Id. at 327 (Justice Brennan, with White, Marshall, and Blackmun).
[33] Id. at 361.
[34] Id. at 306.

with those who joined the Brennan opinion, concluded that the race-conscious affirmative action plan proposed by Harvard (which used race as a "plus" factor) did meet their various constitutional standards, leaving open the possibility that race-conscious plans were permissible and that the "color blind" model should not be read too strictly to preclude that possibility.

Nearly thirty years later, the Court's equal protection jurisprudence is still ambiguous as to whether it fully embraces the formal equality model or permits some recognition of anti-subordination principles to justify race-conscious policies. In its 2007 opinion in *Parents Involved in Community Schools v. Seattle School District,*[35] the Supreme Court continued to straddle that line. The issue in that case was whether school districts in Seattle, Washington, and Louisville, Kentucky, could select students to various public schools, in part, on the basis of racial criteria to avoid racial isolation of African-American children in certain low-performing schools. Justice Kennedy's vote was the necessary fifth vote for a majority determination that the school districts had violated the Equal Protection Clause. Nonetheless, as the Powell opinion in the *Bakke* decision does, his opinion makes it clear that "race may be one component" of an attempt to attain racial diversity and prevent racial isolation in the public schools. Justice Kennedy does not join Part IV of Chief Justice Roberts's opinion in which the Chief Justice makes a bold formal equality statement with the proclamation "The way to stop discrimination on the basis of race is to stop discriminating on the basis of race."[36] As in 1978, the Court sends an ambiguous signal as to whether it is willing to adopt a pure formal equality approach that would preclude all uses of race-conscious measures by state actors.

Justice Breyer's dissent in *Seattle School District,* which was joined by three members of the Court, argues for an approach to equality that

---

[35] 127 S. Ct. 2738 (2007).
[36] Id. at 2768.

is more grounded in an anti-subordination approach. He reminds us that the segregation outlawed in *Brown* "perpetuated a caste system rooted in the institutions of slavery and 80 years of legalized subordination." The use of race in the two cases before the Court in the *Seattle* litigation "does not approach, in degree or in kind, the terrible harms of slavery, the resulting caste system, and 80 years of legal racial segregation." Not all race-based distinctions are the same. Some are vestiges of subordination while others reflect attempts to remedy societal subordination. Justice Stevens (who ironically had joined the opinion invalidating the university's affirmative action program in *Bakke*) makes a similar point in his concurrence when he notes that only black schoolchildren at the time of the *Brown* decision were told where they could lawfully attend school: "Indeed, the history books do not tell stories of white children struggling to attend black schools." An anti-subordination approach, unlike a formal equality approach, is grounded in a historical understanding of the meaning of race-specific policies.

At the time *Brown* was decided, it was widely celebrated in the civil rights community as a landmark decision that would transform American education. Its formal equality language seemed to be the correct antidote to the history of subordination faced by African Americans. With the rise of the critical race movement and frustrations with implementation of integration, however, that enthusiasm waned within the civil rights community. Derrick Bell argued in 1976 that civil rights attorneys' "single-minded commitment" to maximum integration led them to ignore parents' interests in quality education.[37] Charles Ogletree even insists that many African Americans viewed integration with suspicion at the time of the *Brown* decision and "would have welcomed something less than the full integration demanded by the civil rights lawyers."[38] In retrospect, many African Americans have argued that

---

[37] Derrick A. Bell Jr., *Serving Two Masters: Integration Ideals and Client Interests in School Desegregation Litigation*, 85 Yale L. J. 470, 516 (1976).

[38] Charles J. Ogletree Jr., *All Deliberate Speed: Reflections on the First Half Century of Brown v. Board of Education* 296 (2004).

integration has failed to achieve the ideals envisioned by *Brown* as the gap between black and white educational achievement has not narrowed in recent years.[39]

Thus, the formal equality model has suffered from two problems that have impeded its effectiveness in helping to remedy a history of race-based subordination in our society. First, its formalistic definition of equality makes it difficult to distinguish between the use of race for positive purposes versus its use for detrimental purposes. Second, it makes integration an end in itself without respect to whether such integration attains higher-quality education for African Americans. I will return to the *Seattle* decision in Chapter 7; for now, however, we can see that the conflict between formal equality and anti-subordination has plagued the Court for more than thirty years in the race context. I argue that the Court should embrace an anti-subordination approach in the disability context because of the problematic nature of defending "special treatment" under a formal equality model.

II. DISABILITY EQUALITY THEORY

As the previous section has argued, the Supreme Court has struggled with how to justify race-conscious practices under a formal equality model. Disability rights advocates should learn from this history and not embrace a pure formal equality model in the disability context because of the importance of principles like "reasonable accommodation" in that context. Further, disability rights advocates should even be cautious in embracing the integration-style remedies that have become commonplace in the racial context because those remedies do not always help achieve substantive equality. An examination of

---

[39] See, e.g., Drew S. Days III, *Brown Blues: Rethinking the Integrative Ideal*, 34 Wm. & Mary L. Rev. 53. 54 (1992); Alex M. Johnson Jr., *Bid Whist, Tonk and United States v. Fordice: Why Integrationism Fails African-Americans Again*, 81 Cal. L. Rev. 1401, 1402–3 (1993).

disability equality theory can show how there has been insufficient skepticism of integration as disability equality theory has developed.

An important figure in raising awareness of the subordination of individuals with disabilities and the need for effective remedies was Jacobus tenBroek, who in a 1966 article calling for tort reform argued for individuals with disabilities to have "the right to live in the world."[40] He argued for "integrationism," which he described as "a policy entitling the disabled to full participation in the life of the community and encouraging and enabling them to do so," which should guide the decisions of legislatures and courts.[41]

TenBroek's plea for integrationism made sense at a time when individuals with disabilities were excluded from juries, had few educational opportunities, were disenfranchised, were often housed in inhumane warehouses, and had no "right to live in the world." As in the days before the Court decided *Brown*, separation was synonymous with inequality. Formal equality was an appealing doctrine during such days of absolute exclusion.

Similarly, Stanley Herr, who was the lawyer who argued many of the early cases that sought to secure access to the public school system for children with disabilities, adopted a formal equality, integrationist approach. He insisted that children with intellectual impairments be educated in the regular classroom.[42] Separation was considered inherently unequal. His work is often credited as being a precursor to the standards found in the landmark Education for All Handicapped Children Act of 1975, which required that children with disabilities be taught in the regular classroom wherever possible.

Since 1966, at the urging of disability advocates, the law of disability discrimination has developed under the formal equality, integrationist rubric. Mark Weber has praised Congress's most recent

---

[40] Jacobus tenBroek, *The Right to Live in the World: The Disabled in the Law of Torts*, 54 Cal. L. Rev. 841, 917 (1966).

[41] Id. at 843.

[42] See, e.g., *Mills v. Bd. of Education*, 348 F. Supp. 866, 878 (D. D.C. 1972).

anti-discrimination measure as "a classic integrationist measure."[43] Hence, special education is considered intrinsically degrading and is disfavored as the mechanism for delivering educational services to children with disabilities. Disability-based institutionalization is considered an inhumane way to deliver health care services. Segregated voting practices for individuals with disabilities are considered to be a denial of basic citizenship rights.

Integration is overwhelmingly the preferred remedy in the disability area. Samuel Bagenstos, for example, uses an anti-subordination perspective in theorizing about disability discrimination but also adopts integration as the preferred remedy. He says that "antidiscrimination law responds to these harms of social inequality by promoting the integration of workplaces and other important areas of civil life. Such integration helps to remove the stigmatic injury that results from exclusion."[44] Bagenstos is correct that integration *can* help remove the stigmatic injury that results from exclusion, but the connection between equality and integration is more complicated than he acknowledges.

While integration is frequently the appropriate mechanism to overcome a history of discrimination and subordination against individuals with disabilities, this single-minded focus on integration has ignored or even silenced those who might want to argue for other options. In particular, it has stifled an empirical approach to determining what kind of remedies might be most appropriate. For example, in 1985, when the Office of Special Education Programs at the Department of Education sought to fund studies of the effectiveness of full inclusion for children with disabilities, proponents of full inclusion objected to the funding of the research itself.[45] They argued that integration, in the

---

[43] Mark C. Weber, *Home and Community-Based Services, Olmstead, and Positive Rights: A Preliminary Discussion*, 39 Wake Forest L. Rev. 269, 279 (2004).

[44] Bagenstos, supra note 15, at 843–44.

[45] See Genevieve Manset & Melvyn I. Semmel, *Are Inclusive Programs for Students with Mild Disabilities Effective?: A Comparative Review of Model Programs*, 31 J. Special Educ. 155, 156 (1997) (discussing critics of Will's funding proposal).

disability context as in the race context, is a moral imperative and does not need to be justified by empirical research.

Although disability advocates drew their argument from the racial civil rights experience, many critical race theorists were finding it appropriate to criticize the integration mandate because they were unsatisfied with the quality of education attained by African Americans in integrated schools. One of the leading proponents of criticizing the pure integration approach was Derrick Bell, who employed a fictional dialogue in 1987 in which the characters "speculate about policies that might have more effectively improved the quality of education provided for black children, but were rarely attempted because of the civil rights community's commitment to achieving school desegregation through racial balance."[46] The racial civil rights community has engaged in a vigorous exploration of remedies other than racial balance to improve the quality of education for African-American children while the disability community has uniformly supported integration.

An anti-subordination approach can offer a more nuanced discussion of the appropriate remedies in the disability context to redress a history of profoundly unequal treatment in our society of individuals with disabilities. This approach does not ignore the benefits that can be attained through integration. It simply suggests that we have a more open-minded approach that does not reflexively choose integration when other approaches might be better. We can make decisions based on empirical data rather than unfounded presumptions. A brief example from the topic of public education, which will be discussed more extensively in later chapters, should help the reader see the advantages of an anti-subordination approach. This topic is a good place to start because the disability integration perspective was borrowed from *Brown*, which, itself, was a case about public education.

---

[46] Derrick Bell, *And We Are Not Saved: The Elusive Quest for Racial Justice* 102–22 (1987).

The history of our treatment of children with disabilities within the public education system is horrific. Until the nineteenth century, most individuals with disabilities received no education whatsoever, because they were feared and shunned by society.[47] In response to this exclusion, Thomas Hopkins Gallaudet and Samuel Gridley Howe proposed residential facilities for "deaf and dumb persons," for "the blind," and for "the idiotic and feeble-minded."[48] These schools were residential facilities that did not seek to educate children who used wheelchairs, who were not toilet-trained, or who were considered uneducable. Thus, they served a small subsection of the disability community although they were created out of humanitarian impulses.

Meanwhile, the compulsory education movement resulted in increased class size in regular public school classrooms. Teachers resented the "undesirables," who included both students with disabilities and immigrants, and insisted that these students be dumped into separate classrooms. Intelligence testing began to develop, and some of these children were classified as "morons." Educational segregation was a mechanism to remove undesirables from the regular classroom rather than offer them high-quality education.

For example, Merritt Beattie, who was paralyzed at birth, was educated in the public schools until the fifth grade. He was "normal mentally" and "kept pace with the other pupils." Nonetheless, after a visit to the school by a representative of the state department of public instruction, he was excluded from the regular public schools because "his physical condition and ailment produces a depressing and nauseating effect upon the teachers and school children; that by reason of his physical condition he takes up an undue portion of the teacher's time and attention, distracts the attention of other pupils, and interferes generally with the discipline and progress of the school."[49] Educational

---

[47] Robert L. Osgood, *The History of Inclusion in the United States* 18 (2005).
[48] See Scott B. Sigmon, *Radical Analysis of Special Education* 21 (1987).
[49] *State ex rel. Beattie v. Bd. of Educ.*, 172 N.W. 153 (Wis. 1919).

segregation was therefore justified as a means to benefit "normal" students by removing disruptive elements.

Disability segregation began to decline in the 1930s and 1940s but not for humanitarian reasons. The impulse was financial pressure. Because little learning took place when children with cognitive disabilities were returned to the regular classroom, parents pushed for the resurrection of special classes after World War II and were often pleased with the return to that educational alternative. In addition to separate schooling for children with disabilities, more residential institutions began to emerge during the 1950s. In fact, 75 percent of the residential institutions that served individuals with disabilities that existed in 1970 had been built since 1950. Despite the construction boom, these residential facilities suffered from severe overcrowding, and their educational functions "became clouded by the institutions' multiple roles as school, hospital, penal institution, and warehouse."[50] Investigations during the 1960s revealed that many of these institutions were deplorable and offered little or no education to children.

A debate about the benefits of integration versus segregation began to emerge within the disability community in the 1940s and 1950s. In 1945, the International Council for Exceptional Children held a panel entitled "Segregation versus Non-Segregation of Exceptional Children."[51] Although many people began to support integration as a superior educational option, Arthur S. Hill, education director of United Cerebral Palsy and an associate editor of the journal *Exceptional Children*, criticized the pursuit of integration as the "pursuit of a 'cliché' for its own sake."[52] In the 1970s, the prevailing view, even among those who ardently argued for integration of children with mild mental retardation, was that children with severe disabilities should be educated in nonresidential special education programs.[53] The National

---

[50] See Sigmon, supra note 48, at 55.
[51] Osgood, supra note 47, at 42.
[52] Id. at 53.
[53] Id. at 96–97.

Association for Retarded Citizens supported a continuum approach under which nonresidential separate education would play an important role along with integration.

Despite this debate within the disability community, the integration approach soon became predominant under federal law. Several forces converged to achieve this result. First, advocates for full integration overstated the conclusions drawn in an important article by Lloyd Dunn.[54] Dunn explored what educational options work best for children with mild mental retardation. He concluded that mainstreaming was the best option for these children although he supported special education for children with more severe disabilities.

Dunn's conclusions about integration were drawn, in part, out of concern that poor and minority children were misclassified as mentally retarded in order to remove them from the regular classroom. He said: "We are not arguing that we do away with our special education programs for the moderately and severely retarded, for other types of more handicapped children, or for the multiply handicapped. The emphasis is on doing something better for slow learning children who live in slum conditions, although much of what is said should also have relevance for those children who are labeling [*sic*] emotionally disturbed, perceptually impaired, brain injured, and learning disordered." Furthermore, the emphasis of the article is on children, in that no attempt is made to suggest an adequate high school environment for adolescents still functioning as slow learners.[55] Nonetheless, Dunn's work was soon cited as evidence that children with severe impairments be educated in a fully integrated environment.[56]

Second, the race civil rights movement provided the basis for supporting a strong integration paradigm. A report by the United States

---

[54] Lloyd Dunn, *Special Education for the Mildly Mentally Retarded: Is Much of It Justifiable?*, 35 Exceptional Child 5 (1968).

[55] Id. at 6.

[56] See Garry Hornby et al., *Controversial Issues in Special Education* 68–70 (1997).

Department of Health, Education and Welfare identified the *Brown* decision as serving as a model for federal disability policy.[57]

Finally, some people jumped on the integration bandwagon for financial reasons. "The total per capita annual expenditure is considerably less for a nonclassified student, and in this sense, mainstreaming saves money. So in this political era of fiscal austerity, the concept of mainstreaming is welcomed by many."[58] This fact caused one commentator to note: "It is indeed paradoxical that mentally handicapped children having teachers especially trained, having more money (per capita) spent on their education, and being enrolled in classes with fewer children and a program designed to provide for their unique needs, should be accomplishing the objectives of their education at the same or at a lower level than similar mentally handicapped children who have not had these advantages and have been forced to remain in the regular grades."[59] Of course, the regular classroom could be the best site for their education, but it is important to recognize that fiscal concerns could also cloud that judgment.

When the integration approach first appeared in a federal judicial decision, it supported the argument that children with mental retardation should not be excluded entirely from the public schools.[60] The opinion, however, never made findings in support of an integrationist approach. Oddly, the court itself seemed unaware of the scope of its decision when it approved the consent decree. A class action was

---

[57] See State Program Implementation Studies Branch of the Bureau of Education for the Handicapped, U.S. Department of Health, Education & Welfare, Publication No. (OE) 79-05003, *Progress toward a Free Appropriate Public Education: A Report to Congress on the Implementation of Public Law 94-142: The Education for All Handicapped Children Act* 31 (1979).

[58] Sigmon, supra note 48, at 32.

[59] Orville Johnson, *Special Education for the Mentally Handicapped – a Paradox*, 29 Exceptional Children 62, 65–66 (1962).

[60] See *Pennsylvania Association for Retarded Children (PARC) v. Pennsylvania*, 343 F. Supp. 279, 302 (E.D. Pa. 1972); *Mills v. Board of Education*, 348 F. Supp. 866, 878 (D.D.C. 1972).

brought against the Commonwealth of Pennsylvania, arguing that its system of denying a public education to children with mental retardation violated the Due Process and Equal Protection Clauses of the Fourteenth Amendment.[61] In entering a consent decree on behalf of the plaintiffs, the court noted:

> Plaintiffs do not challenge the separation of special classes for retarded children from regular classes or the proper assignment of retarded children to special classes. Rather plaintiffs question whether the state, having undertaken to provide public education to some children (perhaps all children), may deny it to plaintiffs entirely. We are satisfied that the evidence raises serious doubts (and hence a colorable claim) as to the existence of a rational basis for such exclusions.[62]

Despite this statement from the court, the language of the consent decree did challenge the appropriateness of a placement in a special class or special school. The consent decree, entered by the court, stated:

> It is the Commonwealth's obligation to place each mentally retarded child in a free, public program of education and training appropriate to the child's capacity, within the context of the general educational policy that, among the alternative programs of education and training required by statute to be available, placement in a regular public school class is preferable to placement in a special public school class and placement in a special public school class is preferable to placement in any other type of program of education and training.[63]

Although this litigation was limited to the issue of the education of children with mental retardation, federal statutes soon went even further in favoring mainstreaming for all children with disabilities, not

---

[61] *PARC*, 343 F. Supp. at 283.
[62] Id. at 297.
[63] Id. at 307.

simply those with mental retardation. Citing the Pennsylvania litigation in its reports, Congress enacted the Education for All Handicapped Children Act of 1975 (EHCA), in which it required that children with disabilities be educated with children who are not disabled to the maximal extent possible.[64]

The progression from Dunn's work on children with mild mental retardation to the broad consent decree from the Pennsylvania Association for Retarded Children (PARC) litigation to the EHCA is fascinating. An integration remedy was chosen not on the basis of empirical research about the educational needs of children with disabilities but on the basis of a perceived moral imperative borrowed from the racial civil rights community. In fact, as Chapter 4 will indicate, the empirical literature on the education of children with disabilities is quite complex and better supports the continuum approach reflected in Dunn's scholarship, in which a range of options would be tailored to the specific educational needs of individual children. While the work of Dunn and others should certainly be used to argue for the mainstreaming of children with mild mental retardation, it does not support an integration approach for all children with disabilities.

To be clear, I am *not* suggesting that integration is never appropriate. In fact, integration *is* often appropriate because it is likely to result in a qualitative improvement in the lives of individuals with disabilities and is also likely to yield better results than more segregated options. Our nation has a sordid history, which will be discussed in subsequent chapters, of segregating individuals with disabilities and providing them with inferior and degrading treatment. Unfortunately, however, many of our integrated options have also been inferior and degrading. The question should be how to improve the quality of life for individuals with disabilities, and remedies should be chosen that are likely to achieve that end. By presumptively insisting that those remedies are

[64] Education for All Handicapped Children Act of 1975, Pub. L. No. 94-142, § 612(d)(A)(i), 89 Stat. 773, 780. See also H.R. Rep. No. 94-332, at 5 (mentioning this requirement).

integrated remedies, we may be disserving some individuals with disabilities.

I will discuss the educational context in greater detail in Chapter 4 and show how certain categories of children, such as children with autism or learning disabilities, are likely to attain better educational results in less integrated environments and that the law of special education, with its integration presumption, has often impeded their parents' efforts to attain a good education for them. Nonetheless, I am not suggesting we abandon integration remedies for those for whom those remedies make sense. I am simply suggesting that an anti-subordination perspective might open our eyes to other remedies as well. In the next section, I will briefly discuss the deinstitutionalization movement to show how a more nuanced perspective on integration might help attain better policy outcomes there as well.

III. THE DEINSTITUTIONALIZATION MOVEMENT

The deinstitutionalization movement has arguably been one of the most important civil rights campaigns for individuals with disabilities. This movement reflects recognition of the connection between segregation and subordination. While the creation of institutions for individuals who are mentally ill may have had some benign roots, those roots were quickly transformed into horrific practices. Nonetheless, as this section will argue, one needs to be cautious in structuring desegregation programs. Desegregation does not magically solve a historical problem of subordination. The advantage of an anti-subordination approach over a formal equality approach is that it keeps the appropriate focus on ending subordination rather than naively confusing integration with substantive equality.

In the late nineteenth century, some disability rights advocates succeeded in persuading states to allocate funds for the construction of public psychiatric hospitals for individuals with mental illness; that option was considered better than the streets, almshouses, or jails.[65] Although the impulse behind these institutions may have been benign, the institutions soon better represented incarceration than treatment. "By the late nineteenth century, the educational optimism of the founding era succumbed to racial and ethnic mythology, spearheaded by a nativistic fear of the 'menace of the feebleminded' and a professional turn to eugenic control."[66] Segregation constituted subordination.

When some of these institutions were subject to legal attack in the 1970s, they seemingly shocked the judges who heard these cases. For example, in *Wyatt v. Stickney*,[67] the district court describes the inhumane conditions in an Alabama state mental institution six months after defendants were required to institute improvements. The plaintiffs were housed in unsanitary, dangerous living conditions where fifty cents per day was spent on their food, and virtually no medical treatment was offered to the patients.[68] On appeal, Judge Wisdom recounted the conditions in graphic terms. "The patients suffered brutality, both at the hands of the aides and at the hands of their fellow patients; testimony established that four Partlow residents died due to understaffing, lack of supervision, and brutality."[69] "One of the four died after a garden hose had been inserted in his rectum for five minutes by a working patient who was cleaning him; one died when a fellow patient hosed him with scalding water; another died when soapy water was forced into his mouth; and a fourth died from a self-administered overdose of drugs which had been inadequately secured."[70]

---

[65] See E. Fuller Torrey, *Out of the Shadows: Confronting America's Mental Illness Crisis* 81 (1997).

[66] John G. Richardson, *Common, Delinquent and Special* 33 (1995).

[67] 334 F. Supp. 1341 (M.D. Ala. 1971), aff'd, 503 F.2d 1305 (5th Cir. 1974).

[68] Id. at 1343.

[69] *Wyatt v. Aderholt*, 503 F.2d 1305, 1311 (5th Cir. 1974).

[70] Id. at 1311 n.6.

In addition to the conditions of confinement being horrific, many people were institutionalized who did not even arguably suffer from mental illness. For example, an Illinois statute "allowed married women and infants to be committed on the request of a husband or guardian."[71] As a result of these loose commitment standards, 679,000 persons were confined in mental institutions in 1963 and 250,000 persons were involuntarily incarcerated.[72]

Conscientious objectors who had been assigned to work in public hospitals in the 1940s called the deplorable conditions of these institutions to the public's attention.[73] A grand jury was convened in Cleveland in 1944 to investigate the conditions at Cleveland State Hospital and reported that it was "shocked beyond words that a so-called civilized society would allow fellow human beings to be mistreated as they are at the Cleveland State Hospital."[74] This kind of evidence started the deinstitutionalization movement. Consequently, the number of patients at Cleveland State Hospital declined from 2,200 in 1944 to 140 in 1994.[75] The deinstitutionalization movement benefited many individuals who had been living in state mental institutions. A study of individuals discharged from a Rhode Island state hospital into well-structured community settings found that "94 percent expressed a preference for life in the community" even though 55 percent of people in the study required rehospitalization at least once.[76] Hence, the

---

[71] See *Lessard v. Schmidt*, 349 F. Supp. 1078, 1086 (E.D. Wis. 1972) (describing situation in Illinois). The court's order in *Lessard* was reversed on appeal. See *Schmidt v. Lessard*, 414 U.S. 473 (1974) (overturning rule ordered by lower court as insufficient to meet the requirements of a rule and presenting an inadequate foundation for review).

[72] Id. at 1090.

[73] See Torrey, supra note 65. The 1946 publication of *The Snake Pit* and its 1948 movie version (starring Olivia de Havilland) stunned many people into learning about the inhumaneness and coerciveness of lunatic asylums. See Mary Jane Ward, *The Snake Pit* (1946).

[74] Torrey, supra note 65, at 83.

[75] Id. at 85.

[76] Id. at 85.

favored solution to the problem of institutionalization was to seek to return people to integrated, community settings.

Deinstitutionalization, however, occurs against a backdrop in which society is not always willing to devote enough resources to make such efforts successful. A 1994 report by a Cleveland newspaper found that many mentally ill people were living within the prison system rather than in state mental hospitals – there had been an "explosion in the number of mentally ill inmates" because of "repetitive incarceration of nonviolent offenders on scant mental health services in the home counties."[77] Rather than ending institutionalization, the deinstitutionalization movement caused many people to be housed in jails rather than state mental institutions. As E. Fuller Torrey has argued, "Deinstitutionalization has been a psychiatric *Titanic*" for a "substantial minority." "The 'least restrictive setting' frequently turns out to be a cardboard box, a jail cell, or a terror-filled existence plagued by both real and imaginary enemies."[78] Torrey argues that there were 2.2 million Americans with untreated severe mental illnesses in 1995, 150,000 of them "homeless, living on the streets or in public shelters" and 159,000 incarcerated for crimes committed because of their mental illness. Similarly, Steven Raphael concludes that deinstitutionalization of state and county mental hospitals resulted in an increase of 48,000 to 148,000 of inmates in state prisons in 1996.[79]

While the history of institutionalization is horrific, the solution of deinstitutionalization has often created its own set of problems. A Delaware study that followed the results of individuals moved from an institution for the developmentally disabled into the community noted that the movement of people with developmental disabilities from institution to community has been generally more successful than the movement from institution to community for people with mental

---

[77] Id. at 85.

[78] E. Fuller Torrey, supra note 65, at 1.

[79] See Steven Raphael, *The Deinstitutionalization of the Mentally Ill and Growth in the U.S. Prison Population: 1971 to 1996* (manuscript 2000).

illness.[80] The challenge, as described in a 1989 report by the National Institute of Mental Health, is to find the "appropriate balance between liberty and paternalism that will maximize individual and societal rights to physical safety and well-being."[81]

One deinstitutionalization complication is that the population that was released from state institutions after living there for a long period is not the same as the population that has never lived in an institutional setting. Richard Lamb notes that "persons who have been hospitalized for long periods have been institutionalized to passivity." When they are placed in community settings they "tend to stay where they are placed and to accept treatment." But what he calls the "new generation of severely mentally ill persons" do not have this culture of passivity and find it difficult to fare well in community settings.[82] Lamb does not argue for returning the mentally ill to "the back wards of state hospitals," but he also argues that we need to be realistic, in some cases, and promote a "restricted lifestyle" for some people who are severely mentally ill that will help them enjoy the liberty of staying in the community.[83] He also supports the relaxation of involuntary commitment laws so that states can order outpatient civil commitment rather than commitment to a state mental hospital.[84] Finally, he supports the appointment of a conservator for individuals who cannot care for themselves without supervision. The conservator "has the authority to place the conservatee in any setting . . . and to require that he or she participate in psychiatric treatment and take medications in order to remedy or prevent the recurrence of severe disability."[85]

---

[80] James W. Conroy & James Garrow, *Initial Outcomes of Community Placement for the People Who Moved from Stockley Center*, available at www.outcomeanalysis.com.

[81] Id. at 87.

[82] H. Richard Lamb, *Deinstitutionalization at the Beginning of the New Millennium*, in *Deinstitutionalization* 4–5 (H. Richard Lamb & Linda E. Weinberger, eds., 2001).

[83] Id. at 7.

[84] Id. at 9.

[85] Id. at 9.

This book cannot resolve the issue of how states should proceed in seeking to deinstitutionalize as many individuals with disabilities as possible; that issue raises complicated resource and other questions that are beyond its scope. This book simply seeks to suggest that formal equality mantras like "The Constitution is color blind" or "Separate is inherently unequal" are too simplistic to serve as the foundation for effective social policy. Institutionalization was evil as practiced in the nineteenth and twentieth centuries, and those practices unquestionably need to be abandoned. But if we focus on the vision of substantive equality, we will also be aware that integrated solutions are likely to have their own set of problems if not accompanied by a commitment to attain substantive equality. This book suggests that anti-subordination rather than integration should be the measure of equality. Properly constructed integration *can* be an invaluable tool to the attainment of equality. But, in some instances, more segregated options can also be a tool to the attainment of equality. This book will proceed from an agnostic perspective in considering the tool of integration rather than presume that integration is always the most appropriate remedy. Anti-subordination rather than formal equality should be the measure of equality. And empirical data, whenever possible, should guide those measurements, rather than unfounded presumptions.

3

The Mythic 43 Million Americans with Disabilities at the Workplace

O NE OF THE PRIMARY CHALLENGES OF AN anti-subordination perspective is defining who is in the covered class. How would we define the group in society that has faced a history of subordination and deserves legally mandated remedies? The answer to that question will depend, in part, on the area of the law in which we seek to legislate. The purpose of legislation should be to remedy the conditions of subordination within a particular context.

This chapter will focus on one group that has been the target of Congress's assistance – those who are disabled and need protection from discrimination at the workplace. In 1990, Congress sought to provide legal remedies for those individuals under Title I of the Americans with Disabilities Act (ADA). It defined disability as constituting "a physical or mental impairment that substantially limits one or more major life activity."[1] Further, Congress stated that it would protect those who are disabled under that definition, have a record of disability (but are no longer disabled), or are falsely regarded as having a disability. Finally, Congress stated that it intended to cover "some

---

As this book was going to press, Congress was considering amending the definition of disability in the Americans with Disabilities Act (ADA). This chapter discusses the definition of disability as found in the original ADA, enacted in 1990.

[1] 42 U.S.C. § 12102(2).

43,000,000 Americans" and recognized that "this number is increasing as the population as a whole is growing older."[2]

Although one could criticize Congress's definition of disability under the ADA, and its intention to provide protection against workplace discrimination to only 43 million Americans, this chapter will assume that Congress made a reasonable policy judgment to protect a subset of workers with disabilities. The decision to protect 43 million Americans from disability discrimination is an important first step to remedying a history of discrimination at the workplace. As we shall see, that approach would cover the individuals who Census data indicate are moderately disabled but able to work with some accommodations. Moreover, it covers those who are not disabled at all but who stereotypically are treated as if they are disabled, and thereby precluded from working. If we are to make substantial improvement in the employment opportunities for individuals with disabilities, Congress's approach would appear to be a sound one. Nonetheless, as we will see later, the Supreme Court has interpreted Congress's anti-subordination approach as only covering an extremely small segment of the population – those who are usually too disabled to attain employment. By narrowing coverage to that small group, the Court undermined the effectiveness of ADA Title I to help individuals attain economic self-sufficiency through meaningful employment, thereby assisting far fewer than the 43 million Americans whom Congress said it intended to assist.

As with many of the other chapters of this book, this chapter will use an empirical approach in thinking about these issues. Congress used an empirical approach in stating that it intended to cover at least 43 million Americans. This chapter will consider the available empirical evidence to see whether the courts' decisions have resulted in the protection of those individuals with disabilities who would benefit from protection. The answer is a resounding no.

[2] 42 U.S.C. § 12101(1).

I. THE ANTI-SUBORDINATION APPROACH IN STATUTORY FORM

The Americans with Disabilities Act adopts an anti-subordination approach by defining a class that needs legal protection. The ADA prohibits discrimination only against those who are classified as "individuals with disabilities." Congress stated that "individuals with disabilities are a discrete and insular minority who have been faced with restrictions and limitations, subjected to a history of purposeful unequal treatment, and relegated to a position of political powerlessness in our society."[3] Hence, Congress made it clear that it only wanted to protect those who have historically faced a history of subordination.

Congress also explicitly envisioned that "reasonable accommodations" would be available to individuals with disabilities and that such preferential treatment would be consistent with its anti-subordination statutory model. Reverse discrimination cases are not permissible under the ADA because individuals who are *not* disabled may not bring lawsuits to challenge the preferential treatment of individuals with disabilities. Only individuals with disabilities can bring lawsuits in which they allege that they have faced "discrimination," which is defined to include a failure to provide reasonable accommodations. In other words, employers who do *not* provide reasonable accommodations to individuals who are qualified to perform a particular job may find themselves liable for damages under the ADA. Some forms of preferential treatment are *required* under the ADA, whereas preferential treatment is *rarely permitted* under Title VII's formal equality model.

Unfortunately, the courts have resisted implementing the ADA as intended by Congress. They narrowed Congress's anti-subordination protection to cover such a narrow class that they rendered much of Congress's work ineffective. Although Congress identified the goal of "economic self-sufficiency" through employment as a key goal

---

[3] 42 U.S.C. § 12101(a)(7).

of the ADA, the statute has not been able to live up to that promise, in part, because of the way the courts have undermined Congress's basic intentions. The next section will trace how the courts weakened the ADA to the point of rendering it ineffective in the employment area.

II. THE AMERICANS WITH DISABILITIES ACT: SCOPE OF COVERAGE

Unlike Title VII of the Civil Rights Act of 1964, which potentially covers all employees, the ADA only covers individuals who meet the definition of "disability." Congress specified in its first finding that "some 43,000,000 Americans have one or more physical or mental disabilities, and this number is increasing as the population as a whole is growing older."[4] It then defined disability to include

(a) a physical or mental impairment that substantially limits one or more of the major life activities of an individual;
(b) a record of such an impairment; or
(c) being regarded as having such an impairment.[5]

Congress chose not to cover everyone who had any sort of impairment at all; instead, it only covered those who had a moderate impairment that might interfere with their daily activities either because of their actual limitations or because of limitations that are inaccurately perceived by others. The definition also covers those who have a "record of" disability but who are no longer disabled. This chapter will focus on Congress's intent to cover both those who actually have an impairment as well as those who are falsely regarded as having an impairment because court decisions have undermined Congress's desire to cover these categories of people. While it is true that the courts have also undermined the "record of" prong, this result has been more modest and will not be discussed.

---

[4]   42 U.S.C. § 12101(a)(1).
[5]   42 U.S.C. § 12102(2).

A. "Actually Disabled" Prong

Because the United States population was around 250 million when the ADA was enacted in 1990, Congress envisioned that it was covering about one-sixth of the population when it stated its intent to cover 43 million Americans. Congress was not limiting coverage to those who might be considered "severely disabled" because, as we will see, that number is probably around 13.5 million Americans. By also covering those who are moderately disabled, Congress hoped to help reach the goal of economic self-sufficiency by assisting individuals to secure and retain employment.

Despite Congress's clear intentions, the courts have interpreted the ADA to mean that Congress intended to cover *no more* than 43 million Americans. In fact, as a result of the approach chosen by the courts, only about 13.5 million Americans qualify for statutory coverage, and those individuals are typically so disabled that they are not qualified to work, even with reasonable accommodation. This narrow interpretation, which contradicts the plain statutory language, essentially erases the statute's employment discrimination provisions and makes it ineffective as a tool to remedying the problem of subordination.

1. The Social Security Laws

When Congress stated in its first finding that it sought to protect at least 43 million Americans from disability discrimination, it intended to cover those with moderate disabilities as well as those with severe disabilities. It sought to protect more than those already protected under the Social Security laws or labeled as "severely disabled" by the Census Bureau and who were unable to obtain employment. Otherwise, it would have signaled a more narrow statutory scope by stating that it intended to cover no more than 13.5 million Americans.

Because I will argue that the courts have misinterpreted the ADA to parallel the more narrow definition of disability used under the Social

Security laws, it is necessary to understand the scope of protection offered under these laws. Because the purpose of the Social Security laws, with respect to its coverage of those who are "disabled," is to provide a social safety net for those unable to work as a result of disability, Congress used a more narrow scope of coverage under the Social Security laws than under the ADA. In enacting the ADA, by contrast, Congress sought to provide protection to those who are disabled but qualified to work. The Social Security definition does not fit that purpose.

In 1935, Congress made the historic decision to create a federally funded pension system through the Social Security program for workers who became age sixty-five. At that time, individuals could only receive Social Security benefits if they had previously been in the workplace until age sixty-five. From the outset, some people suggested that benefits should also be extended to people who retired early on an involuntary basis because of disability. In 1954, Congress introduced the concept of disability into the Social Security structure by making benefits available to workers who had paid into the Social Security system but retired between the ages of fifty and sixty-five as a result of disability. The term *disability* was also expanded to include mental as well as physical impairments. In 1960, the minimum age requirement was eliminated, and the disability no longer had to be of "long-continued and indefinite duration." Instead, in 1965, it merely had to be a condition that was "expected to last for a continuous period of not less than 12 months." Finally, in 1972, the program was expanded to include those were disabled and had not contributed to the Social Security system through what is termed Social Security Disability Insurance (SSDI).

The disability rosters greatly expanded after Congress eliminated the minimum age requirement as well as the requirement that the individual have been previously employed so that, by 1975, the disability program became larger than the Social Security program for individuals over the age of sixty-five. This growth continued despite a narrowing of the definition of disability in 1968 to require that a claimant "is not only unable to do his previous work but cannot, considering his age, education, and work experience, engage in any other kind of substantial gainful work which exists in the national economy, regardless of whether such work exists in the immediate area in which he lives, or whether a specific job vacancy exists for him or whether he would be hired if he applied for work."[6]

The 1968 amendment reflected Congress's interest in reducing the disability rosters by encouraging individuals with disabilities to obtain work. Congress attempted further tinkering with the Social Security disability laws through "ticket to work" and other measures, but the Social Security disability rosters stayed very large.[7] By 1990, when Congress passed the ADA, approximately 5 million Americans were receiving benefits under SSDI.[8] By 2004, nearly 9 million Americans received SSDI benefits.[9]

The ADA was passed, in part, in an attempt to help remove some individuals from the Social Security rosters. Hence, Senator Riegle stated: "I am currently developing legislation which would protect certain benefits for beneficiaries of the Social Security Disability Insurance Program to facilitate their ability to enter the work force," and Senator Harkin noted, "I believe that the ADA will substantially reduce the costs of dependency of individuals with disabilities."[10] Unfortunately, those hopes were unrealistic. Nonetheless, Congress would

---

[6] P.L. 90-248 (1968) (section 158 amending section 223(c) of the Social Security Act).

[7] See generally Paul Armstrong, *Toward a Unified and Reciprocal Disability System*, 25 J. Nat'l A. Admin. L. Judges 157 (2005).

[8] See Social Security Administration, *Annual Statistical Report on the Social Security Disability Insurance Program, 2004* (released: March 2006) (Table 1 reporting that 4.9 million Americans received disability benefits in 1990, of whom 3 million qualified for those benefits as "workers").

[9] Id. at Table 1 (reporting that 8.8 million Americans received disability benefits in 2004, of whom 6.2 million qualified for those benefits as "workers").

[10] See 133 Cong. Rec. S. 11,182 (May 16, 1988) (Senator Riegle); 134 Cong. Rec. S4984 (May 9, 1989) (Senator Harkin).

have understood in 1990 that the 5 million Americans who received disability-related Social Security benefits were a small minority of the 43 million it expected to cover under the ADA. By picking the figure of 43 million to signal its scope of protection, Congress was signaling that it intended to cover a much larger group than had been covered under the Social Security laws.

2. Census Bureau Figures

The available evidence strongly suggests that Congress relied on estimates from the Census Bureau, not the Social Security Administration, for its conclusion that the ADA's definition of disability would protect 43 million Americans. Deriving the 43 million figure, however, requires one first to derive a 36 million figure because Congress began its discussion of the ADA in 1988 with a bill that defined the number of Americans with disabilities as 36 million.[11]

In 1986, the United States Department of Commerce, Bureau of the Census, published a report entitled "Disability, Functional Limitation, and Health Insurance Coverage: 1984/85."[12] This report was based on a survey of houses during the May–August 1984 period, in which they were asked a set of questions on disability status. These questions focused on physical impairments that might impose functional limitations on individuals who are over the age of fifteen.

The 36 million figure from the 1988 version of the ADA is consistent with the Census Bureau report. The drafters of the ADA were clearly aware of the report because the 1988 version of the ADA was based on a report from the National Council on Disability, and that report repeatedly referred to the Census Bureau data. The bureau found that 37.3 million persons 13.5 years of age or older had a

---

[11] See Congressional Record – Senate 9379 (April 28, 1988).

[12] U.S. Bureau of the Census, Current Population Reports, Series P-70, No. 8, *Disability Functional Limitation, and Health Insurance Coverage: 1984/85*, U.S. Government Printing Office, Washington, D.C. 1986.

functional limitation in one or more of the nine areas that they measured: seeing, hearing, speech, lifting or carrying, walking, using stairs,
getting around outside, getting around inside, and getting into and out
of bed. Of those 37 million Americans, only 8 million of those between
the ages of sixteen and sixty-four years said they had a disability that
prevented them from working. Thirteen million of the 37 million
Americans with disabilities were over the age of sixty-five and not likely
to be working irrespective of their disability status. These figures suggest that Congress would have been aware that about 24 million of the
individuals covered by the ADA could be expected to be covered by
ADA Title I (employment title) if they faced discrimination in the
workplace because they appeared to be both moderately disabled
and qualified to work.

The estimate that at least 24 million Americans covered by the ADA
would be qualified to work is also consistent with the modest nature of
the functional limitation definition used by the Census Bureau in its
survey. The Census Bureau had a "limitation" category and a "severe
limitation" category. Although 37.3 million Americans were found to
have a limitation, 13.5 million were found to have a "severe limitation."
That 13.5 million figure was consistent with those who reported that
they were too disabled to work – 8.0 million between the ages of sixteen
and sixty-four combined with 4 million between the ages of sixty-five
and seventy-two – and reported that they had a disability that "prevented them from working." By contrast, nearly 24 million Americans
reported they had a disability that did *not* preclude their working. In
fact, of the 18.2 million between sixteen and sixty-four who reported
that they had a disability that did not prevent them from working, 11.6
million reported that they were in the labor force.

What do those statistics reveal? They suggest that Congress would
have had to use a "moderate disability" definition in 1990 rather
than a "severe disability" definition if it sought to protect more than
36 million Americans from disability discrimination. When Congress
revised the ADA, during the legislative process, to cover 43 rather than

36 million Americans, it could not have intended to protect only those covered by the Social Security Administration (about 5 million) or only those covered by the Census Bureau's definition of "severe disability" (13.5 million).

The legislative record does not reveal why the estimate of the number of individuals with disabilities was raised from 36 million in 1988 to 43 million in 1990 when the ADA was enacted. Raising the figure may have been a way for Congress to signal that it understood that the number of individuals with disabilities was expected to grow as the population became older. The fact that the figure was raised suggests that there was some concern that a 36 million figure could be construed to cover an insufficient number of individuals with disabilities. The Census report actually mentioned a 37.3 million figure rather than a 36 million figure, so there was good reason for the disability community to be concerned that a 36 million figure was too conservative an estimate of who was entitled to coverage. The decision to raise the figure from 36 to 43 million must, at a minimum, demonstrate an attempt to cover *at least* as many people as are included in the Census Bureau definition of moderate disability.

Moreover, one should remember that Congress intended the 43 million to be a *floor* rather than a *ceiling*. Congress stated, in its first finding, that the number of Americans with disabilities is growing as the population ages. The 1997 Census Bureau report, which relied on similar categories of functional limitations, concluded that 52.6 million individuals had a disability.[13] Unlike the 1984/85 data, this report included 4.6 million Americans who were below the age of fifteen. Nonetheless, it reflects an increase in the disabled population from 37 million to 48 million in a little more than a decade. As the 1984/85 report does, it also reflects that more than 20 million Americans have moderate disabilities that frequently do not preclude them from working. Yet, as we will see,

---

[13] U.S. Census Bureau, *Americans with Disabilities: Household Economic Studies, 1997* (issued February 2001).

the Supreme Court's definition of disability rarely appears to cover someone who is both disabled and qualified for employment.

In any event, these statistics only reflect estimates of who might be covered by the "actually disabled" definition of disability. The ADA also includes those who have a "record of" disability and those who are "regarded as" disabled. Those definitions should raise coverage to *more* than 43 million or even more than the 51.2 million people found to be actually disabled in the 1997 Census Bureau report.

3. Supreme Court Cases Defining "Disability" under "Actually Disabled" Prong

As discussed previously, Congress's choice of the 43 million figure reflected an intention to cover those with both moderate and severe disabilities. Yet, the Court has interpreted the ADA inconsistently with that intent, with the result that the ADA only covers those too disabled to work. The Supreme Court's decisions in three cases decided on June 22, 1989, helped achieve that narrow scope of coverage under the "actually disabled" prong.

a. Sutton v. United Airlines Karen Sutton and Kimberly Hinton argued that United Airlines violated the ADA by denying them an opportunity to be hired as pilots when their uncorrected vision could not meet United's visual acuity standard of 20/100.[14] Their uncorrected vision was 20/200 in one eye and 20/400 in the other eye. They argued that their corrected vision – 20/20 – rendered them qualified for employment but that United Airlines failed to hire them because of their vision in its uncorrected state.

They lost at all levels because the courts considered that they were not "disabled" under the ADA. District Court Judge Daniel Sparr's opinion reflects a common judicial perspective under the ADA – that

---

[14] See *Sutton v. United Airlines, Inc.*, Civ. A. No. 96-S-121 (D. Colo. Aug. 28, 1996) (available at 1996 WL 588917).

the ADA only covers those who are severely disabled and those who need reasonable accommodations. Judge Sparr granted United Airlines's motion to dismiss, concluding that the ADA cannot be interpreted to include individuals with "slight shortcomings that are both minor and widely shared."[15] He found that "millions of Americans suffer visual impairments no less serious than those of the Plaintiffs. Under such an expansive reading, the term 'disabled' would become a meaningless phrase, subverting the policies and purposes of the ADA and distorting the class the ADA was meant to protect."[16] He overlooked the fact that plaintiffs' uncorrected vision placed them in the bottom 2 percent of the United States population and was neither minor nor widely shared.[17]

Judge Sparr also assumed that the statute would only cover those who are visually impaired and who need reasonable accommodations. To justify the conclusion that plaintiffs were not covered by the statute, because their visual impairment was insufficiently disabling, he quoted a sentence from the ADA's legislative history that listed the kind of accommodations that might be needed by some individuals with visual impairments.[18] He did not seem to understand that the statute also covered individuals with mild impairments who did not need accommodations but faced discrimination due to the stereotypical attitudes of others.

The next court to consider Sutton and Hinton's case was the Tenth Circuit Court of Appeals. As the district court had, this court also

---

[15] Id. at *5.

[16] Id. at *5.

[17] See J. Roberts, *Binocular Visual Acuity of Adults, United States, 1960–1962* 3 (National Center for Health Statistics, Series 11, No. 30 Department of Health and Welfare, 1968).

[18] *Sutton v. United Airlines, Inc.*, Civ. A. No. 96-S-121 (D. Colo. Aug. 28, 1996) (available at 1996 WL 588917) at *5 ("For blind and visually-impaired persons, reasonable accommodations may include adaptive hardware and software for computers, electronics [*sic*] visual aids, Braille devices, talking calculators, magnifiers, audio recordings and brailled material.")

assumed that the statute only covered those with severe disabilities. It affirmed the district court's motion to dismiss.[19]

In justifying its decision, the Tenth Circuit cited a Fifth Circuit case and an unpublished decision from the Southern District of New York in which plaintiffs with visual impairments were found not to be handicapped under section 504 or the ADA. The Fifth Circuit case was *Chandler v. City of Dallas*.[20] One of the two plaintiffs in this case was Adolphus Maddox. He had impaired vision in his left eye that could not be corrected to better than 20/60 and he had a horizontal field of vision in that eye that was less than 70 degrees. The vision in his right eye, however, was normal. Maddox prevailed at trial, but the Fifth Circuit overturned that decision on appeal, finding that he was not an individual with a disability under section 504 of the Rehabilitation Act.

The Fifth Circuit's reasoning in *Chandler* was based on an unpublished Fifth Circuit opinion, *Collier v. City of Dallas*, in which the Fifth Circuit had concluded in 1986 that an individual whose vision in one of his eyes could only be corrected to 20/200 was not disabled under section 504.[21] Since 20/60 vision is better than 20/200 vision, the Fifth Circuit reasoned that Maddox was also not disabled for the purposes of section 504. Reliance on *Chandler*, which, in turn, relied on *Collier*, was wrong. Unpublished opinions have no precedential value in the Fifth Circuit. Furthermore, the *Collier* reasoning was simply wrong.

---

[19] *Sutton v. United Airlines*, 130 F.3d 893 (10th Cir. 1997).

[20] 2 F.3d 1385 (5th Cir. 1993).

[21] See *Chandler v. City of Dallas*, 2 F.3d 1385, 1390 (5th Cir. 1993)(citing *Collier v. City of Dallas*, No. 86-1010 (5th Cir. August 19, 1986)). The Moritz Law Library acquired a copy of the *Collier* opinion from the Fifth Circuit archives. It is an unpublished opinion with the following notation: "Local Rule 47.5 provides: 'The publication of opinions that have no precedential value and merely decide particular cases on the basis of well-settled principles of law imposes needless expense of the public and burdens on the legal profession.' Pursuant to that Rule, the court has determined that this opinion should not be published." *Collier v. City of Dallas*, No. 86-1010 (5th Cir. August 19, 1986) (copy on file with Moritz Law Library).

There is no arguable basis for concluding that someone whose vision is only correctable to 20/200 is not disabled. Such vision constitutes legal blindness for the purpose of the Social Security laws and meets the Census Bureau's definition of severe disability. The Tenth Circuit's reference to *Chandler* reflects that it had no manageable standard for determining which visually impaired individuals should be covered by the ADA, because the 20/200 holding from *Collier* cannot be correct.

In further support of its reasoning, the Tenth Circuit in *Sutton* cited *Sweet v. Electronic Data Systems, Inc.*,[22] an unpublished decision of the Southern District of New York. This case involved Bryant Sweet, who as the result of an accident had vision that was correctable to 20/80 in one eye and 20/20 in the other eye. Without glasses, his vision in the weak eye would be 20/200. District Court Judge Michael B. Mukasey granted defendant's motion for summary judgment on the ground that Sweet was not an individual with a disability under the ADA. Judge Mukasey reached his determination, in part, on the basis of standards for visual impairment used by various professional organizations. He noted that the Social Security Administration defines blindness as vision worse than 20/200 and defines visual impairment as vision between 20/40 and 20/200, and that the World Health Organization defines blindness as vision worse than 20/400 and defines visual impairment as between 20/60 and 20/400. Because "plaintiff's corrected visual acuity of 20/80 in his left eye is at the strong end of either scale," and he was able to participate in a broad range of activities without difficulty, the court found that he was not "substantially impaired" in the major life activity of seeing.[23] Judge Mukasey then concluded that "plaintiff's restricted reading capacity does not require a different result."[24]

Judge Mukasey's reasoning, however, was flawed. Congress did not limit the visual impairment category to those who are legally blind. The evidence that Sweet's uncorrected vision was only 20/80 coupled with

---

[22] No. 95 Civ. 3987 (S.D. N.Y. April 26, 1996), available at 1996 WL 204471.
[23] Id. at *6.
[24] Id. at *6.

the evidence of his difficulties with reading would have easily put him within the category of visual impairment used by the Census Bureau in its 1984/85 household survey on disability. An impairment in *reading* was a part of the Census Bureau definition of visual impairment. The problem with the reasoning in *Sweet*, like the problem with the reasoning in *Chandler*, is that it precludes coverage for those with less than "severe" visual impairments. Nothing short of legal blindness in both eyes would appear to suffice.

The Supreme Court followed the path of the lower courts in construing the "actually disabled" prong of the ADA to apply to only a very narrow category of individuals with visual impairments. Unlike the lower courts, however, the Supreme Court closely examined the 43 million figure to arrive at its conclusion.[25] It traced the derivation of the 43 million figure to the reports by the National Council on Disability and the Census Bureau data. On the basis of these data, it concluded that Congress could not have intended to cover people when the limitations imposed by their disabilities could be reduced through the use of mitigating measures. This test is commonly called the "mitigating measures rule." The Court noted, for example, that 100 million Americans use corrective lenses – a figure that, in itself, exceeds the 43 million estimate.[26] It then concluded that Congress did not intend to cover *anyone* who benefited substantially from mitigating measures.

While the Court was correct to conclude that Congress did not intend to cover everyone who uses corrective lenses, the Court was wrong to conclude that Congress did not intend to cover *anyone* who benefited from corrective lenses or other corrective measures. The Census Bureau report found that 12.8 million Americans had visual impairments.[27] Only 1.7 of the 12.8 million individuals with a visual impairment who were surveyed by the Census Bureau indicated that they were not able to see letters or words at all, and were therefore

---

[25] *Sutton*, 527 U.S. at 484–86.
[26] Id. at 486.
[27] Census Bureau Report, at 2 (Table A).

placed in the "severe disability" category.[28] But Congress used the 12.8 million figure, rather than the 1.7 million figure, to attain its 43 million estimate, as discussed earlier. The Census Bureau estimate of 12.8 million Americans with visual impairments constitutes about 5 percent of the population at the time of the Census Bureau survey, although far short of the 100 million who wear corrective lenses.

Rather than broadly ruling that *no one* who uses mitigating measures to attain 20/20 vision can be covered by the statute, the Court had other options available that could have resulted in coverage closer to 43 million Americans. For example, the Court could have presumptively covered anyone whose vision was "significantly" worse than the general population's in a statistical sense. The generally accepted standard for statistical significance is two standard deviations from the mean (which is the bottom 2.5 percent of the population). That approach is currently used to determine which children are presumptively entitled to services under the Individuals with Disabilities Education Act. The statistical significance approach, in fact, is arguably too narrow because the Census Bureau's 12.8 million figure for visual impairment includes about *5 percent* of the 1986 population. Nonetheless, application of a statistical significance test would clearly cover the plaintiffs in the *Sutton* case because their uncorrected vision placed them in the bottom 2 percent of the population. Alternatively, the Court could have limited the mitigating measure rule to cases involving visual impairments because of the easy availability of corrective lenses. Instead, the Court offered an overly rigid standard under which few Americans who would be seeking employment could qualify as individuals with disabilities when they rely on mitigating measures to be qualified to work. The rigid mitigating measure rule carved out by the Supreme Court in *Sutton* was closer to the definition used under the Social Security Act for those too disabled to work rather than the one used under the Census data to form the basis for the 43 million figure.

[28] Id.

Another problem with the way the Court used the 43 million figure is that it did not seem to appreciate that individuals could have more than one disability. It observed, for example, that 100 million Americans wear corrective lenses, 28 million have hearing impairments, and 50 million have high blood pressure. By implication, the Court suggested that a broad definition of disability could cover nearly every American if we add those various figures together to arrive at 178 million Americans. But the Census Bureau arrived at a 37.3 million figure in 1984/85 of the number of people with limitations even though three of the subcategories (lifting or carrying, walking, and using stairs) included 18 to 19 million Americans.[29] Many individuals were in all the categories, resulting in the cumulative figure of 37 million.

One might say that it is not fair to blame the Court for this overly restrictive approach because the parties only gave it two stark options – accept the Equal Employment Opportunity Commission's (EEOC's) broad rule to disregard *all* mitigating measures or impose mitigating measures in all cases. Arguably, it is hard to expect the Court to craft a rule, such as the two standard deviation rule, if that rule is not suggested by a party. But Justice Stevens's dissenting opinion did observe that the plaintiffs in *Sutton* had vision that placed them in the bottom 2 percent of the population.[30] Thus, the Court was aware that middle grounds were possible that might cover the plaintiffs while not covering *everyone* who wore corrective lenses. Further, the Court did not need to create a rule that extended beyond the category of visual impairment. Under the guise of limiting statutory coverage to 43 million, the Court went out of its way to pick an approach that it must have realized would cover far fewer than 43 million. A genuine commitment to substantive equality would have precluded that result.

---

[29] See Census Bureau Report at 2, Table A.
[30] 527 U.S. at 507 n. 4.

b. Albertson's v. Kirkingburg   Hallie Kirkingburg had been a commercial truck driver since 1979.[31] He has amblyopia, and his corrected vision is 20/20 in one eye but only 20/200 in his other eye.

Albertson's hired Kirkingburg as a truck driver in 1990. In order to be hired, he passed both a physical exam and a sixteen-mile road test. His visual acuity was tested twice – before he was hired and several months thereafter. Even though his visual acuity in his left eye was 20/200, he was found qualified for the job. After he had been on the job for a year, he suffered a nondriving, work-related injury when he fell from a truck. When he sought to return to work after a long-term absence, Albertson's required him to be recertified under Department of Transportation (DOT) regulations. This time, the physician determined that he did not meet the DOT's regular visual acuity standard of at least 20/40 in each eye and binocular acuity.

When Kirkingburg learned that he had not met DOT's visual acuity standards, he sought to satisfy their standards through a waiver program created by the Federal Highway Administration. This program was created to bring DOT's standards into compliance with the ADA without sacrificing highway safety. Under this program, an individual can obtain a vision waiver if

> he has three years of recent experience driving a commercial vehicle without (1) license suspension or revocation, (2) involvement in a reportable accident in which the applicant received a citation for a moving violation, and (3) more than two convictions for any other moving violation in a commercial vehicle.[32]

The individual must also present a report from an optometrist that he is "able to perform the driving tasks required to operate a commercial motor vehicle."[33] Kirkingburg was able to obtain a waiver. Albertson's,

---

[31] See generally *Kirkingburg v. Albertson's, Inc.*, 143 F.3d 1228 (9th Cir. 1998). All the facts recited in the following are stated in the Ninth Circuit opinion.

[32] 143 F.3d at 1231.

[33] Id. (quoting 57 Fed. Reg. 31,458 (1992)).

nonetheless, terminated Kirkingburg's employment and refused to rehire him after he obtained a waiver from the Federal Highway Administration. Albertson's explained that it had a policy of employing only drivers who "meet or exceed the minimum DOT standards."[34]

Kirkingburg brought suit against Albertson's, arguing that it discriminated against him in violation of the ADA. Albertson's moved for summary judgment, arguing that Kirkingburg had not established a prima facie case under the ADA. It argued that he was not qualified to perform the job of truck driver because he could not meet the basic DOT vision standards. The district court granted its motion.[35] On appeal, Albertson's made the additional argument that it was entitled to summary judgment because Kirkingburg did not have a disability within the meaning of the ADA.[36]

The Ninth Circuit reversed the district court's determination that Kirkingburg was not disabled as a matter of law. But its reasoning was sloppy. It ruled that he was disabled because "the *manner* in which he performed the major life activity of seeing was different"[37] than for other people. Although that observation was correct, Kirkingburg met the statutory definition of being disabled because his vision in his left eye, with correction, was only 20/200. That vision placed him in the bottom 2 percent of the population.

The Supreme Court reviewed the Ninth Circuit's decision but offered little clarity on what standards would need to be met in order for an individual to have a visual disability under the ADA. The Supreme Court chided the Ninth Circuit for discussing whether Kirkingburg had "different" vision rather than "impaired" vision in concluding that he was disabled.[38] After reviewing some of the general evidence about the visual limitations of individuals with monocular

---

[34] Id. at 1231.
[35] See generally *Albertson's Inc. v. Kirkingburg*, 527 U.S. 555, 561 (1999).
[36] Id.
[37] 143 F.3d at 1232.
[38] *Albertson's*, 527 U.S. at 566–67.

vision, the Court suggested that "our brief examination of some of the medical literature leaves us sharing the Government's judgment that people with monocular vision 'ordinarily' will meet the Act's definition of disability"[39] but, nonetheless, reversed the Ninth Circuit. In fact, the Court's decision has led to other decisions in which individuals with amblyopia or monocular vision have been found not to satisfy the definition of disability under the ADA. If the Court had adopted a manageable standard, like a "statistical significance solution" for those with visual impairments, lower courts (and employers) would have been able to conclude that individuals with monocular vision are disabled.[40] Under that standard, the focus of the case would have been whether he was qualified for employment, not whether he was an individual with a disability.

c. Murphy v. United Parcel Service, Inc. Vaughn Murphy was diagnosed with high blood pressure when he was ten years old. For over twenty years, he performed mechanic jobs despite the fact that he used a lever to lift heavy objects, did not run to answer the telephone, did not work above his head, and did not perform heavy or very heavy work.[41]

Murphy applied for a mechanic job at United Parcel Service (UPS) in August 1994. One aspect of this mechanic job was to drive tractor trailers and package cars to perform "road tests" and "road calls." He was hired by UPS on August 18, 1994, and performed road tests on

---

[39] Id. at 567.

[40] In fact, the dissenting opinion cited a well-regarded medical source to observe that only 2 percent of the population suffers from myopia that is worse than 20/200. See *Sutton*, 527 U.S. at 507. The majority, by contrast, cited a different source for the proposition that more than 100 million Americans need corrective lenses to see properly. *Sutton*, 527 U.S. at 487. The question in the case was not how many Americans wear corrective lenses; instead, it was how many Americans have vision worse than 20/200. The majority and dissenting opinions, nonetheless, reflect that it is possible to use scientific sources for common impairments to evaluate who is in the bottom 2 percent of the population.

[41] See generally *Murphy v. United Parcel Service, Inc.*, 946 F. Supp. 872 (D. Kan. 1996).

UPS vehicles between twelve and eighteen times. In order to perform those road tests, a mechanic was supposed to have a DOT commercial driver's license. To obtain such a license, one must have blood pressure less than or equal to 160/90 or obtain temporary certification.

Although Murphy took medication to reduce his blood pressure, he was not able to get his blood pressure below 160/100 without suffering severe side effects such as stuttering, loss of memory, impotence, lack of sleep, and irritability. His blood pressure, even when treated, placed him in the bottom 2 percent of the adult population.[42]

UPS mistakenly certified Murphy as qualified to obtain a DOT commercial license despite his high blood pressure. When this error was detected a month later, his employment was terminated. Although Murphy's blood pressure was not low enough to qualify him for a one-year certification, it was sufficient to qualify him for optional temporary DOT health certification with his employer's cooperation.[43] Nonetheless, UPS did not allow Murphy to attempt to obtain the optional temporary certification so that he could retain his employment.

The trial court held that Murphy was not disabled because his high blood pressure did not limit him substantially. The court of appeals and the Supreme Court affirmed.

The Supreme Court dodged the question of whether Murphy was "actually disabled" even after taking medication because certiorari was only granted on the more narrow question of whether his disability should be assessed in its unmedicated state. Having ruled in *Sutton* that one's disability should be assessed *after* the use of mitigating measures – an assessment that was not made by the lower courts in Murphy's case – the Supreme Court did not interject its own conclusion in this matter. Nonetheless, the framework offered by the Court to resolve this question is not likely to cover many individuals who are both disabled and

---

[42] See U.S. Dept. of Health and Human Services, *Blood Pressure Levels in Persons 18–74 Years of Age in 1976–80, and Trends in Blood Pressure from 1960 to 1980 in the United States* 31 (July 1986) (Table 1).

[43] 527 U.S. at 522.

qualified to work. The Court suggested that the focus on the inquiry, under the *Sutton* mitigating measure rule, is "whether petitioner is 'disabled' due to limitations that persist despite his medication or the negative side effects of his medication."[44] Because he was able to work with medication, he was unlikely to meet that definition of disability.

A "statistical significance" approach rather than such a nebulous standard, however, would have been more likely to reach the correct result. That rule is especially appropriate because Murphy is the kind of individual who was counted in the Census Bureau's disability determination because of his self-imposed limitations in the performance of daily tasks. Murphy had learned over the years to self-accommodate by avoiding heavy lifting and activities that would raise his blood pressure so that he could work as a mechanic. Murphy would have indicated on the Census form that he had difficulty walking one-quarter of a mile, difficulty walking stairs without resting, and difficulty carrying objects as heavy as a full bag of groceries. To be moderately (rather than severely) disabled, an individual was not required by the Census Bureau to be *unable* to perform those tasks. It merely required that an individual could only perform them with *difficulty*. Murphy provided ample evidence of such difficulties, yet not one court that heard his case ruled in his favor. Those rulings are inconsistent with the Census Bureau data that formed the basis for the 43 million estimate of individuals with disabilities.

As in *Sutton*, the focus on whether the plaintiff was disabled allowed the Court to avoid entirely the question of whether he was qualified for employment. Vaughn Murphy is exactly the kind of person whom Congress thought it might assist through passage of the ADA. He was already employed as a mechanic before the ADA went into law. But he wanted to improve his employment situation with a higher-paying mechanic job with UPS. UPS certified him as qualified and had no problems with his job performance, before it began to focus on

---

[44] *Murphy*, 527 U.S. at 521.

his blood pressure. The Court's twisted interpretation of disability prevented someone who was clearly terminated because of the employer's stereotypical perception that he was too disabled to do the job from demonstrating that he was qualified for employment. The ADA is not likely to make an impact on the employability of individuals with disabilities if such individuals are outside the scope of statutory coverage.

d. The Statistical Significance Solution   If one accepts the premise that the Court carved out too narrow a definition of disability in *Sutton* to attain substantive equality, then one is left with the difficult task of constructing an interpretation of the term *disability* that covers a reasonable, but not unlimited, number of Americans. One solution is to suggest that the Court merely repeal the "mitigating measures" rule. But, as the Court notes, this could cause 100 million Americans who wear corrective lenses to be covered by the statute if they face discrimination on that basis. If the statute also covered everyone who takes medication for high blood pressure and other common conditions, then such an approach could result in the statute's covering 150 or even 200 million Americans.

In theory, such a change is possible. Title VII covers the entire population because we each have a race and a gender. But Congress did not take the same approach with the ADA that it took with Title VII. It chose a "limited class" model under which only individuals who were "disabled" rather than individuals who faced discrimination on the basis of a physical or mental characteristic were covered by the statute. Most likely, it made that choice because it wanted to make "reasonable accommodations" available to the covered class without worrying about reverse discrimination lawsuits. It also wanted to limit the expenses associated with reasonable accommodation through a limited class model.

In any event, Congress did choose a "limited class" model for the ADA. It created a definition consistent with a limited class model and drafted a first finding that suggested that that definition would not cover much more than one-sixth of the population. So is there a manageable way to get rid of the mitigating measures rule while also keeping statutory coverage around 43 or 50 million (today's equivalent of one-sixth of the population)?

One possible way to cover common, *measurable* impairments[45] such as poor vision or high blood pressure would be to protect those individuals whose conditions place them at the bottom 2.5 percent of the population irrespective of the effectiveness of mitigating measures. Instead of the ADA's covering all 100 million Americans who wear corrective lenses, it would only cover the 2–3 million Americans whose vision is two standard deviations below the mean, even if their vision is correctable with lenses. That figure does not threaten to cause the ADA to cover nearly the entire population but allows those like the plaintiffs in *Sutton* or *Kirkingburg* to receive statutory protection. One advantage of a statistical significance approach for common, measurable disabilities is that we would have a group of individuals, who both plaintiffs and defendants would know with certainty were covered by the statute. Statutory coverage would also have to be available to others whose impairments are not readily measurable but who have "substantial limitations" as required by the statute. A definition of statistical significance, however, is consistent with the meaning of the word *substantial* as used in the statute; in fact, the ADA regulations use the term *significant* to define the term *substantial*.[46] Hence, it makes sense to use a common statistical test to help define the term *substantial* in the statute. It should be emphasized, however, that a statistical significance test is likely to *understate* the number of individuals with disabilities in our society. That test should be a floor rather than a ceiling and should only be applied to common impairments whose existence can be considered statistically normal.

---

[45] This test would not work for psychological impairments that are not readily measurable. Instead, such impairments should be covered without regard to the mitigating measure rule.

[46] See 29 C.F.R. § 1630.1(i).

Because of the possibility that a statistical significance test would cause the statute *not* to cover even 43 million, it is important to limit its application to common, measurable impairments. Further, one must remember that the "record of" and "regarded as" definitions of disability would still be available to those with common, measurable impairments that did not meet the two standard deviation requirement. If they are treated *as if* their impairment is severe when it is mild, they still might be "regarded as" disabled.

One major challenge in fashioning a legal definition of disability is that the word is an arbitrary term that seeks to fit a wide range of people. People with mental impairments have little in common with people with visual impairments or hearing impairments or mobility impairments. Hence, it was arguably a mistake for the Court to try to develop an overarching definition that would readily apply to all types of disabilities. A more cautious approach would have allowed the Court to see what type of definition worked in a variety of different contexts. But, unfortunately, the definition chosen by the Court in *Sutton* does not even work well in the context of visual impairments even though the case involved plaintiffs with visual impairments.

If the Court had not crafted such a broad holding in *Sutton*, which applied to a range of disabilities not yet before the Court, its decision could have promoted dialogue about the appropriate legal standard. Instead, the *Sutton* opinion has inappropriately closed the door until the Court acknowledges its error and reexamines the issue, or Congress amends the statute. The Court's current analysis of disability under the "actually disabled" prong leaves far fewer than 13.5 million Americans protected by the ADA, and individuals like the Sutton twins, Vaughn Murphy, and Hallie Kirkingburg outside the scope of statutory protection. For the ADA to provide effective protection in the workplace, it needs to protect such individuals whose disability is relatively mild yet who still fall within the bottom 2.5 percent of the population.

B. "Regarded as" Disabled Prong

If the Supreme Court's interpretation of the "actually disabled" prong is correct, then other tools must be available to broaden the scope of statutory coverage beyond the 13.5 million severely disabled individuals covered under that prong in order to attain substantive equality. One option would be for the "regarded as" prong in subsection (c) to be such a vehicle. The "regarded as" prong seeks to protect individuals in three different categories:

(1) The individual may have an impairment which is not substantially limiting but is perceived by the employer or other covered entity as constituting a substantially limiting impairment;

(2) the individual may have an impairment which is only substantially limiting because of the attitudes of others toward the impairment; or

(3) the individual may have no impairment at all but is regarded by the employer or other covered entity as having a substantially limiting impairment.[47]

Consistently with the anti-subordination approach, this prong should assist those who face a history of discrimination while not covering all Americans who simply may be displeased with employment decisions. An "anti-subordination" approach is a limited class model whereby only a subset of society is provided protection. Under subsection (c), the courts could reach individuals with no impairments or mild impairments who do not meet the "actually disabled" definition of disability but who face discrimination due to the stereotypes of others. Because those individuals rarely, if ever, are eligible for reasonable accommodations, liberal interpretation of subsection (c) could help protect Americans who cannot meet the standards imposed under the "actually disabled" prong without imposing costs on defendants

---

[47] 29 C.F.R. § 1630.2(l) App.

through accommodations. Nonetheless, the *Sutton* decision also makes subsection (c) unavailable for such plaintiffs.

Subsection (c) requires that an individual be treated *as if* that individual had an impairment that substantially limits one or more major life activities. This stereotypical treatment can occur in one of two ways: (1) the individual could be treated as if he or she has an impairment that he or she does not have at all, or (2) the employer could exaggerate the consequences of a real (but modest) impairment that a person does have. As we will see later, this second type of stereotypical treatment is the most common in the existing case law. The courts' treatment of this category of cases has virtually erased this category of protection from the statute. Hence, the "regarded as" prong has done little to achieve protection of at least 43 million Americans who face disability-related discrimination.

1. *Sutton* and *Murphy*

The *Sutton* plaintiffs also argued that they were entitled to bring a claim under subsection (c) because the employer exaggerated the scope of the limitations imposed by their visual physical impairment. They contended that United Airlines "mistakenly believes their physical impairments substantially limit them in the major life activity of working."[48] They alleged that United Airlines "has a vision requirement that is allegedly based on myth and stereotype."[49]

At first glance, the *Sutton* case should have easily fallen within the "regarded as" definition of disability under the first theory. There was no dispute in the case that they were rejected for employment because of a physical attribute. Although the Court, in its earlier discussion of the "actually disabled" prong in subsection (a), concluded that their vision was not a "disabling condition" as defined by the ADA, the

[48] 527 U.S. at 490.
[49] Id.

employer appeared to regard it as a disabling condition in denying them employment. One only proceeds to subsection (c), under the first theory, if one has a condition that has been determined not to meet the definition of disability under subsection (a). Hence, the argument under subsection (c) will be that an employer treated a condition as disabling when, in fact, it was not.

The complication in this case arose from the "class of jobs" rule that the EEOC crafted for cases brought under subsection (a) ("actually disabled" prong). The Supreme Court erroneously applied this rule (which is not required by the statutory language) to the subsection (c) context ("regarded as" prong).

In the regulations defining "substantially limits," the EEOC states that with respect to the major life activity of working that "the term substantially limits means significantly restricted in the ability to perform either a class of jobs or a broad range of jobs in various classes as compared to the average person having comparable training, skills and abilities. The inability to perform a single, particular job does not constitute a substantial limitation in the major life activity of working."[50] Hence, a plaintiff who contends that he or she has a physical or mental impairment that substantially limits the major life activity of "working" has to establish that he or she is limited in the performance of a class of jobs, not merely the specific job in question.

According to Professor Chai Feldblum,[51] the EEOC drafted this regulation in response to concerns raised by Christopher Bell, an attorney working for the EEOC, which were embraced by the House Judiciary Committee during its consideration of the ADA. The committee noted in its report that someone should not be able to use subsection (a) if the person is limited "in his or her ability to perform only a particular job, because of circumstances unique to that job site

---

[50] 29 C.F.R. § 1630.2(j)(3).
[51] Chai R. Feldblum, *Definition of Disability under Federal Anti-Discrimination Law: What Happened? Why? And What Can We Do About It?*, 21 Berkeley J. Emp. & Lab. L. 91, 133 (2000).

or the materials used."[52] But the committee made it clear in its report that the confined nature of the "substantially limits" rule in the context of the major life activity of working only applied to subsection (a). It did *not* apply to subsection (c):

> A person who is rejected from a job because of the myths, fears and stereotypes associated with disabilities would be covered under this third test, whether or not the employer's perception was shared by others in the field, and whether or not the person's physical or mental condition could be considered a disability under the first or second part of the definition.[53]

The EEOC interpretive guidance makes a similar statement. The interpretive guidance states: "Therefore, if an individual can show that an employer or other covered entity made an employment decision because of a perception of disability based on 'myth, fear or stereotype,' the individual will satisfy the 'regarded as' part of the definition of disability."[54] There is no suggestion in the legislative history or regulations that the "class of jobs" rule applies outside the subsection (a) context.

It makes no sense to apply the "class of jobs" rule to a subsection (c) case. Presumably, the "class of jobs" regulation was drafted to help limit an employer's reasonable accommodation expenses when an individual's impairment only limited his or her ability to perform a particular job. In a subsection (a) case, an individual who alleges that she is disabled because she is substantially limited in the major life activity of working would necessarily request accommodations that would allow her to be a *qualified* worker. By requiring that the plaintiff demonstrate that her physical or mental impairment substantially limits her in a broad class of jobs, the EEOC limits the number of individuals who can qualify as disabled under that definition of disability.

---

[52] H.R. Rep. No. 485 (III) at 29.
[53] Id. at 30.
[54] 29 C.F.R. § 1630.2(l). App.

In turn, the rule would then limit the number of cases in which defendants would be asked to spend money on reasonable accommodations. Those concerns, however, are not applicable to a subsection (c) case. In the subsection (c) case, the plaintiff takes the position that she *is* qualified for employment but has been stereotypically denied employment because the employer has exaggerated the consequences of her physical or mental impairment. She is typically not requesting accommodations; she is merely requesting an opportunity to demonstrate that her impairment does not preclude her from being qualified. Thus, the cost of reasonable accommodation is not an issue.

This class of jobs rule is not even operative in the subsection (c) context, because it would impose an unrealistic burden of proof on the plaintiff. The only evidence the plaintiff has available is that the defendant considered her unable to perform the particular job for which she applied because of an exaggerated understanding of her physical or mental impairment. She would have no basis to demonstrate that the defendant considered her unqualified for a broad class of jobs because the defendant need not have an opinion with respect to a broad class of jobs. In the *Sutton* case, for example, the plaintiffs would have no way to know or establish that the defendant considered them unable to fly any airplanes, drive any vehicles, or participate in various other occupations. The plaintiffs only knew that the defendant viewed them as unqualified to perform the discrete job of global airline pilot for which they applied.

The *Sutton* Court applied the class of jobs rule to these subsection (c) cases without even pausing to consider whether the "class of jobs" rules should apply to cases brought under both subsection (c) and subsection (a). It held that the plaintiffs could not establish that they were being substantially limited in the major life activity of working because they could merely allege that the defendant regarded them as unqualified to work in the position of global airline pilot.[55] But, of course, United

[55] 527 U.S. at 493–94.

Airlines had no reason to have or express an opinion about their qualifications for a position other than the one to which they applied.

Similarly, Vaughn Murphy lost in the Supreme Court under his subsection (c) theory because he could only demonstrate that the employer perceived him as unable to perform the particular job as a mechanic at UPS because of his high blood pressure. It is, of course, possible that the employer *also* thought his high blood pressure made him unable to perform *any* mechanic jobs. But Vaughn Murphy would have no way of knowing those facts. All he knew was that the employer considered his high blood pressure to render him unqualified to work as a mechanic for UPS even though he could obtain the proper medical clearance from DOT to test drive their trucks.

In light of the limited evidence available about the employer's perceptions, the Court found in the *Murphy* case: "At most, petitioner has shown that he is regarded as unable to perform the job of mechanic only when the job requires driving a commercial motor vehicle – a specific type of vehicle used on a highway in interstate commerce."[56] Thus, "in light of petitioner's skills and the array of jobs available to petitioner utilizing those skills, petitioner has failed to show that he is regarded as unable to perform a class of jobs."[57] The Court used the "class of jobs" regulation to avoid asking the question of whether UPS exaggerated the scope of Murphy's impairment to deny him employment opportunities. UPS, for example, insisted that DOT certification was necessary for Murphy to perform the essential functions of his job. But DOT certification was only required if the vehicle was to be used on a highway in interstate commerce.[58] Driving a truck around a parking lot or local road does not even implicate this requirement. Because the case was decided on summary judgment, there are no facts in the record about the necessity of Murphy's having the DOT certification.

[56] 527 U.S. at 524.
[57] Id. at 525.
[58] 49 C.F.R. § 390.5 (1998).

The "class of jobs" rule, as this chapter will demonstrate later, has been devastating to plaintiffs in subsection (c) cases because employment discrimination plaintiffs who bring cases under subsection (c) will nearly always allege that they meet the definition of disability due to the major life activity of working. By definition, subsection (c) plaintiffs take the position that they are *not* disabled but are being treated by others as disabled. In the employment context, that evidence of adverse treatment is most likely going to involve an employer's misperception of their ability to perform a particular job. It is possible that the employer also has misperceptions about their inability to perform other major life activities (or other jobs), but plaintiffs have no way of producing such evidence.

2. Post-*Sutton* Case Law

The case law reflects that subsection (c) has been useless in ADA employment cases and that it has little application outside the employment context. The EEOC's class of jobs rule coupled with the *Sutton* Court's narrow interpretation of that rule have been fatal to plaintiffs' subsection (c) claims in the employment context. Before the Supreme Court decided *Sutton*, courts were mixed with respect to how strictly they applied the "working" rule in "regarded as" cases.

Of the fifty or so appellate cases that have proceeded under the "regarded as" theory since *Sutton* was decided, only a few have been successful. Ronald Foore, who had uncorrectable vision of 20/400, was placed on involuntary disability retirement from his position as a police officer and was unable to meet the definition of disability under the "actually disabled" or "regarded as" definitions. The city did not discharge him until it discovered his visual impairment, seven years after his vision became impaired. While acknowledging that the *Albertson's* Court said that individuals with monocular vision will "ordinarily" meet the "actually disabled" test, the Fourth Circuit found that Foore's self-compensation for his monocular vision made him not the "ordinary case."[59] He also could not meet the "regarded as" definition because police officer was not considered to be a broad enough class of jobs.[60] He was removed from his position merely because he could not meet a vision requirement (even though the court found he had no significant vision problems) and although his job performance as a police officer had been entirely satisfactory. Foore could only establish that the employer found him unqualified to perform the job he had held; that evidence was insufficient to meet the "class of jobs" rule. Without the "class of jobs" rule, Foore had the perfect case of being treated unfairly as a result of a false assumption about his physical abilities. A jury had awarded him $50,000, finding that he had been inappropriately terminated.[61] The Fourth Circuit overturned that decision. The "class of jobs" technicality precluded a jury from awarding him damages for what it considered to be unlawful disability discrimination.

The "class of jobs" problems prevented many other plaintiffs from obtaining relief. In the First Circuit, Steven Lessard's work as a "mounting employee" could not meet the "class of jobs" rule and there were not sufficient job openings for him to demonstrate a perception of unqualification for all jobs requiring repetitive work.[62] In the Second Circuit, Christina Peters lost her claim at trial because school guidance counselor was found not to meet the "class of jobs" rule.[63] The court of appeals overturned that decision on another ground.[64] The Fourth

---

[59] *Foore v. City of Richmond*, 6 Fed. Appx. 148, 153 (4th Cir. 2001).

[60] Id. at 154.

[61] Id. at 151.

[62] *Lessard v. Osram Sylvania, Inc.*, 175 F.3d 193 (1st Cir. 1999) (plaintiff who had suffered shrapnel wounds in his left hand not able to demonstrate that he was regarded as unable to do all jobs involving repetitive work because a broad category of jobs was not available to the plaintiff when he unsuccessfully applied for work).

[63] *Peters v. Baldwin Union Free Sch. Dist.*, 320 F.3d 164, 168 (2nd Cir. 2003) (summarizing trial court decision).

[64] Id. at 168 ("A mental illness that impels one to suicide can be viewed as a paradigmatic instance of inability to care for oneself").

Circuit affirmed the decision of the trial court that an employee, Tess Rohan, who allegedly suffered from posttraumatic stress disorder and severe depression, was not "regarded as" disabled by her employer merely because it perceived that she could not work as an actress in a touring theater company.[65] In the Fifth Circuit, an emergency room doctor, who allegedly received adverse treatment after being exposed to hepatitis C, could not meet the "class of jobs" rule.[66] The hospital administrator allegedly said "that he didn't think that I could work in the Emergency Room with hepatitis C, that he wouldn't go to a dentist with hepatitis C and he would not let me suture his child."[67] That remark was insufficient to sustain the "regarded as" theory. Similarly, the Sixth Circuit held that John Swanson did not sufficiently allege that he was "regarded as" disabled in a class of jobs because of his depression when the employer "perceived Swanson as a capable physician, just not a capable surgeon under its program."[68] The Seventh Circuit affirmed the dismissal of Robert Tockes's suit against Air-Land Transport Services for not meeting the "regarded as" definition of disability even though the evidence indicated that he was told he was being fired because "he was crippled, and the company was at fault for having hired a handicapped person."[69] The Eighth Circuit rejected a case brought by Albert James Conant, who sought a general laborer position with the city of Hibbing, because he had no evidence to demonstrate how the employer would have treated him with regard to other laborer positions within the city.[70] A plaintiff did succeed on the "regarded

---

[65] *Rohan v. Networks Presentations LLC*, 375 F.3d 266, 277–78 (4th Cir. 2004) (touring theater company actress not a broad class of jobs). The court relied on a prior Fourth Circuit case in which a subsection (a) plaintiff could not meet the "class of jobs" rule in a case involving a utility repair worker. Id. at 278 (citing *Forrisi v. Bowen*, 794 F.2d 931 (4th Cir. 1986).

[66] *Gowesky v. Singing River Hospital Systems*, 321 F.3d 503 (5th Cir. 2003).

[67] Id. at 506.

[68] *Swanson v. University of Cincinnati*, 268 F.3d 307, 318 (6th Cir. 2001).

[69] *See Tockes v. Air-Land Transport Services, Inc.*, 343 F.3d 895 (7th Cir. 2003).

[70] *Conant v. City of Hibbing*, 271 F.3d 782 (8th Cir. 2001).

as" theory in the Tenth Circuit but only because she was able to demonstrate that the employer refused to consider her for a wide range of jobs in the Sheriff's Department despite ten years of service when she sought to return to work after having sought treatment for posttraumatic stress disorder.[71] It is not clear that the plaintiff, McKenzie, would have prevailed if the defendant had merely found her unqualified to work as a patrol officer given the adverse decisions on that fact pattern from other circuits.

Hence, the courts have found that plaintiffs have not met the "class of jobs" test in "regarded as" cases when they were perceived as unable to be emergency room doctors, surgeons, laborers, senior management, a bus driver, police officer, school counselor, and an actress in a touring company. Even evidence that they were subjected to derogatory terms like "cripple" did not lead a court to speculate that the defendant generally regarded them as disabled. Plaintiffs can only prevail in the exceptional case where the defendant foolishly offers a view on a wide range of jobs that happen to be available.

The Sixth Circuit has recently recognized that the existing rules make a "regarded as" case in the context of working "extraordinarily difficult."[72] It observed that "it is safe to assume employers do not regularly consider the panoply of other jobs their employees could perform, and certainly do not often create direct evidence of such considerations, making the plaintiff's task even more difficult. Yet the drafters of the ADA and its subsequent interpretive regulations clearly intended that plaintiffs who are mistakenly regarded as being unable to work have a cause of action under the statute."[73] Recognizing the difficulty posed by such cases, in a case involving a salesperson who developed a bad back, the Sixth Circuit found that evidence of pretext could help establish the required level of

---

[71] *McKenzie v. Dovala*, 242 F.3d 967 (10th Cir. 2001).
[72] *Ross v. Campbell*, 237 F.3d 701, 709 (6th Cir. 2001).
[73] Id.

proof.[74] In a subsequent decision, the Sixth Circuit found in favor of an administrator who was discharged because of an alleged misperception that he was an alcoholic.[75] There was no direct evidence that the employer viewed him as being unable to perform any particular job except the one he held. But the Sixth Circuit was willing to speculate to meet the "class of jobs" rule that there was a "reasonable inference" that the plaintiff's purported alcoholism "rendered him incapable of performing a substantial number of managerial jobs."[76] Despite noting the "extraordinary" difficulty of the class of jobs rule, however, the Sixth Circuit has not questioned whether the statute should even be interpreted to require that rule.

3. Further Retrenchment: *Toyota* Decision

It is time for the courts to reject the "class of jobs" rule, especially in the "regarded as" context, and restore the ADA to the protection of at least 43 million Americans. Unfortunately, the Supreme Court does not appear to be going in that direction. If anything, its recent decisions suggest that it is further constricting the scope of the ADA so that it can only protect the 13.5 or so million people whom the Census Bureau defines as being "severely disabled." This fact became most evident in its 2002 decision in *Toyota Motor Manufacturing v. Williams*.[77] In this case involving a woman who the Sixth Circuit had found was "actually disabled" under subsection (a),[78] the Supreme Court reversed and remanded with instructions that the lower court should determine whether the plaintiff's physical impairment "prevents or *severely restricts*

---

[74] Id. at 709. ("In cases such as this one, where there is substantial evidence that an individual's medical status played a significant role in an employer's decision to fire that individual, combined with evidence that the employer concocted a pretextual justification for that firing . . . the resolution of that issue is properly left to the jury.")

[75] 398 F.3d 469 (6th Cir. 2005).

[76] Id. at 484.

[77] 534 U.S. 184 (2002).

[78] *Williams v. Toyota*, 224 F.3d 840, 842 (6th Cir. 2000).

the individual from doing activities that are of central importance to most people's daily lives."[79] Neither the statute nor regulations, however, contain a "severely restricts" requirement. The statute refers to a *substantial limitation*, which the regulations define as including a "significant" restriction." The regulations state that *substantially limits* means "significantly restricted as to the condition, manner or duration under which an individual can perform a major life activity as compared to the condition, manner, or duration under which the average person in the general population can perform the same major life activity."[80] The Court offered no explanation for why it raised the requirement from "significant" to "severe."

The Court's statement in *Toyota* that the plaintiff seeking to prove that she is disabled under subsection (a) must demonstrate that she is "severely" limited is consistent with this chapter's thesis that the Court has used the Census Bureau's "severe" limitation definition, which, according to the Census Bureau, covers no more than 13.5 million Americans, most of whom are too disabled to work. The ADA, however, does not impose a "severe limitation" requirement under the definition of disability. And the ADA purportedly protects far more than the 13.5 million Americans whom the Census Bureau considers to be severely disabled. There are numerous devices that the Court has used to limit coverage of the ADA to a group far fewer than 43 million. The "regarded as" theory coupled with the "major life activity of working" rule is a major part of that problem, and together they preclude the statute from being an effective remedy to the problem of employment discrimination.

III. CONCLUSION

The ADA was historic legislation that sought to embody an anti-subordination perspective to provide protection for a class of individuals

[79] 534 U.S. at 198 (emphasis added).
[80] 29 C.F.R. § 1630.1(i).

in society. Congress clearly stated in its findings and purpose sections that it sought to protect a discrete and insular minority, and that it considered the size of that group to be at least 43 million Americans. Further, Congress stated that it wanted this statute to provide meaningful protection in the area of employment discrimination. The Supreme Court has undermined this basic intention by construing the protected class so narrowly that it has virtually become a nullity in the employment context.

The problems that individuals with disabilities face in the employment sector are twofold. Some individuals with disabilities could engage in employment if they received accommodations. They often need to use the ADA as a vehicle to gain such accommodations. Other individuals have more mild physical or mental impairments and could engage in employment if they were given a chance to demonstrate their capabilities rather than their disabilities. They do not seek accommodations; they seek an opportunity to overcome myth and stereotype about their disabilities. The first group needs to be within the statute's "actually disabled" prong to obtain effective assistance in maintaining employment. The second group could be within the "actually disabled" or "regarded as" prong to attain assistance. They have only become disabled through the attitudes of others. It is essential that the ADA provide protection to this second group of individuals, like the Sutton twins, Hallie Kirkingburg, and Vaughn Murphy, if it is to have a meaningful impact on the employment opportunities of individuals with disabilities. It is critical that the courts keep that larger objective in mind when interpreting the scope of the definition of disability under the ADA.

One response to this story of overly narrow judicial protection is to suggest that Congress enact corrective legislation to restore its original intentions. Given the Court's hostility to the ADA's antisubordination perspective, however, no good option is available to Congress. Congress could seek to overturn the *Sutton* mitigating measure rule, but a sweeping reversal of *Sutton*, without something like the statistical significance solution proposed by this chapter, would cause nearly every American to be covered by the statute and able to request reasonable accommodations. Even if the business community tolerated such an amendment, we can anticipate that the courts would seek to find other narrowing devices to limit such a broad statutory scope, such as narrowly interpreting the reasonable accommodation requirement.

Another alternative is for Congress to abandon the anti-subordination approach and make statutory protection available to anyone who faces discrimination on the basis of a physical or mental condition. As would the first alternative, this alternative would provide a potential cause of action to nearly every individual in society. Further, by entirely abandoning the protected class approach, it would open up the possibility of "reverse discrimination" lawsuits, which would limit the effectiveness of the reasonable accommodation requirement.

The drawbacks of both approaches reflect what a masterful job Congress did in 1990 by defining a protected class that was also entitled to reasonable accommodation. That approach posed challenges when plaintiffs had a common impairment, like poor vision, because it was not clear whether Congress intended such individuals to be within the scope of statutory coverage. But the Court did not have to undermine the effectiveness of the statute's ability to respond to employment discrimination problems to respond to this challenging fact pattern. It should have adopted something like the statistical significance solution and otherwise left intact Congress's masterful work. There should be no need to amend the 1990 statute. Instead, the Court should honor Congress's basic purpose to provide a "clear and comprehensive national mandate for the elimination of discrimination against individuals with disabilities" by revising the mitigating measure rule and abandoning the class of jobs rule in subsection (c) cases.[81]

---

[81] 42 U.S.C. § 12101(b)(1).

4

K–12 Education

IN CHAPTER 3, I ARGUED THAT CONGRESS CORRECTLY adopted an anti-subordination approach in defining who should be covered by the Americans with Disabilities Act but that the courts have undermined that intention through an exceedingly narrow interpretation of the term *disability*. Consequently, ADA Title I has been ineffective in improving the employment opportunities of individuals with disabilities who are qualified to work with or without reasonable accommodations. Because the courts disallowed claims of discrimination altogether by concluding that the plaintiffs were not even covered by the statute, that chapter did not discuss whether the remedies adopted by the courts were effective under an anti-subordination perspective.

The problems with legal protections for children with disabilities who desire an effective education are quite different from the problems faced by adults with disabilities who desire employment. As under the ADA, Congress used an anti-subordination approach in defining the scope of the covered class in the education area. Only children who meet the definition of *disability* are covered by the relevant federal statute – the Individuals with Disabilities Education Act (IDEA). Congress used different definitions of *disability* under the IDEA and the ADA. On the whole, the definition adopted by Congress under the IDEA is appropriate and consistent with an anti-subordination approach. Further, the courts have generally interpreted the IDEA consistently with Congress's intent, so the statute does offer protection to many children with disabilities. Hence, this chapter will not offer an extensive critique of Congress's or the courts' decisions with regard to the scope of coverage.

The problem with the IDEA is at the stage of remedy. Congress adopted a remedy model under which it presumes that children benefit from the most integrated education possible. This presumption causes school districts and courts to prefer a more mainstream education for a child even if the available evidence suggests that the child would attain more educational benefit from a more segregated educational environment. This presumption particularly makes it difficult for many parents who have children with autism and want to place their child in a special class or school for children with autism. The statute requires them to overcome unnecessary hurdles to achieve that outcome because of its formal equality underpinnings. Rather than favoring integrated remedies, I suggest that courts should be agnostic as to whether integrated remedies are the most appropriate. Instead, I suggest that Congress and the courts adopt what I call a "continuum model," under which school districts must have available a range of educational options so that students can receive the most appropriate educational program. Then, parents and school districts can choose a segregated or integrated option depending on what is more appropriate for an individual child. As with the other chapters of this book, I will look closely at empirical data to justify the remedies that should be available.

In Part I of this chapter, I will first discuss the scope of coverage under the IDEA and show how, as does the ADA, it reflects a "limited class model" consistent with the anti-subordination approach. In Part II, I will discuss the evolution of the integration presumption under the IDEA. I will show how this presumption arose from a history of stark subordination under which children with disabilities were excluded or segregated from the educational environment. The integration presumption made sense in that context even though it no longer makes sense today. Part III will discuss how the integration presumption has operated in practice. Part IV will argue that the integration presumption no longer is justified because the empirical evidence suggests that well-funded, segregated programs may be as effective for the individual child as well-funded, integrated programs. In the conclusion, I will argue that a "continuum of services" approach rather than an integration presumption makes more sense as an effective remedy at this time. To be clear, I am not suggesting that integration is *never* the appropriate remedy or even that it *typically* is not the appropriate remedy. My argument is simply that the appropriate educational environment should be considered on an individual basis without a presumption in favor of or against integration. Empirical data and a child's demonstrated individual needs should guide decisions rather than unwarranted presumptions.

I. SCOPE OF COVERAGE

As the Americans with Disabilities Act does, the IDEA defines whom it intends to cover under a "limited class" model, presumably for the purpose of diverting resources to those children most in need of extra educational resources to make adequate educational progress. In general, the term *child with a disability* means a child

> (i) with mental retardation, hearing impairments (including deafness), speech or language impairments, visual impairments (including blindness), serious emotional disturbance . . ., orthopedic impairments, autism, traumatic brain injury, other health impairments, or specific learning disabilities; and
>
> (ii) who, by reason thereof, needs special education and related services.[1]

For children ages three through nine, or any subset of that age range, including ages three through five, the state or local education

---

[1]   20 U.S.C. § 1401(3)(A).

agency can also include within the category "child with a disability" a child

(i) experiencing developmental delays, as defined by the State and as measured by appropriate diagnostic instruments and procedures, in 1 or more of the following areas: physical development; cognitive development; communication development; social or emotional development; or adaptive development; and
(ii) who, by reason thereof, needs special education and related services.[2]

Finally, the statute also defines an *infant or toddler with a disability* as "an individual under 3 years of age who would be at risk of experiencing a substantial developmental delay if early intervention services were not provided to the individual."[3]

The rationale behind these three definitions makes a great deal of sense. In general, Congress decided to provide extra funding for children with disabilities who needed special education and related services. If their disability does not affect them academically, then Congress saw no need to provide extra educational resources to them. Further, Congress understood the importance of early intervention in the lives of children with disabilities. Although public education does not typically begin until age five when children enter kindergarten, Congress allocated funds for children below the age of five even when they could not meet the more rigorous standards set forth for school-age children. Although it is difficult to measure developmental disabilities in young children, Congress allocated money to children with developmental disabilities without requiring that they have a precise diagnosis. In euphemistic terms, Congress called these disabilities "developmental delays," but many of these children will never "catch up" and may be more properly characterized as developmentally disabled.

---

[2] 20 U.S.C. § 1401(3)(B).
[3] 20 U.S.C. § 1432(1).

These definitions are not perfect. For example, Congress gives states the discretion of whether to provide extra resources to children, ages three through nine, who do not have a diagnosis of a precise disability but who have what the statute calls "developmental delays." Most states use that discretion to cover children with developmental delays in preschool but require proof of a specific diagnosis for continued intervention in grade school. Given the research on the benefits of early intervention, it would have been more effective for Congress to insist that states cover all children who meet the definition of "developmental delay" through age nine. But, at least, Congress has tried to identify and provide funding for those most in need of assistance. Early intervention services are required for children less than three years of age who are "at risk of experiencing a substantial developmental delay"; that, from an anti-subordination perspective, is consistent with providing assistance to those most in need of assistance.

Unlike the ADA, the courts have not undermined Congress's intention to cover a broad range of children under the IDEA. Most of the case law speaks to the issue of what kinds of remedies are appropriate, not whether children are covered by the statute. It is hard to know why there have been far fewer coverage issues under the IDEA than the ADA, but a few explanations come to mind. First, the IDEA is an older statute and school districts have grown accustomed to having certain children covered by the statute. Second, school districts may have somewhat less sophisticated legal teams assisting them and are less likely to take aggressive legal positions because of the difficulty of bearing litigation expenses under the IDEA compared with the ADA. When the ADA was enacted, the defense bar decided to make a concerted attempt to limit the scope of coverage. School district lawyers do not appear to have followed that path. Third, there is simply much less case law under the IDEA than under the ADA because parents have few incentives or opportunities to litigate decisions with which they disagree. Litigation can take a long time and children can rarely afford to wait a long time to attain an appropriate educational arrangement. Hence, there is a strong incentive for parents to cooperate with school districts rather than litigate. Also, parents cannot recover attorney fees for using lawyers to attend most prelitigation meetings with school district personnel, and that fact limits litigation as a strategy. Finally, school districts have a modest financial incentive to classify children as disabled to obtain some additional state or federal financial resources. For whatever reasons, there has been only limited litigation over coverage issues.

In sum, Congress identified who was in most need of intervention and created a funding statute to provide school districts with extra resources for those students. That program has worked pretty well within the funding limits set by Congress. The challenge, as I will discuss next, is identifying what kinds of educational resources are appropriate for these students. At that stage, as I will argue, Congress used an integration presumption that has undermined the effectiveness of the statute even though that presumption may have been appropriate when it was initially developed.

II. EVOLUTION OF THE INTEGRATION PRESUMPTION

A. Background

Until the nineteenth century, most individuals with disabilities received no education whatsoever, because they were feared and shunned by society.[4] One of the earliest cases affirming this principle is *Watson v. City of Cambridge*,[5] in which the court permitted the exclusion of a child who is "weak in mind" from the public schools. That principle

---

[4] Robert L. Osgood, *The History of Inclusion in the United States 18* (2005) ("patterns of response grounded in fear, suspicion, contempt, and cruelty").

[5] 32 N.E. 864, 864–65 (Mass. 1893).

was approved as recently as 1958, when an Illinois court found that the "feeble minded" had no right to public education.[6]

Thomas Hopkins Gallaudet was among the earliest American reformers to argue for the education of individuals who are deaf. He helped found the Connecticut Asylum for the Education and Instruction of Deaf and Dumb Persons in Hartford, Connecticut, in 1817.[7] Samuel Gridley Howe played a similar role in Massachusetts, helping to found the Massachusetts Asylum for the Blind in 1832 and the Massachusetts Asylum for Idiotic and Feeble-Minded Youth in 1848.[8] Howe argued that such institutions should be considered part of the public school system.[9] Both Gallaudet and Howe had to overcome enormous barriers even to suggest that individuals with disabilities should be educated. Robert Osgood has suggested that educational institutions for individuals with disabilities came into being "amid intense scrutiny and skepticism on the part of the public."[10] These schools were residential facilities that did not seek to educate children who used wheelchairs, who were not toilet-trained, or who were considered uneducable.[11] Thus, they served a small subsection of the disability community.

Gallaudet and Howe had humanitarian reasons for seeking to create separate residential facilities for individuals who were deaf, blind, or mentally disabled. By the early 1900s, however, such institutions became much more problematic. Attitudes toward disability became more negative "with the disabled facing near as much ostracism, contempt, and misunderstanding as ever."[12]

---

[6] See *Dep't of Pub. Welfare v. Haas*, 154 N.E.2d 265, 270 (Ill. 1958) (finding no right to public education for the "feeble minded").

[7] See Scott B. Sigmon, *Radical Analysis of Special Education* 21 (1987).

[8] Id. at 23.

[9] Osgood, supra note 4, at 21.

[10] See generally Osgood, supra note 4, at 21.

[11] Sigmon, supra note 7, at 22.

[12] Osgood, supra note 4, at 22.

A case from 1919 reflects this ostracism. Merritt Beattie, who was paralyzed at birth, was educated in the public schools until the fifth grade. The record indicates that he was "normal mentally" and "kept pace with the other pupils."[13] Nonetheless, after a visit to the school by a representative of the state department of public instruction, he was excluded from the regular public schools. The school district's rationale for the exclusion was that

> his physical condition and ailment produces a depressing and nauseating effect upon the teachers and school children; that by reason of his physical condition he takes up an undue portion of the teacher's time and attention, distracts the attention of other pupils, and interferes generally with the discipline and progress of the school.[14]

In addition to separate residential facilities for children with hearing, sight, or intellectual disabilities, states also began to educate children with disabilities in nonresidential public school classrooms beginning in the late 1800s.[15] They began to develop segregated education classrooms. The development of special education classrooms must be understood in relationship to the development of compulsory education and hostility to immigrants.[16] Compulsory education laws were enacted in each state between 1852 and 1918.[17] The compulsory education movement increased class size in regular public school classes and put pressure on the public school system to discard the undesirables (who included the disabled and immigrants) by dumping them into special education classrooms. Large public schools began to exist in urban areas in the United States in the early 1800s. These classes often had eighty or ninety students. In the second half of the century, schools instituted grade placement whereby students were

---

[13] *State ex rel. Beattie v. Bd. of Educ.*, 172 N.W. 153 (Wis. 1919).
[14] Id.
[15] Sigmon, supra note 7, at 22.
[16] Id.
[17] See id. at 20.

assigned according to their chronological age but differed dramatically with respect to background, interests, skills, abilities, and preparation.[18] Faced with broad differences among students in the classroom, teachers began to request "segregated settings for children who were different, uncooperative, or unsuccessful in school."[19] School districts developed generic ungraded classes for these children, which were "dumping grounds."[20] The primary population for these generic ungraded classes was immigrants, although the developing interest in intelligence testing also gave rise to the classification of many of these immigrants as in the "moron" range of intelligence.[21] Thus, educational segregation was a mechanism to remove undesirables from the regular classroom rather than offer them high-quality education.

Meanwhile, school districts also began to open some day schools for subcategories of individuals with disabilities – primarily students who were deaf or mentally retarded.[22] By 1932, 75,000 children with mental retardation were being educated in special classes. Ironically, the category of mental retardation received little attention until compulsory education raised the literacy rate; children who had trouble learning to read then became more visible.[23] The rise of the mental retardation category called attention to the need to create a formal identification process. Students classified as mentally retarded were typically male immigrants of all races.[24]

Justifications for segregation of these various populations in the late nineteenth and early twentieth centuries into separate schools in urban school districts were (1) that separate schools benefited "normal"

---

[18] Osgood, supra note 4, at 22–25.

[19] Id. at 24.

[20] Id.

[21] Id. at 25.

[22] Sigmon, supra note 7, at 21.

[23] Id. Similarly, a focus on "intelligence" has been historically a mechanism to limit the franchise. See *Dunn v. Blumstein*, 405 U.S. 330, 356 (1972) ("The criterion of 'intelligent' voting is an elusive one, and susceptible of abuse").

[24] Osgood, supra note 4, at 26–27.

students by removing disruptive elements and (2) that segregated settings benefited children with disabilities because they would be surrounded by "mutual understanding, helpfulness and sympathy."[25] Special schools arose from a mixture of bureaucratic interest in controlling the classroom and a humanitarian interest in developing appropriate educational programs for children with a wide variety of disabilities.[26] Special schools were largely an urban phenomenon; rural school districts with one-room schoolhouses typically sought to exclude or expel children who presented problems.[27]

The movement toward special classes in public day schools or separate disability-only institutions, however, declined from 1930 to 1940 as a result of financial pressures.[28] Children with mental retardation returned to the regular classrooms, where little learning took place. Parents pushed for the resurrection of special classes after World War II and were often pleased with the return to that educational alternative.[29] By 1948, more than 439,000 children were educated in special settings; those numbers increased by 47 percent between 1948 and 1953.[30] Although separation was the primary method of educating children with disabilities, some parents and practitioners began expressing concern about separation in the 1940s and 1950s. As early as 1945, the International Council for Exceptional Children held a panel entitled "Segregation versus Non-Segregation of Exceptional Children."[31] Efficacy studies were conducted to determine which educational configuration made the most sense for children with mild mental retardation.[32] The dominant view continued to support segregation. Studies

---

[25] Id. at 28 (quoting J. E. Wallace Wallin, *The Education of Handicapped Children* 94–97 [1924]).
[26] Id. at 31.
[27] Id. at 32–33.
[28] Id. at 37–38.
[29] See Sigmon, supra note 7, at 22.
[30] Osgood, supra note 4, at 42.
[31] Id. at 44.
[32] Id. at 47.

suggested that children with disabilities suffered rejection and isolation in mainstream classrooms. "Such rejection, it was thought, underscored the judgment that physical proximity did not necessarily lead to true integration, nor did a primarily separate setting condemn an exceptional child to permanent isolation."[33] Arthur S. Hill, education director of United Cerebral Palsy and an associate editor of the journal *Exceptional Children,* criticized the pursuit of integration as the "pursuit of a 'cliché' for its own sake."[34] His sharp critique of integration responded to an emerging mainstreaming movement.

In addition to separate schooling for children with disabilities, more residential institutions began to emerge during the 1950s. In fact, 75 percent of the residential institutions that served individuals with disabilities that existed in 1970 had been built since 1950.[35] These institutions varied widely with respect to how much education occurred within their walls. "The wide range of ages and severity of disabilities made provision of formal schooling problematic, and the educational functions of each became clouded by the institutions' multiple roles as school, hospital, penal institution, and warehouse."[36] Although this construction boom was supposed to alleviate serious overcrowding problems, those problems persisted in the 1970s.[37]

Until 1967, state and federal legislation did not focus on placing children with disabilities in the regular classroom.[38] The focus was on creating universal and compulsory educational opportunities for children with disabilities. Many disability advocates considered integration to be a less expensive and less satisfactory option than special schools or classrooms.

---

[33] Id. at 51.
[34] Id. at 53.
[35] Id. at 54–55.
[36] Id. at 55.
[37] Id.
[38] Sigmon, supra note 7, at 24.

In the 1960s and 1970s, educators began to publish articles questioning the effectiveness of self-contained schools and special education classes.[39] Their work laid the foundation for the concept of "least restrictive alternative" – that children should be educated in the most integrated setting possible.[40] The proponents of integration presented evidence that special schools and separate classrooms did not necessarily achieve better outcomes than regular classrooms with appropriate support. Further, as one proponent of integration has noted:

> Not all of those jumping on the mainstreaming bandwagon are doing so for solely egalitarian reasons. The total per capita annual expenditure is considerably less for a nonclassified student, and in this sense, mainstreaming saves money. So in this political era of fiscal austerity, the concept of mainstreaming is welcomed by many.[41]

In fact, one of the best-known critiques of the effectiveness of special education identified monetary concerns as one problem with special education. G. Orville Johnson argued:

> It is indeed paradoxical that mentally handicapped children having teachers especially trained, having more money (per capita) spent on their education, and being enrolled in classes with fewer children and a program designed to provide for their unique needs, should be accomplishing the objectives of their education at the same or at a lower level than similar mentally handicapped children who have not had these advantages and have been forced to remain in the regular grades.[42]

The disability rights movement, in some sense, became strange bedfellows with school districts that sought a less expensive way to

[39] Id. at 27–28; see also Osgood, supra note 4, at 78–84 (discussing critiques of special education).
[40] See *Welsch v. Likins*, 550 F.2d 1122, 1125 (8th Cir. 1977) (at the time, the concept was referred to as "least restrictive environment").
[41] Sigmon, supra note 7, at 32.
[42] Osgood, supra note 4, at 80 (quoting 6 Orville Johnson, *Special Education for the Mentally Handicapped – a Paradox*, 29 Exceptional Child. 62, 65–66 (1962)).

educate children with disabilities. Motivations other than attaining anti-subordination spurred some school districts to adopt integration for children with disabilities.

The racial civil rights movement also influenced the disability rights movement toward integration. Educators began to argue that there were parallels between the treatment of African Americans and that of individuals with disabilities, and that integration was necessary to eliminate negative stereotypes.[43] Increased attention to disability, especially mental retardation, arose during John F. Kennedy's presidency, particularly because of his personal family experience with mental retardation.[44] Federal funding became available to the states to support special education.

Further, disability advocates began to identify the horrific nature of many of the residential institutions for school-age children with disabilities. The number of children enrolled in such institutions rose from 40,000 in 1958 to 127,000 in 1966.[45] Investigations during the 1960s revealed that many of these institutions were deplorable and offered little or no education to children.[46] The "normalization" or deinstitutionalization movement sought to move these individuals out of disability-only institutions.[47]

Although the movement toward normalization and deinstitutionalization reached its initial impetus on behalf of individuals who were mentally retarded and who lived in institutional settings, it soon spread to concerns about other categories of disability and to children who

---

[43] Osgood, supra note 7, at 60–61.

[44] Id. at 64–66 (noting that Kennedy's sister Rosemary was identified as mentally retarded).

[45] Id. at 67.

[46] Id.

[47] "[T]he normalization principle means making available to all mentally retarded people patterns of life and conditions of everyday living which are as close as possible to the regular circumstances and ways of life of society." Id. at 94 (quoting Doug Fuchs and Lynne Fuchs, *Evaluation of the Adaptive Learning Environments Model*, 55 Exceptional Child. 155 (1988)).

received special education outside the residential institutional setting. In the 1970s, the prevailing view, even among those who ardently argued for integration of children with mild mental retardation, was that children with severe disabilities should be educated in nonresidential special education programs.[48] The National Association for Retarded Citizens supported a continuum approach under which nonresidential separate education would play an important role along with other educational alternatives.[49] Nonetheless, the continuum approach took a backseat to a presumption that children should be educated in the most integrated environment possible. Lloyd Dunn's article on the benefits of integrated education for young children with mild mental retardation[50] was used to support an integration presumption for all children with disabilities, although Dunn himself supported special education for children with more severe disabilities.[51] Dunn asserted:

> We are not arguing that we do away with our special education programs for the moderately and severely retarded, for other types of more handicapped children, or for the multiply handicapped. The emphasis is on doing something better for slow learning children who live in slum conditions, although much of what is said should also have relevance for those children who are labeling [*sic*] emotionally disturbed, perceptually impaired, brain injured, and learning disordered. Furthermore, the emphasis of the article is on children, in that no attempt is made to suggest an adequate high school environment for adolescents still functioning as slow learners.[52]

This brief history of special education reflects that it went through many stages of development. Initially, children with disabilities were excluded entirely from the school system. Then, humanitarian

[48] Id. at 96–97.
[49] Id. at 98.
[50] See Lloyd Dunn, *Special Education for the Mildly Retarded: Is Much of It Justifiable?* 35 Exceptional Child. 5 (1968).
[51] Id. at 6.
[52] For further discussion, see Osgood, supra note 7, at 80–84, 96–98.

reformers supported the creation of residential institutions for subcategories of individuals with disabilities. These humanitarian impulses were soon co-opted by those who wanted to separate out the "undesirables," including immigrants as well as individuals with disabilities. The institutions became dumping grounds or warehouses for society's outcasts. During a period of fiscal austerity in the 1930s, some children with mental retardation were returned to the regular classroom with negative results. Parents then pushed for the development of well-funded disability-only institutions in the 1950s as the United States recovered financially. Parallel to the development of disability-only institutions was the development of special education classes. This mode of education for children with disabilities was popular until the 1970s, when the separate nature of these programs was called into question. The legal discourse soon moved to an integration presumption even though many educators, in fact, called for a continuum of programs and services for individuals with disabilities.

Advocates for children with disabilities have been able to find many examples of abuse during this period. Many disability-only institutions were substandard warehouses. Many special classrooms for individuals with disabilities did not do an effective job. Nonetheless, children with disabilities who were integrated into the regular classroom did not always fare well because of negative attitudes and inadequate support. Every alternative has been problematic. As we will see in the next subpart, success in the education area has been measured by the extent to which children are educated in the most integrated setting possible rather than by whether they have received the most effective education possible.

B. Legal Developments

In response to this and other evidence of substandard educational practices for children with disabilities in the special education context, courts began to insist that such practices be ended. Because many of the children receiving a substandard education were African American, the law of special education developed alongside the law of race discrimination. This was particularly true for students who were labeled as "mentally retarded" and placed in special education rather than the regular classroom. In 1967, Judge Skelly Wright authored an opinion for the United States District Court for the District of Columbia in which he concluded that ability tracking was a mechanism to maintain de facto segregation after de jure segregation was ended in D.C. public schools.[53] He concluded that the tracking system was "tainted" by race discrimination because "of all the possible forms of ability grouping, the one that won acceptance in the District was the one that – with the exception of completely separate schools – involves the greatest amount of physical separation by grouping students in wholly distinct, homogeneous curriculum levels."[54] Throughout the opinion, Judge Wright referred to "retarded" students who were assigned to the lowest tracking level so that they could be placed with a curriculum that they could understand.[55] This track was called "special academic" and was for students who had "emotionally disturbed behavior, an IQ of 75 or below, and substandard performance on achievement tests."[56] Originally, placement in this track was mandatory for qualifying students; over time, it became possible only with parental consent. Judge Wright was very critical of the implementation of this tracking system. He found that the methodology used to place children in the lowest track was culturally biased and that assignments in early grades tended to be permanent and offered students no opportunity to take classes outside their track. Further, the special academic track was supposed to offer students remedial education, yet he found that little remedial education

[53] *Hobson v. Hansen*, 269 F. Supp. 401, 513 (D.D.C. 1967).
[54] Id. at 443.
[55] See, e.g., Id. at 444.
[56] Id. at 448.

was available in that track. Hence, the effect of being subjectively placed in the lowest track was to consign poor and African-American students to a low-skill vocational track.[57] His hundred-page opinion was a ringing indictment of the relationship between ability tracking and racial segregation.

Similar litigation was brought in Georgia, but the court did not find that the disproportionate placement of African-American children in the educable mentally retarded category violated federal law.[58] In more recent litigation, a Georgia district court found that ability tracking, even though it yielded racially disparate results, did not violate federal law or the Constitution.[59] On appeal, however, the Eleventh Circuit reversed, finding that the district court had failed to determine whether the placements were "based on present results of past segregation."[60]

Further D.C. litigation focused on the failure of the public schools to provide any education to a subclass of children with disabilities – those with mental or cognitive impairments.[61] Some of these children were never allowed to enroll in the public school system; others were suspended or expelled after they enrolled. Each of the named plaintiffs was African American.[62] Hence, disability status and race were commingled, as with the lawsuit challenging tracking.

This litigation was consistent with Lloyd Dunn's critique of special education as reflecting institutional racism. He argued: "In my best judgment, about 60 to 80 percent of the pupils taught by these teachers are children from low status backgrounds. . . . This expensive

[57] Id. at 512–13.

[58] See *Ga. State Conference of Branches of NAACP v. Georgia*, 775 F.2d 1403, 1412–13 (11th Cir. 1985).

[59] See *Thomas County Branch of the NAACP v. City of Thomasville Sch. Dist.*, 299 F. Supp. 2d 1340, 1358–59 (M.D. Ga. 2004), aff'd in part, rev'd in part sub nom. *Holton v. City of Thomasville Sch. Dist.*, 425 F.3d 1325 (11th Cir. 2005).

[60] *Holton*, 425 F.3d at 1346.

[61] See *Mills v. Bd. of Educ.*, 348 F. Supp. 866, 874 (D.D.C. 1972).

[62] Id. at 870.

proliferation of self contained special schools and classes raises serious educational and civil rights issues which must be squarely faced. It is my thesis that we must stop labeling these deprived children as mentally retarded. Furthermore, we must stop segregating them by placing them into our allegedly special programs."[63]

Lawsuits in other states challenged both exclusion and tracking. One of the earliest lawsuits challenging exclusion was brought in Pennsylvania.[64] The lawsuit was brought by the parents of thirteen children with mental retardation, alleging that they were excluded from the educational system. Under Pennsylvania law, children could be excluded from the state's compulsory education law if they were deemed "uneducable and untrainable" or had not attained a mental age of five years.[65] The case resulted in a consent decree under which the state agreed to provide all mentally retarded children with a free public education.[66] The parents wanted their children to receive a free public education; some of these parents had paid for their children to attend a private residential school during the pendency of the litigation. The focus of this litigation was ending the practice of exclusion rather than creating integrated education within the regular classroom,[67] yet the consent decree included the presumption that "placement in a regular public school class is preferable to placement in a special public school class."[68]

Similar lawsuits were brought elsewhere. Unlike the Pennsylvania case, these cases also alleged racial bias in the placement of children in the mentally retarded category. Overrepresentation of African

---

[63] See Dunn, supra note 50, at 6.

[64] See *Pa. Ass'n for Retarded Children v. Pennsylvania (PARC)*, 343 F. Supp. 279 (E.D. Pa. 1972).

[65] Id. at 282–83.

[66] Id. at 288.

[67] Id. at 297 ("Plaintiffs do not challenge the separation of special classes for retarded children from regular classes or the proper assignment of retarded children to special classes").

[68] Id. at 307.

Americans in special education continues today.[69] In 1971, six African-American children in California filed suit challenging as unconstitutional the use of standardized intelligence tests for the placement of children in classes for the "educable mentally retarded."[70] Although their case began as one brought under the Constitution, it soon expanded to include allegations of violations of race-based and disability-based federal statutes.[71] Similar litigation was brought in Chicago.[72] This litigation was unsuccessful; disagreeing with the result in the California litigation, the court concluded that the tests were not culturally biased and did not discriminate against African-American children.[73]

As in the earlier D.C. litigation, the California case provided strong evidence of how the separate, special education program was used to remove African Americans from the regular classroom through the mentally retarded label. There were three categories of children in this

[69] See generally Robert A. Garda, Jr., *The New IDEA: Shifting Educational Paradigms to Achieve Racial Equality in Special Education*, 56 Ala. L. Rev. 1071 (2005) (arguing that the Individuals with Disabilities Education Improvement Act of 2004 is a necessary, though not sufficient, step in addressing the overrepresentation of African Americans in special education programs); Daniel J. Losen & Kevin G. Welner, *Disabling Discrimination in Our Public Schools: Comprehensive Legal Challenges to Inappropriate and Inadequate Special Education Services for Minority Children*, 36 Harv. C.R.-C.L. L. Rev. 407 (2001) (advocating a combination of Title VI and disability law to combat overrepresentation of African Americans in special education programs).

[70] *Larry P. v. Riles*, 343 F. Supp. 1306, 1307 (N.D. Cal. 1972), aff'd, 502 F.2d 963 (9th Cir. 1974); see also Larry P. v. Riles, 495 F. Supp. 926 (N.D. Cal. 1979), aff'd in part, rev'd in part, 793 F.2d 969 (9th Cir. 1984) (expanding claims in earlier litigation and reaching a decision on the merits in favor of Larry P.).

[71] *See Larry P.*, 495 F. Supp. at 978–79. The intervening Supreme Court decision in *Washington v. Davis*, 426 U.S. 229, 239 (1976), in which the Court concluded that disparate impact alone did not demonstrate a constitutional violation, put pressure on statutory approaches to disparate impact arguments in the special education context. Ultimately, the *Larry P.* court concluded that federal law, but not the Fourteenth Amendment, was violated by the disproportionate enrollment of African-American children in classes for the "educable mentally retarded." *See Larry P.*, 793 F.2d at 984.

[72] *Parents in Action on Special Educ. v. Hannon*, 506 F. Supp. 831, 833 (N.D. Ill. 1980).

[73] *Hannon*, 506 F. Supp. at 882.

school system: typical children, the "educable mentally retarded," and the "trainable mentally retarded."[74] African Americans were statistically overrepresented in the "educable mentally retarded" category but not in the "trainable mentally retarded" category. If genetic or socioeconomic factors caused African Americans, in general, to have lower IQ scores than whites, then one would have expected African Americans to be disproportionately represented in *both* of the below-average IQ categories.[75] Instead, the evidence strongly suggested that the educable mentally retarded category was used to take African Americans out of the regular classroom. The separate classrooms for the educable mentally retarded were described as "dead-end" classes, which did *not* try to teach these children the regular curriculum or prepare them to reenter mainstream classes.[76]

These cases drew attention to two problems: (1) the misidentification of some children as mentally retarded and (2) the inadequate education made available to those who were identified as mentally retarded. Initially, the courts focused on the first problem. Schools that had a racial disparity in placement in the classes for children with mental retardation were required to devise a remedial plan to equalize placements.[77] So long as the appropriate racial balance existed, California could maintain its system of "dead-end" classes for children with mental retardation.

This misidentification focus continues today.[78] Schools are required to keep program data by race, ethnicity and limited English proficiency status, gender, and disability categories[79] so that the

---

[74] See Cal. Educ. Code § 56515 (West 1978) (repealed 1980).

[75] *See Larry P.*, 793 F.2d at 976.

[76] Id. at 980.

[77] Id. at 984.

[78] For a recent case involving this issue, see *Lee v. Butler County Board of Education*, No. CIV.A.70-T-3099-N, 2000 WL 33680483, at *3 (M.D. Ala. Aug. 30, 2000) (continuing to monitor overrepresentation of African-American children in the mental retardation and emotional disturbance categories and underrepresentation in the specific learning disabilities and gifted and talented special education classifications).

[79] 20 U.S.C. § 1418 (Supp. IV 2004).

government, as well as plaintiffs, can ascertain whether certain groups are disproportionately represented in certain disability categories or certain types of education programs. The assumption underlying this misidentification problem is that special education programs are inferior programs where children should not be educated unless they are genuinely mentally retarded. Separation is equated with invidious segregation. The concept that "separate is inherently unequal" has passed back and forth between disability- and race-based civil rights cases because of the historical connection between special education and racial segregation in the mental retardation context. This early case law in which courts were critical of the relationship between special education and racial segregation led, in part, to the content of the IDEA. The next section will trace the legal development and application of the integration presumption.

III. THE INTEGRATION PRESUMPTION IN PRACTICE

In response to evidence that children with disabilities were receiving a substandard education, Congress enacted the Education for All Handicapped Children[80] Act, which later was renamed the Individuals with Disabilities Education Act.[81] An "integration presumption" has been part of these statutes since 1974.[82] In order for states to receive funding under the IDEA, they must meet various criteria, including compliance with the integration presumption rule, which states:

> To the maximum extent appropriate, children with disabilities, including children in public or private institutions or other care facilities, are educated with children who are not disabled, and special classes, separate schooling, or other removal of children with

---

[80] Pub. L. No. 94-142, 89 Stat. 773.
[81] 20 U.S.C.A §§ 1400-1487 (West Supp. 2005).
[82] See Education of the Handicapped Amendments of 1974, Pub. L. No. 93-380, §613(a)(13)(B), 88 Stat. 579, 582.

disabilities from the regular educational environment occurs only when the nature or severity of the disability of a child is such that education in regular classes with the use of supplementary aids and services cannot be achieved satisfactorily.[83]

Neither the House Report nor the Senate Conference Report that accompanied adoption of this rule in 1974 discussed why it was important to the statute.[84] Although the statute has been reauthorized numerous times, with the language of this provision being unchanged, it has never received any congressional attention. On the basis of contemporary circumstances, discussed earlier, it would appear that the integration presumption was a response to reports that children with disabilities were being educated in inhumane disability-only warehouses. There was little discussion in 1974 of the more complicated question of how to configure educational resources between regular classrooms and special education classrooms within a public school building, or how to determine whether a private school that specializes in the needs of children with disabilities is the most appropriate placement for an individual child. The language of the integration presumption would appear to apply to *all* educational decisions, not simply decisions to close inhumane disability-only warehouses.

[83] 20 U.S.C.A § 1412(a)(5) (West Supp. 2005). The integration presumption is not the same as a local school presumption. Sometimes, school districts are better able to integrate children into the mainstream classroom if they do not attend their local public school. This problem may be particularly true in rural school districts, where schools are spread out and it is impossible to concentrate many specialists in each of the schools. See, e.g., *Flour Bluff Indep. Sch. Dist. v. Katherine M.*, 91 F.3d 689, 695 (5th Cir. 1996) (upholding school district's decision to place a child at a school sixteen miles away from her home rather than nine miles away from her home because of the broader range of services available at the school farther from her home). As has the Fifth Circuit, the Tenth Circuit has held that the integration presumption does not include the right to be educated at the local public school. *Murray v. Montrose County Sch. Dist. RE-1J*, 51 F.3d 921, 929 (10th Cir. 1995). This book does not question that decision.

[84] See S. Rep. No. 93-1026, at 91–96 (1974) (Conf. Rep.); H.R. Rep. No. 93-805, at 52–66 (1974).

Modern implementation of the integration presumption has been complicated, with disputes frequently arising concerning the education of children with significant cognitive or mental health impairments. The courts have varied in their willingness to implement the integration presumption in these contexts. As we will see, the Sixth Circuit has been the strictest in implementing the integration presumption – applying it even in a case in which there arguably was evidence that the more segregated educational alternative was the better choice for the individual child.[85] When faced with a similar case, the Fifth Circuit allowed the school district to overcome the disability presumption.[86] Both the Fifth and Sixth Circuits appear to have taken the integration presumption seriously, helping it to achieve some of its intended structural reforms even if the courts' decisions did not necessarily reach the right educational result for the children in the litigation. By contrast, the Fourth and Eighth Circuits appear to be applying a weak version of the integration presumption that is not achieving the integration presumption's desired structural reforms or benefiting the individual child.[87] These inconsistent results suggest the need for clearer nationwide guidelines that are consistent with sound educational policy.

The integration presumption appears to have worked better for children who do not have impairments in learning – children with mobility impairments or serious illnesses – because there is general agreement between parents and the school district that these children should be educated in a regular classroom. For such children, the dispute between parents and school districts has frequently been which regular public school a child should attend to attain a fully inclusive education rather than whether he or she should be mainstreamed into a regular public school. Courts have sometimes

---

[85] *Roncker ex rel. Roncker v. Walter*, 700 F.2d 1058, 1063 (6th Cir. 1983).

[86] *Daniel R. R. v. State Bd. of Educ.*, 874 F.2d 1036, 1048 (5th Cir. 1989).

[87] *DeBlaay ex rel. DeVries v. Fairfax County Sch. Bd.*, 882 F.2d 876, 879 (4th Cir. 1989); *N. W. ex rel. A. W. v. Nw. R-1 Sch. Dist.*, 813 F.2d 158, 163 (8th Cir. 1987).

approved the school district's decision to place the child in a regular, but not local, public school because of the greater provision of medical or other specialized services at the nonlocal public school.[88] Rather than involving the integration presumption, these cases have involved the question of whether children are entitled to be educated at their local public school.

The neighborhood public school problem can also arise in cases involving children with visual or auditory impairments. These children may need various kinds of services to enhance their ability to learn, although there is general agreement that they can be taught in a regular classroom for most, if not all, of the schoolday.[89] A school district, however, may not be able to afford to include all of the specialized services for each child in each public school. In such circumstances, the courts have typically sided with the school districts while noting that the cases do not involve the integration presumption because the

---

[88] See, e.g., *Kevin G. v. Cranston Sch. Comm.*, 130 F.3d 481, 482 (1st Cir. 1997) (upholding decision to send a student with several severe medical conditions to a school with a full-time nurse rather than reassigning the nurse to the student's local school); *Schuldt v. Mankato Indep. Sch. Dist. No. 77*, 937 F.2d 1357, 1361 (8th Cir. 1991) (upholding decision to send a child with spina bifida to a fully accessible school that was not the closest school to the student's home).

[89] Nonetheless, the appropriate site for children with hearing impairments has been controversial. There has been a lively debate within the disability community about the deaf culture movement. See generally Harlan Lane, *The Mask of Benevolence: Disabling the Deaf Community*, at xi (1992) (challenging the view that deaf people are disabled and arguing that "the deaf community is a linguistic minority"). The deaf culture community strenuously advocates for schools in which the dominant mode of communication is American Sign Language. Bonnie Tucker, *The ADA and Deaf Culture: Contrasting Precepts, Conflicting Results*, 549 Annals Am. Acad. Pol. & Soc. Sci. 24, 33–34 (1997). This debate has informed my argument that it is important for children and parents to have genuine choices in educational format so that one educational format is not devalued. Hence, a deaf environment, as an educational alternative, should be one option for a deaf child. Even if the child does not choose that educational environment, the existence of the alternative should help send the message that a deaf culture environment is valued.

parents and school district are in agreement about the appropriateness of an education in the regular public classroom.[90]

The question of whether Congress should mandate the education of children with disabilities at their closest neighborhood schools is an important issue that might have profound social implications, but it is beyond the scope of this chapter. For my purposes, it is sufficient to observe that neither parents nor school districts frequently litigate the integration presumption for children who do not have impairments in learning because there is general agreement that these children belong in the regular classroom. In addition, I have found that the presumption is infrequently litigated for children with visual or hearing impairments because school districts often try to place such children in the regular classroom. Parents and school districts are more likely to disagree with respect to the education of children with cognitive or mental health impairments. Thus, I will focus on those children when examining the case law and empirical literature to see what we can learn about the most appropriate educational configuration for them.

A. Rigid Application of the Integration Presumption

The most rigid example of the application of the integration presumption is a Sixth Circuit case in which it appears that application of the integration presumption even trumped evidence that a child with mental retardation regressed in the somewhat more integrated environment.[91] At the time of the relevant Sixth Circuit litigation, Neill Roncker was

---

[90] See, e.g., *Flour Bluff Indep. Sch. Dist. v. Katherine M.*, 91 F.3d 689, 695 (5th Cir. 1996) (child with hearing impairment educated at regional day school rather than regular school closer to the student's home so that the student could have access to a broader range of services); *Barnett v. Fairfax County Sch. Bd.*, 927 F.2d 146, 153 (4th Cir. 1991) (child with a hearing impairment educated at a high school other than the one closer to his home so that he could have access to "cued speech" services).

[91] See *Roncker ex rel. Roncker v. Walter*, 700 F.2d 1058, 1063 (6th Cir. 1983) ("Neill's progress, or lack thereof . . . is not dispositive").

nine years old and severely mentally retarded. His IQ was estimated to be below 50 and his mental age was estimated to be two to three years old with regard to most functions.[92] Although the case involved the meaning of the "least restrictive alternative" rule, the choices available to Neill were pretty limited. He could attend a segregated school, or he could attend a special education class at a regular school and therefore have access to typically developing children for lunch, gym, or recess. At the segregated school, he would be educated with children of the same chronological and developmental age. In the special education program, he would be educated with other children with disabilities, many of whom would most likely be higher functioning. Because the special education program was housed in a regular public school, he would also have limited access to typically developing children.

The school district recommended that Neill be placed in the segregated school. The parents objected and insisted that he be educated in the special education classroom within the regular public school. Everyone "agreed that Neill required special instruction; he could not be placed in educational classes with non-handicapped children."[93] For eighteen months, during the pendency of the litigation, Neill was educated in the program chosen by his parents – in a class for severely mentally retarded children at a regular elementary school. Apparently, Neill made no significant progress, or even regressed, in this classroom setting, and the school district thought he would make more progress in the segregated school because he could be educated with children of his same age and ability.

The district court ruled for the school district, finding that Neill should be educated in the segregated school.[94] The Sixth Circuit reversed the district court, holding that it had not given sufficient weight to the "least restrictive alternative" rule. The court said that

[92]   Id. at 1060.
[93]   Id. at 1061.
[94]   Id. at 1058 (citing the decision of the U.S. District Court for the Southern District of Ohio).

"since Congress has decided that mainstreaming is appropriate, the states must accept that decision if they desire federal funds."[95] Elsewhere, the Sixth Circuit described the mainstreaming rule as "a very strong congressional preference."[96]

In applying this strong congressional preference, the Sixth Circuit gave little weight to the available evidence concerning Neill's education. In the court's words, even in a situation where the "segregated facility is considered superior, the court should determine whether the services which make that placement superior could be feasibly provided in a non-segregated setting."[97] Neill's "progress, or lack thereof" was considered a "relevant factor" but "not dispositive" of the placement issue.[98] If the school district could mimic the services offered at the segregated school at Neill's regular public school, then that was the presumed superior outcome because of the mainstreaming available there. The fact that Neill apparently did not really have the ability to interact with other children was not even a factor in applying the mainstreaming presumption.[99] According to the dissent, Neill's parents argued that he should be educated in the regular school environment even "if the only benefit from such placement is to avoid the stigma of attending a special school."[100] It was not necessary for the evidence to reflect that Neill benefited from the interactions with typically developing children at lunch, recess, and gym. Apparently, Neill did not interact with the typically developing children; he only observed them.[101] His parents simply needed to invoke the mainstreaming presumption for Neill to be placed in a regular school.

[95] Id. at 1062.
[96] Id. at 1063.
[97] Id.
[98] Id.
[99] Id. at 1064 (Kennedy, J., dissenting).
[100] Id. at 1065. It seems unlikely that Neill would have been aware of a concept as abstract as "stigma." Was it his parents who were concerned about the stigma of having a severely disabled child?
[101] Id. at 1065.

The integration presumption appears to have been irrebuttable in *Roncker*. As the court said, "Since Congress has chosen to impose that burden . . . the courts must do their best to fulfill their duty."[102] Had the court required the competing options to be weighed against each other (without operation of a presumption), the outcome might have been different. For example, as I will discuss in Part IV of this chapter, there is empirical evidence that would have supported the school district's assertion that Neill would perform better in a more segregated environment. Coupled with the available evidence about Neill's own performance, the school district might have prevailed in the absence of the operation of the integration presumption.

Supporters of the integration presumption would cite the *Roncker* case as evidence of why an integration presumption is necessary. This was not simply a case of determining which educational configuration made sense within a regular public school. It was a case involving the education of a child at a disability-only institution. It therefore went to the core of the purpose of the integration presumption – encouraging the closure of a disability-only institution.

But the *Roncker* case raises the question of what justifications should be permitted for education at a disability-only institution. In this case, the choice was between having Neill educated in special education classrooms within the public school versus educated in a disability-only institution but among his own peers with respect to age and disability. Does he really benefit from being in a more integrated environment when he is segregated within that environment? The evidence from the disability literature, which I examine in Part IV, suggests that children with severe mental retardation are often unlikely to receive significant educational benefit from being educated in the regular classroom. Neill fits that pattern; no one suggested that he should be educated in the regular classroom.

A strong presumption against education in disability-only institutions makes sense for children who can benefit from spending at least

[102] Id. at 1063.

part of their day in a regular classroom where they are exposed to the regular curriculum. In a case like *Roncker*, however, the integration presumption seems to serve a cosmetic benefit – creating the appearance of integration through the placement in a regular public school – without the child's having a meaningful integrated experience. The purpose of closing disability-only institutions was to close inhumane warehouses that were not serving the educational needs of children with disabilities. The issue in the *Roncker* case should have been whether the disability-only institution was a high-quality institution or a warehouse that provided little educational benefit to children. A strong articulation of the integration presumption diverted attention from that central issue and did not necessarily enhance Neill's education. He was placed in a regular public school irrespective of whether it could offer him more educational benefit than the segregated school. Despite the requirement that he received an "individualized" educational plan, the outcome of the case was decided on the basis of a presumption rather than individualized evidence of what program was most likely to benefit Neill.

B. Overcoming the Integration Presumption

In another case involving a child with mental retardation, the Fifth Circuit in *Daniel R. R. v. State Board of Education*[103] affirmed the school district's decision to place a child with severe mental retardation in a more segregated setting. Unlike in *Roncker*, however, the more segregated setting was not housed in a disability-only institution. This case involved the question of whether the child should be placed in a regular classroom versus a special education classroom. Because of the application of the integration presumption, the court did not, as an initial matter, weigh each educational alternative against the other. Instead, it

---

[103] 874 F.2d 1036 (5th Cir. 1989).

evaluated the available educational programs only after determining that Daniel could not flourish at all in the regular classroom.[104]

Daniel R. R. was a six-year-old boy who was severely mentally retarded. At the time of the litigation, he was in prekindergarten. His parents wanted Daniel to attend a special education class for half the day and a regular prekindergarten class for the other half of the day. The school district initially complied with the request but then decided to move Daniel out of the regular classroom. It proposed to have Daniel spend his entire academic day in the special education classroom, allowing him to mix with typically developing children only during lunch and recess. The parents objected to this change and eventually moved Daniel to a private school. The court's opinion contains no information about the private school – whether it was a regular private school or one devoted to children with disabilities.[105]

The court permitted the integration presumption to be rebutted but only on the basis of very strong evidence. The school district took the position that it need not "mainstream a child who cannot enjoy an academic benefit in regular education."[106] The parents took the position that the school district should mainstream Daniel "to provide him with the company of nonhandicapped students."[107] The court identified several factors that could guide it in determining whether the integration presumption should be overcome in a particular case: (1) "whether the state has taken steps to accommodate the handicapped child in regular education,"[108] (2) "whether the child will receive an educational benefit from regular education,"[109] and (3) "what effect the handicapped

---

[104] Id. at 1050–51.

[105] Id. at 1040.

[106] Id.

[107] Id.

[108] Id. at 1048.

[109] Id. at 1049. That "inquiry must extend beyond the educational benefits that the child may receive in regular education" when assessing whether the child will "suffer from the [mainstreaming] experience" and may consider the benefits of integration on other areas of development. Id.

child's presence has on the regular classroom environment and, thus, on the education that the other students are receiving."[110]

The court found that the evidence was so stark that the school district could overcome the integration presumption. It concluded that Daniel received no educational benefit from the regular classroom even with supplemental assistance because the curriculum would have to be modified "beyond recognition" for Daniel to benefit.[111] Further, the court found that Daniel did not participate in any class activities; thus, mainstreaming merely resulted in giving Daniel an "opportunity to associate with nonhandicapped students."[112] Arguably, the mainstream classroom even caused some harm to Daniel because he was so exhausted from the full day of programming that he sometimes fell asleep at school and might have developed a stutter from the stress.[113] Applying the final factor, the court found that Daniel's presence harmed the other students because of the disproportionate amount of time that the teacher had to devote to Daniel's needs. The court found that the "instructor must devote all or most of her time to Daniel."[114]

The court was correct to take the integration presumption seriously because the option proposed by the school district resulted in the segregation of the child within the regular public school building. The parents preferred a more genuinely integrated approach under which their child was educated in the regular classroom. The evidence from the experience with racial integration in the United States suggests caution in considering whether proposed tracking in a segregated environment within the public school is warranted. But disability is dissimilar to race, and there can be strong, legitimate reasons for a different style of teaching and curriculum for a child with a disability. The requirement that the school district demonstrate that Daniel could attain no

---

[110] Id. at 1049.
[111] Id. at 1050.
[112] Id.
[113] Id. at 1051.
[114] Id.

educational benefit[115] in the more integrated environment was unwarranted because skepticism about the value of special education for children with mental retardation should not be so profound. As I will discuss in Part IV, there is evidence in support of a segregated educational environment for some children with mental retardation.

In Daniel's case, the school district sought a segregated option and the parents sought a more integrated option. Sometimes, the rules are reversed and the integration presumption becomes an impediment to parents who desire a more segregated option for their child. Such an example involved Thomas Fisher.[116] Thomas was diagnosed as learning disabled in second grade. By fifth grade, a nationally certified school psychologist reported:

> Despite having Thomas as a student for his entire school career, the school district has maintained his placement in an inclusion program, which provided accommodations and assistance but no remediation to improve his functional literacy skills. This has worsened Thomas's situation overall and has resulted in secondary behavior concerns.
>
> Although the school district could have provided Thomas with an appropriate program and placement beginning in the first grade, this was never offered. Rather, the district continued to cling to its inclusion model as the only available option under the least restrictive environment criteria for program and placement.[117]

After several years of litigation, Thomas's parents prevailed and succeeded in placing Thomas in a special school with a very low

---

[115] See *Daniel R. R.*, 874 F.2d at 1050 ("[The court must] determine that education in the classroom cannot be achieved satisfactorily"). The Fifth Circuit used the same approach in *Brillon v. Klein Indep. Sch. Dist.*, 100 Fed. Appx. 309, 315 (5th Cir. 2004), to conclude that the school district court could educate the child, Ethan, in a special education classroom. The court concluded that the second-grade curriculum "would have to be modified beyond recognition" for Ethan to participate in the regular school environment. Id. at 313 (internal quotation marks omitted).

[116] See *Fisher v. Board of Education*, 856 A.2d 552 (Del. 2004).

[117] Id. at 555.

teacher-student ratio, consistent with the psychologist's recommendation. To reach that result, however, the Delaware Supreme Court had to conclude that "Thomas did not receive a meaningful educational benefit from the program provided by the School District."[118] As in *Daniel R. R.*, the court could only consider other educational possibilities after concluding that Thomas regressed in the regular educational program.

The "no educational benefit" standard can have two adverse consequences. First, it can cause school districts to fear recommending a more segregated setting for children with mental retardation or a learning disability even if their educational professionals make that recommendation on the basis of their genuine evaluation of the child's best interests. Second, it can force school districts or parents to exaggerate the facts to support a legal argument. "No educational benefit" is a very harsh standard. A more appropriate approach would be to focus on whether school districts had available a continuum of programs, from which the parents or school district could select the most appropriate placement.

An important feature of the school districts involved in the *Roncker* and *Daniel R. R.* litigation is that the districts appeared to have a full range of educational programs available. Inclusion in a regular classroom, special education programming within the regular public school, and disability-only institutions all appeared to be available. The question should have been which of these programs fit the needs of Neill and Daniel. These cases stand in contrast to those involving school districts that have not created a range of programming for children with disabilities, where the integration presumption has not served its structural purpose of encouraging the creation of such a range. These cases will be discussed in the next section, which will show that the integration presumption needs to continue to serve its core, structural purpose while also better serving children within school districts that offer a continuum of services.

[118] Id. at 559.

C. Disregarding the Integration Presumption

The strongest argument for implementing the integration presumption is that it hastens structural reform by making educational opportunities other than disability-only institutions available for children with disabilities. Nonetheless, some courts have failed to implement the integration presumption to achieve this structural end. Examples from the Fourth and Eighth Circuits demonstrate the continuing need for operation of the integration presumption as a means of increasing the available educational options for children with disabilities.

The facts in *N. W. ex rel. A. W. v. Northwest R-1 School District*,[119] an Eighth Circuit case, are similar to those in *Roncker*. A. W. was an elementary school–aged boy with Down's syndrome who the school district contended had severe mental retardation. The school district sought to place him in State School No. 2, while his parents wanted him to be educated in House Springs Elementary School. As in *Roncker*, everyone agreed that it did not make sense for A. W. to take academic classes with typically developing children. If he attended House Springs, he would be educated in a special, self-contained classroom with a teacher trained to meet his special needs.[120] Nonetheless, were A. W. to attend House Springs, he could interact with typically developing children on the bus to school, at lunch, at recess, and in activities such as physical education. The trial court had concluded, however, that A. W. would merely observe, rather than participate with, typically developing children during these various encounters.[121]

Although the record is unclear in *A. W.*, it appears as if the school district did not have a well-developed special education program at House Springs. In order to educate A. W., the school district would have

---

[119] 813 F.2d 158 (8th Cir. 1987).
[120] Id. at 161 n.4.
[121] Id. at 161 n.5.

to offer him a new room designed for his specific needs. That, in turn, raised the specter of substantial costs. As described by the trial court:

> The specific difficulty with placement at the House Springs School is that there is no teacher who is certified to teach severely retarded children like A. W. The addition of a teacher is not an acceptable solution here since the evidence before the Court shows that the funds available are limited so that placing a teacher at House Springs for the benefit of a few students at best, and possibly only A. W., would directly reduce the educational benefits provided to other handicapped students by increasing the number of students taught by a single tacher [*sic*] at [State School No. 2].[122]

The district court ruled for the school district, and the Eighth Circuit affirmed the district court opinion, finding that the district court could consider the cost to the school district of A. W.'s attendance at House Springs.[123] Consideration of cost therefore trumped the integration presumption. The integration presumption did not become a vehicle to require the school district to educate children with disabilities in integrated settings rather than exclusively in separate schools. Possibly, the Eighth Circuit did not understand the structural purpose behind the integration presumption rule and therefore allowed the cost of creating alternative placements to trump the integration presumption.

Similarly, the Fourth Circuit has been too eager to overcome the integration presumption without a demonstration that a school district has made available a range of educational programs for children with disabilities. Michael DeVries was a seventeen-year-old boy with autism and a measured IQ of 72.[124] Despite low academic achievement, Michael had successfully worked for three hours every other day as a hamburger assembler at a Burger King and commuted to work without assistance on public transportation. His mother wanted him to attend the

---

[122] Id. at 161.

[123] Id. at 163.

[124] *DeBlaay ex rel. DeVries v. Fairfax County Sch. Bd.*, 882 F.2d 876, 879 (4th Cir. 1989).

local public high school, which served 2,300 students, but the school district insisted that he attend either a private day school for children with disabilities or a local vocational school. DeVries's attorney sought to enter into evidence the fact that no autistic children, and only a small percentage of multihandicapped and retarded children, attended their home-based school within the school district.[125] The district court excluded the proffered evidence and the court of appeals concluded that the refusal was a harmless error because there was unlikely to be any substantial probative value from that evidence.[126] If true, however, that evidence would have helped demonstrate that the school district was not making available a continuum of services in the public schools and was not engaging in an individualized decision about what services were appropriate for children with significant cognitive or mental health impairments.

This case did not involve a fact pattern where a rural public school system could not realistically place specialists at each of its schools and therefore sought to place children with disabilities at only some of its regular public schools. Instead, a public school system had apparently decided not to allocate resources for children with autism or cognitive impairments at its large public high school. This is exactly the type of problem that the integration presumption is supposed to solve. Had the court been more aware of the purpose behind the integration presumption, it might have used it more effectively to attain that structural reform.

In sum, the case law is unsatisfactory. On the most basic level, the integration presumption does not always lead to structural reforms that would ensure that school districts offer children with cognitive or mental health impairments the opportunity to be educated in a regular public school. In addition, none of the leading circuit court cases does a satisfactory job in determining what educational configuration makes sense

[125] Id. at 880.
[126] Id.

for a child with mental retardation. The integration presumption argu-ably interfered with the Fifth and Sixth Circuits' evaluations because it precluded an even-handed analysis, while in the Fourth and Eighth Cir-cuits the presumption was not given sufficient weight. The results in the Fourth and Eighth Circuits make it clear that there is a significant risk that more school districts might seek to educate children in disability-only institutions in the absence of an integration presumption.

The integration presumption worked well to avoid that problem recently in the Tenth Circuit. Despite evidence that the child, who had an autistic spectrum disorder, would benefit from placement in a regular educational program, the school district only offered to place her in a preschool populated predominantly by children with disabil-ities.[127] That limited option was found unacceptable. It is important for courts to continue concluding that school districts are in violation of the IDEA when they do not offer a continuum of placements for children with disabilities, instead offering only a segregated placement. As I will discuss in Part V, my approach would achieve this result because school districts would not be permitted to offer only one edu-cational option. The integration presumption should be restored to its original purpose by being a vehicle to encourage school districts to create more than disability-only options for children while not displac-ing sound educational choices at school districts that have available a full continuum of educational options for children with disabilities.

There are at least three ways that these background norms can change. Congress could amend the IDEA to soften the articulation of the integration presumption. The Department of Education could promulgate regulations that provide a more flexible interpretation of the existing integration presumption. Or, the courts could try to inter-pret the integration presumption in a way that is more consistent with Congress's intentions. School districts are likely to be risk-averse and

---

[127] See *L. B. ex rel. K. B. v. Nebo Sch. Dist.*, 379 F.3d 966, 968 (10th Cir. 2004) ("Although Nebo considered the mainstream setting of Appellants' choice, Nebo offered Park View as the only school placement that it thought appropriate for K. B.").

follow federal law rather than seek litigation if these changes were made. At present, the background norm is a strong integration presumption that neither school districts nor parents are likely to challenge even if it is not serving the child's best interests. Parents are likely to be risk-averse in the education setting and are not likely to challenge the school district's decision. They are unlikely to take a lawyer to an Individualized Educational Plan (IEP) meeting, and, as people who have to work cooperatively with the school district over time, they are unlikely to risk antagonizing the school system by challenging its educational decisions.[128] Thus, the school district's recommendation is likely to govern the placement of the child in the school even if it is not consistent with sound educational practices.

If Congress, the Department of Education, or the courts were to give school districts more leeway in choosing educational options for children with disabilities, what factors should they require school districts to consider in determining educational placements? In the next two parts, I will examine the literature from the educational field to see what factors would be most appropriate.

IV. DISABILITY-BASED EMPIRICAL LITERATURE

Although Congress has presumed that a fully integrated education is preferable for children with disabilities, education researchers have considered this issue to be an open question for many types of disabilities that affect a child's ability to learn. In Part III, we saw the courts struggle with the integration presumption for children with cognitive impairments or mental health impairments. Should they look for evidence of no educational benefit to overcome the integration

---

[128] See David M. Engel, *Law, Culture, and Children with Disabilities: Educational Rights and the Construction of Difference*, 1991 Duke L.J. 166, 169 (arguing that parents may be unwilling to jeopardize relationship with school officials by challenging educational decisions).

presumption? Or is a more even-handed approach appropriate if the school district has available an array of educational alternatives? In this section, I will survey the literature on children with (A) mental retardation, (B) emotional or behavioral impairments, and (C) learning disabilities, to determine whether a presumption for full inclusion is appropriate and, if not, what factors might guide school districts and courts in thinking about the appropriate configuration of educational resources for these children. These studies support the conclusion that a fully integrated education, with proper support in the mainstream classroom, is appropriate for some children with disabilities, but it makes little sense to presume this result in advance of an individualized evaluation.

A. Mental Retardation

The argument for the integration presumption largely arose in the mental retardation context. Cases involving children with mental retardation resulted in the first consent decrees, which formed the basis for the integration presumption under the IDEA.[129] A close examination of the empirical research underlying those arguments, however, reveals that the researchers did not necessarily argue for full inclusion. Instead, they argued for the closing of disability-only institutions for children with mental retardation.

In 1968, Lloyd Dunn called for the elimination of schools for children with mild mental retardation on the basis of evidence from the racial civil rights movement showing that academically disadvantaged African-American children in racially segregated schools made less progress than those of comparable ability in integrated schools.[130]

---

[129] See *Pa. Ass'n for Retarded Children v. Pennsylvania*, 343 F. Supp. 279 (E.D. Pa. 1972) (involving a class action on behalf of disabled children challenging their exclusion from public schools); supra Part I.A (discussing the history of the IDEA).

[130] Lloyd Dunn, *Special Education for the Mildly Retarded – Is Much of It Justifiable?* 35 Exceptional Child. 5, 7 (1968).

But Dunn did not call for full integration. Instead, he proposed pullout, remedial resource rooms, staffed by special education teachers as a way to achieve a more integrated and effective education, although he did note that full inclusion might work for children with IQs in the 70 to 85 range (mild mental retardation).[131] Dunn's literature review was based on studies of a mentally retarded population with IQs of up to 85, and he only argued against special class placements for children in the IQ range of 70 to 85, but his work was soon applied to arguments for full inclusion for children with IQs in the 50 to 70 range.[132]

More recently, Douglas and Lynn Fuchs questioned studies that argue for full inclusion for children with mental retardation.[133] They contended that such studies were seriously flawed because "the researcher rarely assigned the disabled students at random to special education and mainstream classes. . . . School personnel had assigned students to programs to suit their own pedagogic purposes long before the researcher showed up, with the consequence that the mainstreamed students were stronger academically from the study's start."[134]

Similarly, Bryan Cook argued that students with mental retardation frequently need the skills of a special education teacher that a regular classroom teacher is unlikely to have.[135] Although students with severe and obvious disabilities may be well accepted in the

---

[131] Garry Hornby et al., *Controversial Issues in Special Education* 70 (1997) (noting that Dunn's argument applies to children with IQs between 70 and 85).

[132] For a general discussion of this problem, see id. at 68–70 (reviewing the development of more recent theories that extend Dunn's work to lower-IQ groups). Carlberg and Kavale corroborated Dunn's conclusions, finding that students with mental retardation in regular class placements performed as well, academically, as those placed in special classes. Conrad Carlberg & Kenneth Kavale, *The Efficacy of Special Versus Regular Class Placement for Exceptional Children: A Meta-Analysis*, 14 J. Special Educ. 295, 304 (1980).

[133] Douglas Fuchs & Lynn S. Fuchs, *What's "Special" about Special Education?*, 76 Phi Delta Kappan 522 (March 1995).

[134] Id. at 526.

[135] Bryan G. Cook, *A Comparison of Teachers' Attitudes toward Their Included Students with Mild and Severe Disabilities*, 34 J. Special Educ. 203, 210 (2001).

regular classroom, Cook argued that surveys of regular classroom teachers reveal that they "do not know how to provide instruction that meets the unique needs of students with obvious disabilities."[136] Teachers "feel ill-prepared to discuss a student [with severe disabilities] with a parent and do not feel they know how to appropriately instruct that student."[137] Prior studies may have found that students with severe disabilities fare well in the regular classroom, but Cook cautioned that those results simply reflected a model of differential expectations. "Because teachers can readily recognize the disabilities of their included students with severe and obvious disabilities (e.g., autism or multiple disabilities), atypical behavior and performance appears to be anticipated, explained, and excused and does not, therefore, engender teacher rejection."[138] Tolerance should not be equated with genuine education.

Researchers of children with mental retardation are not uniform in their generalizations. Possibly, children with mild mental retardation fare better in the regular classroom than children with severe mental retardation. Rather than presume that a particular configuration of educational resources works for such children, however, it would make sense to weigh the evidence in a particular case and to consider whether the regular classroom teacher has the skills necessary to provide the child with an appropriate and adequate education.

B. Emotional or Behavioral Impairments

The education literature does not support a strong presumption that children with emotional or behavioral impairments should be fully included in the regular classroom. Conrad Carlberg and Kenneth Kavale reviewed fifty independent studies comparing special

---

[136] Id. at 211.
[137] Id.
[138] Id. at 209.

education with full inclusion and, in general, found no differences based on type of placement. "Thus, regardless of whether achievement, personality/social, or other dependent variables were chosen for investigation, no differential placement effects emerged across studies."[139] Nonetheless, they did find an effect based on type of disability. "The findings suggest no justification for placement of low-IQ children . . . in special classes. Some justification in the form of positive gain in academic and social variables was found for special class placement of LD [learning disabled] and BD/ED [behaviorally, emotionally disturbed] children."[140] The authors therefore concluded:

> This finding suggests that the present trend towards mainstreaming by regular class placement may not be appropriate for certain children. Special class placement was not uniformly detrimental, but appears to show differential effects related to category of exceptionality. MacMillan (1971) warned that "special educators must not allow the present issue to become one of special class versus regular class placement lest they find themselves in a quagmire analogous to that which resulted from the nature-nurture debate over intelligence."[141]

Similarly, Paul Sindelar and Stanley Deno reviewed seventeen studies and concluded that "resource programs can be effective in improving the achievement of children identified by teachers as exhibiting learning or behavior problems."[142]

The previous two literature reviews were conducted more than twenty years ago. In a more recent article, James Kauffman, Teresa M. Riedel, and John Wills Lloyd offered an anecdotal assessment of what kinds of

---

[139] Carlberg & Kavale, supra note 132, at 304.

[140] Id.

[141] Id. at 304–5 (quoting Donald L. MacMillan, *Special Education for the Mildly Retarded: Servant or Savant?* 2 Focus on Exceptional Child. 1, 8 (1971)).

[142] Paul T. Sindelar & Stanley L. Deno, *The Effectiveness of Resource Programming*, 12 J. Special Educ. 17, 24 (1978).

programs work best for students with severe emotional or behavioral disorders.[143] On the basis of interviews with teachers, administrators, and mental health personnel, the researchers concluded that the following conditions are necessary for educating these students: "1) a critical mass of trained, experienced, and mutually supportive personnel located in close physical proximity to one another and 2) a very low pupil/staff ratio (approximately 5:1 for students in day or residential treatment and 1:1 for the most severely disabled students.)"[144]

Kauffman and his colleagues concluded that regular classrooms are extremely unlikely to meet those criteria. On the other hand, they noted that "special schools and classes can be made safe, accepting, valuing, and productive environments for these students."[145] It is important to note that this study is discussing children with severe emotional or behavioral disorders. Kauffman and his colleagues recognize that children with severe mental health disabilities have historically been institutionalized in inappropriate settings, therefore spurring on calls for inclusion. Nonetheless, they conclude that "overenthusiasm for the regular school and the regular classroom as the sole placement options for students with disabilities has the potential for creating an equal tyranny."[146]

Another category of children who have been the subject of many empirical studies is children with autism. Children with autism spectrum disorders share a pervasive impairment in the development of reciprocal social interaction skills but vary in their verbal and nonverbal communication skills and other characteristics.[147] Much

---

[143] See James M. Kauffman et al., *Inclusion of All Students with Emotional or Behavioral Disorders? Let's Think Again*, 76 Phi Delta Kappan 542, 543–44 (1995) (discussing the common characteristics of the most effective programs for students with emotional or behavioral disorders).

[144] Id. at 544.

[145] Id. at 546.

[146] Id.

[147] See generally National Institute of Mental Health, Autism Spectrum Disorders (Pervasive Developmental Disorders), available at http://www.nimh.nih.gov/publicat/autism.cfm

controversy exists over the most appropriate way to educate these children. Nonetheless, a practice that has helped many children improve their social functioning skills is applied behaviour analysis (ABA).[148] This technique is described as follows:

> Specifically, ABA focuses on teaching small, measurable units of behaviour systematically. Simple (e.g., maintaining eye contact) and complex responses (e.g., social interaction) are analysed and broken down into small steps. Each step is taught, often in a one-to-one situation, by presenting a specific cue or instruction, and by using prompts (e.g., physical guidance, gestures) if necessary.[149]

Because of the emphasis on one-on-one instruction and the need to provide a large number of hours of instruction per week, ABA is often done in a combination of a home and school setting. Early intervention is often considered key to the success of ABA, with educators emphasizing the importance of starting the program when the child is two to three years of age. Parents often want to continue ABA therapy in grade school and sometimes find it difficult to persuade school districts to provide and pay for this kind of direct therapy.

For example, Dr. and Mr. Burilovich contested the school district's decision with regard to the education of their son, B. J., who was diagnosed as autistic at a young age.[150] As a preschooler, B. J. was receiving twenty-five to thirty hours of ABA therapy per week, and his parents had reduced his classroom time to provide more time for ABA therapy. When B. J. entered kindergarten, the parents and school district could not agree on an appropriate program because the school district was not willing to place B. J. in a setting where he could receive ABA therapy throughout the day. The parents' expert testified that B. J. was not ready to attend a mainstream kindergarten class, even

---

[148] See generally Ian Dempsey & Phil Foreman, *A Review of Educational Approaches for Individuals with Autism*, 48 Intl. J. of Disability, Development and Education (2001).
[149] Id. at 108.
[150] See *Burilovich v. Board of Education*, 208 F.3d 560 (6th Cir. 2000).

with the assistance of a paraprofessional, and that he needed to continue to receive one-on-one ABA therapy until he developed better communication skills.[151] Their experts' opinion was consistent with empirical literature that questions the effectiveness of paraprofessionals in working with children with disabilities in the mainstream classroom.[152] Deferring to local education authorities and citing the preference for integrated education, the courts approved the plan proposed by the school district and refused to order the parents reimbursed for their provision of ABA therapy. The preference for mainstream education makes it difficult for parents to offer evidence about the benefits of ABA therapy in a one-on-one situation for their child.

The empirical and educational literature increasingly supports the argument that the most appropriate education for many children with autism spectrum disorders includes "one-on-one behavioral and educational interventions that are delivered for at least 10–15 hours per week."[153] Such intervention "can be very expensive, averaging about $40,000 per child per year for a full-time program."[154] In 1999–2000, it was estimated that school districts typically paid $6,556 per child for children not receiving special education services and $18,790 per child for students receiving special education services in the autism category. One can see that school districts have a financial incentive not to raise those expenses to $40,000 per child by offering intensive one-on-one full-time programs. But it is also not appropriate for the integration presumption to be a vehicle to assist school districts to save money if the empirical evidence suggests that less-integrated environments may

---

[151] Id. at 571.

[152] See Michael F. Giangreco & Stephen M. Broer, *Questionable Utilization of Paraprofessionals in Inclusive Schools: Are We Addressing Symptoms or Causes?* 20 Focus on Autism and Other Developmental Disabilities 10 (2005).

[153] Paul T. Shattuck & Scott D. Grosse, *Issues Related to the Diagnosis and Treatment of Autism Spectrum Disorders*, 13 Mental Retardation & Developmental Disabilities 129, 132 (2007).

[154] Id. at 133.

often attain better results. If the issue is cost, then cost is what should be on the table in the discussion, but an integration presumption should not be used to hide a discussion of cost.

Thus, we can see that the empirical evidence does not support the assumption that the most integrated environment possible is the most appropriate educational environment for some children with emotional or behavioral impairments. Even if experts agree that the ultimate goal should be the inclusion of the child in the regular classroom, a period of intensive, one-on-one education may be necessary before that result may be possible. Frustrated parents, such as the Buriloviches, believe that the school district is choosing the integrated program as a means to save money, not as a means to provide a high-quality education for their children.[155] The integration presumption is a tool that school districts can use to argue for mainstreaming over the objection of parents.

C. Learning Disabilities

Studies of children with learning disabilities suggest that they often fare poorly in the regular classroom. Sindelar and Deno found that resource programs were effective in improving the academic achievement of students with learning disabilities as compared with the achievement of students simply placed in regular classrooms without resource support.[156] Similarly, Carlberg and Kavale found that students with learning disabilities in special classes (both self-contained and resource programs) had a "modest academic advantage . . . over those placed in regular classes."[157]

---

[155] See Burilovich, 208 F.3d at 571 ("Plaintiffs reiterate their assertion that the IEP was based on the availability of resources and experience of school personnel, not B. J.'s needs").

[156] Sindelar & Deno, supra note 142, at 24.

[157] Naomi Zigmond et al., *Special Education in Restructured Schools: Findings from Three Multi-Year Studies*, 76 Phi Delta Kappan 531, 532 (1995).

One reason that these early studies reported such poor results for students in regular classrooms is that these students may not have been receiving adequate support in the regular classrooms. By contrast, they were receiving special services if they were in self-contained special education classes or pull-out programs.

Naomi Zigmond sought to examine strong inclusion models to see whether they produced better results than pull-out programs for children with learning disabilities. She examined three inclusion models that focused on restructuring mainstream instruction to increase the classroom teacher's capacity to accommodate learning activities that met a greater range of student needs.[158] These were well-funded programs sponsored by major research universities seeking to incorporate validated teaching techniques. She found that the percentage of students with learning disabilities who made average or better gains than typically developing students was an average of 37 percent across sites.[159] Forty percent of the students in the study recorded gains of less than half the size of the grade level averages – what she described as a "disturbing rate."[160] On the basis of these findings, she concluded "that general education settings produce achievement outcomes for students with learning disabilities that are neither desirable nor acceptable."[161]

Admittedly, the Zigmond study did not compare students in full-inclusion placement with students receiving pull-out services. As Zigmond notes, however, the results from her study are deeply disappointing for full inclusion because the "three projects invested tremendous amounts of resources – both financial and professional – in the enhancement of services for [learning disabled] students in the mainstream setting."[162] It is certainly possible that pull-out programs

[158] Id.
[159] Id. at 533–40.
[160] Id. at 538.
[161] Id. at 539.
[162] Zigmond et al., supra note 157, at 539.

that invested amounts of resources equal to those invested in full-inclusion programs would produce better results.[163]

One problem with many of these studies is that they compare one group of children with disabilities with another group of children with disabilities, rather than comparing them with typically developing children. Children with mental retardation may do better in a regular classroom than in a resource room, but, overall, they may make insignificant academic progress. One goal of special education is to help children with

[163] The Zigmond study focused on the poor results that were achieved for a majority of students in a well-funded full-inclusion program. Critics of this study emphasize that there was no basis upon which to conclude that resource rooms or pull-out programs would have produced better results for these students. Moreover, critics argue that it is unrealistic to expect students with disabilities to make progress comparable to their peers'. Nancy Waldron and James McLeskey argue the following:

> We would concur with several other investigators who contend that the criterion for judging [Inclusive School Programs] should not be whether students with disabilities are making progress that is comparable to grade-level peers (which is tantamount to saying that the disability must be "cured"), but rather a more appropriate criterion should be that students with disabilities make at least as much progress in an inclusive setting as they would make in a non-inclusive setting.

Nancy L. Waldron & James McLeskey, *The Effects of an Inclusive School Program on Students with Mild and Severe Learning Disabilities*, 64 Exceptional Child. 395, 402 (1998) (citations omitted). Using such criteria, Waldron and McLeskey found that students with severe learning disabilities made comparable progress in reading and math in pull-out and inclusion settings, but students with mild learning disabilities were more likely to make gains commensurate with typically developing children's in reading when educated in inclusive environments than when receiving special education services in a resource room. Id. at 402–3. Madhabi Banerji and Ronald Dailey also argue that an inclusive model works well for students with disabilities. See Madhabi Banerji & Ronald A. Dailey, *A Study of the Effects of an Inclusion Model on Students with Specific Learning Disabilities*, 28 J. Learning Disabilities 511, 521 (1995) ("The data . . . were in agreement with regard to certain findings, indicating some clearly beneficial effects of the inclusion SLD [specific learning disabilities] model"). Their sample sizes, however, were small, and they had no comparison group for the study; their study is therefore of limited utility.

disabilities narrow the gap between their performance and that of their typically developing peers. None of these studies was able to report such findings. The goal of the IDEA is to provide children with disabilities an adequate education. It is hard to know whether the education is adequate if one does not measure progress over time, comparing children with disabilities with typically developing children.

Douglas Marston designed a study that overcame that problem. He compared the reading progress of students in three different delivery models: inclusion only, combined services, and pull-out only.[164] In the combined services model, students received special instruction in a pull-out resource room and general education through a team-teaching model.[165] Marston found that students in a combined-services model made the most progress.[166] The students in the combined-services model typically moved from the 15th to the 20th percentile, whereas students in the full-inclusion or resource-only model often made no progress in comparison with typically developing children.[167]

Interestingly, however, Marston found that special education resource teachers did not pursue fully inclusive models when they were given the latitude to do so. "Of the average 946 minutes per week they devoted to direct instruction with students with disabilities, 561 minutes, or 59%, of their instructional time occurred in pull-out settings."[168] Special education teachers, themselves, therefore realized the relative ineffectiveness of full inclusion and tried to incorporate a more collaborative model in full-inclusion programs. Special education teachers also preferred the combined-services model. Of the three teaching models, 71.2 percent showed moderate or significant satisfaction with the combined-services

---

[164] Douglas Marston, *A Comparison of Inclusion Only, Pull-Out Only, and Combined Service Models for Students with Mild Disabilities*, 30 J. Special Educ. 121, 123–24 (1996).

[165] Id. at 123.

[166] Id. at 125–27.

[167] Id. at 125–27.

[168] Id. at 129.

model, 58.9 percent with the pull-out only model, and 40.3 percent with the inclusion-only model.[169] To the extent that we value these teachers as having expertise based on professional experience, the data are not very supportive of a full-inclusion model.

Genevieve Manset and Melvyn Semmel conducted a broad-based review of eight different inclusive models for elementary students with mild disabilities, primarily learning disabilities, and reached a similar result.[170] They compared the results from inclusive programs with those of pull-out programs. Only two of the eight models yielded supportive findings for full-inclusion programs in reading, and only two of the five models found positive results in math.[171] Manset and Semmel concluded that "inclusive programming effects are relatively unimpressive for most students with mild disabilities, especially in view of the extraordinary resources available to many of these model programs."[172] They added "that a model of wholesale inclusive programming that is superior to more traditional special education service delivery models does not exist at present."[173]

Bryan Cook also concluded that inclusive programming may be ineffective for students with mild disabilities.[174] He surveyed the teachers of 173 students with hidden disabilities, as well as students with obvious disabilities, who were receiving inclusive programming.[175] He found that teachers were far more likely to want to exclude students with mild disabilities from their classrooms than children with severe disabilities (16.7 percent compared with 31.8 percent).[176] He explained this

---

[169] Id.

[170] Genevieve Manset & Melvyn I. Semmel, *Are Inclusive Programs for Students with Mild Disabilities Effective? A Comparative Review of Model Programs*, 31 J. Special Educ. 155, 155 (1997).

[171] Id. at 177.

[172] Id.

[173] Id. at 178.

[174] Cook, supra note 135, at 210–11.

[175] Id. at 206–7.

[176] Id. at 209.

difference in terms of a model of "differential expectations." "Students with mild or hidden disabilities are violating expectations and are rejected because they fall outside of teachers' instructional tolerance. . . . In a sense, because they do not appear significantly different from nondisabled classmates, students with hidden disabilities are held responsible and are blamed for aberrant behavior and performance."[177] Cook therefore concludes, "Considering teachers' frequent rejection of students with mild and hidden disabilities, it appears that their inclusion should not be a foregone conclusion, particularly for those students exhibiting attitudinal and behavioral problems."[178]

Researchers who support a presumption for full-inclusion models base their arguments on moral rather than empirical arguments. For example, Waldron and McLeskey conclude from their data that children should be presumptively educated in an integrated setting, although their data only support that conclusion for children with mild disabilities with respect to reading. To draw a broader conclusion, Waldron and McLeskey must rely on a theoretical or moral argument about the benefits of full inclusion. They argue that "if students with disabilities make comparable progress in two settings, then they should be educated in the less restrictive setting, as per the [Least Restrictive Environment] provision of IDEA."[179] If one does not accept as given that the IDEA presumption is appropriate, then one is left with a very limited empirical justification for the integration presumption.

Even Waldron and McLeskey, however, are not so naïve as to suggest that full inclusion is always best for children with disabilities. They note that "poorly designed, bad inclusive programs, which do not meet the needs of students with disabilities are being implemented in many parts of the country."[180] They therefore argue that "it seems to be an opportune time to begin studying how effective inclusive programs are

[177] Id.
[178] Id. at 210.
[179] Waldron & McLeskey, supra note 163, at 402.
[180] Id. at 403.

developed and what barriers exist to the development and implementation of these programs."[181] Alternatively, one could say it is time to begin studying when inclusive programs are likely to be effective and when other kinds of approaches might be more effective. One barrier to the development and implementation of effective programs may be an unwarranted integration presumption.

One justification for a full-inclusion model is that it is considered less stigmatizing to children to be educated in the regular education setting.[182] Jenkins and Heinen, however, found that older students tended to prefer a pull-out program because they considered it to be less embarrassing than inclusion programs.[183] Similarly, Padeliadu and Zigmond reported that children found a special education placement to be a more supportive, enjoyable, and quiet learning environment than their general education classroom.[184] On the basis of a survey of the literature, Lisa Aaroe and J. Ron Nelson concluded that "students tended to support and enjoy receiving instruction in the

[181] Id.

[182] See, e.g., Joseph R. Jenkins & Amy Heinen, *Students' Preferences for Service Delivery: Pull-out, In-Class, or Integrated Models*, 55 Exceptional Child. 516, 516 (1989) (noting that a common criticism of pull-out programs is that they attach "stigmas to the children who are pulled out").

[183] See Id. at 519 (finding that children who prefer pull-out programs do so because they view this option as "less embarrassing than having a specialist come into the classroom"). But see id. (observing that children who preferred inclusion frequently cited embarrassment at being "pulled-out" as the reason for their opposite choice). The authors conclude, however, that the effect of these data is to demonstrate that, "counter to the perception of many educators," students "apparently view pull-out as no more embarrassing and stigmatizing than in-class services." Id. at 520.

[184] See Susana Padeliadu & Naomi Zigmond, *Perspectives of Students with Learning Disabilities about Special Education Placement*, 1 Learning Disabilities Res. & Prac. 15, 22 (1996) (finding that the majority of children "liked going to special education class," because of the extra help they received and the "special treats or games and reinforcement systems" employed in these programs). But see Id. at 21 (explaining that other students noted that pull-out programs caused them to miss instruction on a particular subject or to miss recreation and free-time activities that took place during the scheduled time of the special education classes).

resource classroom," although they also recognized the need to study students' preferences more fully.[185] Examining the preferences of children with disabilities, Marty Abramson also concluded that "many children in special classes prefer to remain in special education programs" because social acceptance did not accompany integration.[186]

The problem is not simply that these children are not accepted by their classmates; they are often not accepted by their classroom teacher. As Abramson notes, "a number of studies have indicated that regular classroom teachers perceive handicapped children to be socially and academically inferior to regular children. However, it is these very teachers who will be required to accept handicapped children into their classrooms."[187] By contrast, special education teachers have usually become educators in order to teach children with special needs. Because of their educational background and interests, they are more likely to have a positive attitude about children with disabilities. In conclusion, there is little theoretical or empirical basis from which to presume that children with disabilities would face less stigmatization in the regular classroom, although more research is certainly warranted on this topic.

Even if one accepts the data that suggest that children with mental and emotional disorders, as well as other disabilities, fare better in special education, one still might ask whether regular education could be transformed to be more effective for these students. Douglas Fuchs and Lynn Fuchs suggest that the answer is no. They conclude, "We have found that the instructional adaptations that general educators make in response to students' persistent failure to learn are typically oriented

---

[185] Lisa Aaroe & J. Ron Nelson, *Views about Key Curricular Matters from the Perspectives of Students with Disabilities*, Current Issues in Educ., Nov. 18, 1998, http://cie.asu.edu/volume1/number8/index.html.

[186] Marty Abramson, *Implications of Mainstreaming: A Challenge for Special Education in The Fourth Review of Special Education* 315, 325 (Lester Mann & David A. Sabatino, eds., 1980).

[187] Id. at 333.

to the group, not to the individual, and are relatively minor in substance, with little chance for helping students with chronically poor learning histories."[188] They observe that although regular education provides a "productive learning environment for 90% or more of all students," it is hard to make it a productive learning environment for the 10 percent who may have a different learning style.[189]

The empirical literature regarding children with mental retardation, emotional impairments, or learning impairments does not support an integration presumption. Instead, these studies suggest that such children often benefit from education by special education teachers for at least some of the day and often attain more educational benefits when not in a fully inclusive environment. The research on effective strategies for children with disabilities, however, is relatively new and has faced serious research design challenges. We would benefit from the continued funding of such research as we seek to design educational configurations that are likely to assist children with a range of disabilities.

V. CONCLUSION

The integration presumption in the disability context has led to some profound changes in our society. The enforced segregation of children with disabilities from mainstream society, whether by refusing to educate them or by warehousing them in disability-only institutions, has typically ended. Nonetheless, about one in four children with disabilities continues to receive an education outside the regular classroom.[190]

---

[188] Fuchs & Fuchs, supra note 133, at 528.

[189] Id. at 529.

[190] See Spencer J. Salend & Laurel M. Garrick Duhaney, *The Impact of Inclusion on Students with and without Disabilities and Their Educators*, 20 Remedial & Special Educ. 114, 114 (1999) ("Approximately 73% of students with disabilities receive their instructional program in general educational classrooms").

Although full inclusion has been shown to pose significant challenges, the disability discussion has not changed to reflect these challenges. Both Congress and the U.S. Department of Education – with no suggestion to the contrary from the disability rights movement – continue to recite the mantra of full inclusion. Congress recently reauthorized the IDEA without even tinkering with the integration presumption.[191]

It is time for us to examine the cold data about the successes and failures of full integration for children with disabilities. The Department of Education can develop checklists or criteria that will help guide school districts and parents in deciding what combination of educational resources is most likely to be effective for an individual child. The department should do so while also monitoring to ensure that disability-only institutions do not reopen and that African-American children are not disproportionately resegregated through disability mislabeling. It is time for the federal government to pay attention to thirty years of research on educational outcomes for children with disabilities and to develop a more nuanced approach to the education of those children.

The Department of Education and the courts should refocus their attention so that the continuum of services regulations should be given greater weight than the integration presumption. The integration presumption should serve its historical purpose of preventing school districts from only offering segregated, disability-only education, but the presumption should not be understood to dictate that a fully inclusive education is necessarily the best educational option when a school district offers a continuum of educational alternatives. The continuum of services regulation should play a bigger role in the IEP process, with a school district failing to meet its procedural

---

[191] See Individuals with Disabilities Education Improvement Act of 2004, H.R. 1350, 108th Cong. § 612(a)(5) (2004) (enacted) (keeping the integration presumption in the "Least Restrictive Environment" paragraph).

requirements if it does not offer a continuum of services within the public school building.[192]

Under the "continuum of services" regulation, the IDEA already requires that:

(a) Each public agency shall ensure that a continuum of alternative placements is available to meet the needs of children with disabilities for special education and related services.

(b) The continuum required in paragraph (a) of this section must –

(1) Include the alternative placements listed in the definition of special education under § 300.26 (instruction in regular classes, special classes, special schools, home instruction, and instruction in hospitals and institutions); and

(2) Make provision for supplementary services (such as resource room or itinerant instruction) to be provided in conjunction with regular class placement.[193]

Greater emphasis on the continuum of services rule, and less emphasis on an integration presumption favoring full inclusion, would often attain better results in these cases.

Roncker, Daniel R. R., and *A. W.* could have been decided correctly with more emphasis on the continuum of services regulation. In *A. W.,* the school district was not offering a continuum of services.[194] Cost should not be a defense to a school district's general obligation to provide an array of educational outcomes. Because an array of options did not exist, the school district could not demonstrate that it had created an individualized educational plan that would serve A. W.'s needs. By contrast, in *Roncker* and *Daniel R. R.,* the school did apparently have an array of available

---

[192] See 34 C.F.R. § 300.551 (requiring a continuum of alternative placements).
[193] Id.
[194] *N. W. ex rel. A. W. v. Nw. R-1 Sch. Dist.,* 813 F.2d 158, 161 n.5 (8th Cir. 1987).

educational options.[195] Because an array of options existed, the courts' tasks should have been to evaluate those options and to determine whether the school district had selected an appropriate educational option. It should not be necessary for a school district to demonstrate that no educational benefit would arise from the most integrated option in order to propose a less integrated option for an individual child.

If a school district satisfies the continuum of services test, then it should be expected to follow a disability-specific checklist prepared by the U.S. Department of Education to determine whether it has chosen the appropriate placement for an individual child. Experts in the field should convene to create such a checklist. The Department of Education has taken a correct step in that direction by issuing disability-specific guidance for children with visual impairments.[196] These guidelines recognize the importance of the continuum of services rule.[197] They do not directly question the validity of the integration presumption but do note problems with its implementation:

> Some students have been inappropriately placed in the regular classroom although it has been determined that their IEPs cannot be appropriately implemented in the regular classroom even with the

[195] *Daniel R. R. v. State Bd. Of Educ.*, 874 F.2d 1036, 1043 (5th Cir. 1989) (finding that El Paso school district had an adequate "continuum of alternate placements" since the district had "experimented with a variety of alternative placements and supplementary services," including mixed placements, instructor adjustments, and placements in special education that included socialization with nondisabled children); *Roncker ex rel. Roncker v. Walter*, 700 F.2d 1058, 1061 (6th Cir. 1983) (examining a school district and finding that various options existed from total integration to total segregation, including mixed placement allowing education in a disabled-only environment, with social activities mixed).

[196] See *Educating Blind and Visually Impaired Students: Policy Guidance*, 65 Fed. Reg. 36,586 (June 8, 2000).

[197] See Id. at 36,592 ("In making decisions . . . it is essential that groups making placement determinations regarding the setting in which appropriate services are provided consider the full range of settings that could be appropriate").

necessary and appropriate supplementary aids and services. In these situations, the nature of the student's disability and individual needs could make it appropriate for the student to be placed in a setting outside of the regular classroom in order to ensure that the student's IEP is satisfactorily implemented. . . . In making placement determinations regarding children who are blind or visually impaired, it is essential that groups making decisions regarding the setting in which appropriate services are provided consider the full range of settings that could be appropriate depending on the individual needs of the blind or visually impaired student, including needs that arise from any other identified disabilities that the student may have.[198]

Although these guidelines hint that there should be an individualized process under which there is no presumption for a fully inclusive education, they never make that direct point. Instead, they recite the integration presumption before making the points noted previously.[199] If the statutory language did not contain an integration presumption, possibly policymakers would feel less constrained by that rule in offering their expert opinion.

Although experts in the field should convene to develop such a checklist, my own review of the literature suggests that the following are some of the factors that should be included:

- Is the child's self-esteem likely to be enhanced by being clustered with children of similar chronological age and ability? If so, what settings offer that kind of clustering?
- Do the teachers have sufficiently high expectations for the child's development?
- Will the child with a disability be a "token" in a particular classroom setting? If so, is that fact likely to lead to adverse consequences?

---

[198] Id.

[199] See Id. at 36,591 ("Before a disabled child can be removed from the regular classroom, the placement team . . . must consider whether the child can be educated in less restrictive settings with the use of appropriate supplementary aids and services").

- Does the school district offer educational programming to children in the regular classroom to improve their tolerance of disability diversity?
- Which teachers have special education training? Do the regular classroom teachers have any special education training? Does the regular classroom teacher know how to adapt the classroom for the child with a disability?
- If "tracking" exists, are we confident that the child with a disability has been placed in the correct "track"? Were accommodations made available so that testing and other measurements were accurate?
- Did racial bias possibly influence the determination of the child's disability status and appropriate placement?
- How old is the child? Is mainstreaming made more or less difficult because of the child's age?
- Are the parents involved in the child's education? Would the parents be more likely to be involved in one kind of educational configuration than another?
- Is one classroom setting or school smaller or larger than another? Is size of the classroom or building likely to be a factor in the child's educational success?
- What is the teacher/student ratio in the various classrooms? Is there reason to believe that a smaller teacher/student ratio would particularly benefit this child?

These factors were not closely examined in any of the leading integration presumption cases. The *A. W.* case would certainly turn out differently under consideration of these factors because the school district could not demonstrate that it had a continuum of services at all.[200] But there is no way to know how the Fifth and Sixth Circuit cases

---

[200] *A. W.*, 813 F.2d at 160 (discussing a school district in which the options for educating a retarded student were limited to regular school or a school specifically designated for and exclusively serving disabled children).

would be decided, given the paucity of the factual records and the limited scope of the issues considered by the courts.

If implemented, these factors would begin to allow us to move toward a goal of developing an individualized and adequate educational program for each child under a continuum of services model. Successful implementation requires courts to consider these factors within the educational alternatives available in a particular case so that the decision can be very concrete. In some cases, the courts appear to have considered many of these factors but at too high a level of abstraction. For example, in *Sacramento City Unified School District Board of Education v. Rachel H.*, the court appeared to make a very individualized assessment of whether Rachel would perform better in the regular classroom or the special education classroom and concluded that the regular classroom offered her the superior learning environment.[201] That conclusion was drawn from appropriate factors. Rachel's social and academic progress was assessed, and the special qualities of her regular classroom teacher were considered.[202] The problem with the decision, however, was that the regular classroom that was evaluated was not the classroom in which Rachel would be educated within the school district; it was a private school classroom from her previous grade. At the end of the opinion, the court recognized this limitation of its analysis when it said, "We cannot determine what the appropriate placement is for Rachel at the present time."[203] But the court insisted that future decisions should be made on the basis of the "principles" set forth in the court's opinion, which included the integration presumption.[204] Thus, in the future, the scales would be tipped in favor of the regular classroom because of Rachel's success in a regular, private school classroom in the hands of an apparently gifted teacher. The court failed to ask which classroom in the regular public

---

[201] 14 F.3d 1398, 1399–1402 (9th Cir. 1994).
[202] Id.
[203] Id. at 1405.
[204] Id.

school environment would best replicate the experience that Rachel had in the private school classroom. It is not clear whether the integrated nature of that classroom led to Rachel's success there, or whether that teacher's particular skills led to that success. The court assumed that all regular, integrated classrooms would be equally beneficial to Rachel without considering the uniqueness of each classroom environment.

School districts that could not demonstrate that they had available a full range of programs would be deemed presumptively in violation of the IDEA if parents were not satisfied with the single educational option made available to their child, especially if that single option were a separate educational facility. If the school district did have available a continuum of services, then courts would presume that it was acting in good faith so long as that district considered the checklist factors in determining the child's placement.

The Supreme Court properly recognized more than two decades ago that the courts "lack the specialized knowledge and experience necessary to resolve 'persistent and difficult questions of educational policy.'"[205] Courts are well equipped, however, to ensure that procedural safeguards are being followed. For that reason, the IDEA is a very process-driven statute. At present, however, the IDEA and its regulations do not contain safeguards sufficient to ensure that school districts choose the most appropriate educational placement for an individual child once the disability-only option has been rejected. The development of a checklist by educational professionals could help guide school districts to make better decisions.

The rigid integration presumption served a useful purpose. It helped us move to a system where only 5 percent of children with disabilities are educated in disability-only institutions. Now, it is time

---

[205] *Bd. of Educ. of Hendrick Hudson Cent. Sch. Dist. v. Rowley,* 458 U.S. 176, 209 (1982) (quoting *San Antonio Indep. Sch. Dist. v. Rodriguez,* 411 U.S. 1, 42 (1973)).

to focus our attention on the 95 percent of children with disabilities who spend their day in the regular public schools. What is the most appropriate configuration of resources for those children? Is the regular classroom the best place for them to be receiving their education? In particular, is the regular classroom the best place for children with significant cognitive or mental health impairments? This chapter has sought to begin, and reshape, the discussion concerning those children so that we can better meet the goals of the IDEA by creating a truly individualized educational program for them. I welcome vigorous debate on what factors school districts should consider in determining the appropriate configuration of educational resources when a continuum of educational alternatives exists and the integration presumption is not needed. As long as educational policy is governed by the integration presumption, however, that discussion is unlikely to occur.

It is disappointing that advocates for individuals with disabilities seem as resistant today as they were in 1985, when Madeleine Will suggested studying the effectiveness of full inclusion. For example, Professor Mark Weber quotes a 1978 statement by Senator Robert Stafford to support the policy basis underlying the integration presumption without questioning what empirical data could have supported that statement in both 1978 and beyond.[206] Weber recognizes that my survey of the existing empirical literature casts doubt on whether the integration presumption is better in the "run of cases."[207] Nonetheless, he insists that the correctness of the integration presumption should be measured by whether it is appropriate in the run of "litigated" cases.[208] Although I have attempted to show the presumption has not worked well in some of the most well known litigated cases, I would also disagree with Weber that that should be

---

[206] See Mark C. Weber, *Reflections on the New Individuals with Disabilities Education Improvement Act*, 58 Florida L. Rev. 7, 44 (2006).

[207] Id. at 45.

[208] Id.

the issue in deciding the appropriateness of the presumption. Litigated cases form only a small fraction of all cases involving IEPs. Yet the background norms reflected in federal education policy as reflected in the text of the IDEA and its regulations inform nearly all IEP meetings. Increased emphasis on the continuum of services regulation and more attention to the appropriate individualized outcome for each child would better serve most children with disabilities without sacrificing the gains that have been made in closing many outmoded disability-only institutions. We need to have the courage to abandon the existing integration presumption when school districts offer a continuum of educational alternatives in order to develop more appropriate individualized education programs for our children in the future.

5

Higher Education and Testing Accommodations

I N CHAPTER 4, I ARGUED THAT THE COURTS SHOULD BE more agnostic in determining whether the appropriate educational placement for a child is in the most integrated setting possible. I offered this argument from an anti-subordination perspective under which one would not presume that segregated tools are more effective than integrated tools in attaining substantive equality. Instead, I insisted that we consider what educational tools are most likely to be effective for each individual child and suggested that a "continuum of services" model under which remedies are chosen from a wide range of options would best serve the individual child.

Regrettably, some people might interpret my recommendations from Chapter 4 to suggest that I am opposed to integrated solutions. In fact, nothing could be further from the truth. When the available evidence suggests that integration is the most appropriate tool, I am an avid fan of integration.

The higher education context can demonstrate how we, in fact, could do a better job of using more integrated tools while also serving the needs of a wide cross-section of students with disabilities. To make this argument, I will focus on one aspect of higher education – testing – with particular emphasis on testing within the law school context. Because I believe that the empirical evidence must be assessed rigorously in deciding what solutions are most appropriate, I have limited myself to that context. Much of my argument, however, would apply to other contexts.

Before I present this specific argument, I would like to make a theoretical observation about what the field of disability theory can teach us about effective integration. One mantra in the disability studies field is the principle of "universal design." This principle is usually applied in the architectural context to show how we can design buildings at the outset under principles of universal design so that later we do not have to retrofit them for individuals with disabilities. Universal design facilitates integration because everyone can enter a building without advance planning.

The principle of universal design, however, does not have to be limited to the architectural context. In this chapter, we will see how the emphasis on accommodations in the testing context could be lessened if tests were developed under more universal design principles. Time-pressured exams, for example, are not just bad for students with learning disabilities. They fail to test what *many* students have learned irrespective of whether those students have learning disabilities. Fewer time-pressured exams could therefore better serve principles of universal design and help us achieve a more integrated society.

This chapter will examine two types of time-pressured tests implemented in the law school context – the Law School Admissions Test (LSAT) and timed, in-class final examinations. Because the LSAT shares many similar features with other standardized tests such as the Scholastic Aptitude Test (SAT), Medical College Admission Test (MCAT), and Graduate Record Examination (GRE), many of the arguments offered in this chapter will apply to those contexts as well. Similarly, law school exams share many similar features with exams offered in college and elsewhere, so those arguments should also translate into those other contexts. The data examined in this chapter, however, will mostly be from the law school context.

This chapter will argue that attention to the field of learning disabilities has caused many advocates for students with disabilities to suggest that they should receive extra time on examinations. This suggestion proceeds from the correct premise that language processing impairments cause some students to take longer than nondisabled students to demonstrate their knowledge and abilities. These students are therefore treated "differently" by being given extra time on examinations. Although it is true that some students proceed more slowly because of a learning disability, it is not true that the empirical literature supports the provision of extra time in the way that extra time is typically allocated. This is one area where a special treatment rather than formal equality model has prevailed in the disability arena although the empirical literature does not fully support the special treatment model.

This chapter will demonstrate that a more integrated solution is possible that would also better attain fairness for all students including students with undiagnosed disabilities who are not receiving extra time under the current model. We should take steps to reduce the speed component of most examinations, because the available empirical evidence does not support the notion that the fastest students have necessarily learned the material best. If we reduced the emphasis on speed in examinations, then there would be less need to give extra time to designated students.

To be clear, I do not dispute that it would be grossly unfair to insist that students with learning disabilities take the examinations that are currently offered in the typical time frame. Extra time for those students is a better solution than insisting that they take an exam under conditions in which they cannot demonstrate their knowledge or abilities. Nonetheless, I am suggesting that we could do *better* if we examined the empirical literature more closely and asked why exams need to have such a significant speed component. Such an approach will reveal that a more integrated solution, in fact, is preferable to the current approach.

The provision of extra time on examinations as an accommodation for some students with disabilities is well accepted. The College Board and the Law School Admissions Council have established procedures for students with disabilities to request extra time as an accommodation.[1]

---

[1] See generally, The College Board, SAT Registering with Accommodations (2007), http://www.collegeboard.com/student/testing/sat/reg/ssd.html, Law School Admissions Council, Accommodated Testing (2007), http://www.lsac.org/LSAC. asp?url=lsac/accommodated-testing.asp.

Most universities and law schools also have procedures by which such requests can be made.

Litigation has also ensued, relating to these requests for extra time. In some litigation, the plaintiff has contested the denial of a request for extra time.[2] In other litigation, the plaintiff has contested how his or her score is reported when extra time has been provided.[3] The issue in those cases is whether the score should be "flagged" to indicate that the test was taken under accommodated conditions.[4] In all of these instances, the background presumption has been that extra time is an appropriate accommodation for some students with disabilities. Similarly, it is presumed that it is appropriate to limit the amount of time provided for examinations so that they may contain a "speededness" component.[5]

[2] See, e.g., *Agranoff v. LSAC*, 17 Nat'l Disability L. Rep. 223 (D. Mass 1999) (challenging denial of extra time on LSAT); *Rothberg v. LSAC*, 28 National Disability Law Reporter 129 (10th Cir. 2004) (challenging denial of extra time on LSAT); *Buhendwa v. University of Colorado*, 34 Nat'l Disability L. Rep. 41 (10th Cir. 2007) (challenging denial of extra time on calculus final exam); *Love v. LSAC*, 34 National Disability Law Reporter 120 (E. D. Pa. 2007) (challenging denial of extra time on LSAT).

[3] See, e.g., *Doe v. NBME*, 199 F.3d 146 (3rd Cir. 1999) (challenging flagging of United States Medical Licensing Exam (USMLE) test results), *Breimhorts v. ETS*, No. C-99-338 (N.D. Calif. 2001) (challenging flagging of Graduate Management Admissions Test (GMAT) scores); see also Stephen G. Sireci, *Unlabeling the Disabled: A Perspective on Flagging Scores from Accommodated Test Administrations*, 34 Educational Researcher 1, 3 (2004).

[4] As will be discussed in Part II.C.2.b, LSAC takes the position that the test results for test takers who receive extra time have not been "validated" and therefore need to be flagged to reflect that result.

[5] The validity of speeded exams is beyond the scope of this chapter but deserves significant attention within the law school community. The psychometric literature has long supported the notion that accuracy and speededness are different variables. See generally Susan Ellerin Rindler, *Pitfalls in Assessing Test Speededness*, 16 J. Educ. Measurement 261 (1979); David J. Scrams & Deborah L. Schnipke, *Making Use of Response Times in Standardized Tests: Are Accuracy and Speed Measuring the Same Thing?*, paper presented at the Annual Meeting of the National Council on Measurement in Education, Chicago, March 1997 at 9 ("For the present data, speed and accuracy are at least separable if not orthogonal"); Jens Forster, E. Tory Higgins & Amy Taylor Bianco, *Speed/Accuracy Decisions in Task Performance: Built-in*

This chapter does not accept those presumptions. Part I assesses the literature that justifies extra time as an accommodation for some students with disabilities. It concludes that the provision of extra time as an accommodation is more controversial than is frequently recognized in the legal literature. Part II applies these observations to the LSAT and Part III applies these observations to law school examinations. Part IV concludes by asking what other approaches we might use in conducting fair exams other than extended time.

As this chapter will argue, the issue of extra time on examinations is a very complicated one. Undoubtedly, certain disabilities cause some people to perform language processing tasks more slowly than others. In other words, it may take some individuals longer to demonstrate their knowledge and understanding in a testing situation because of a disability. If these individuals with disabilities are given an insufficient amount of time to complete an exam, then we have tested for their "disability" rather than their "ability." For example, two students may be given a "reading check" to see whether they have understood material they read for homework on the previous night. If student A completes the test and student B does not complete it, then we do not know whether student B, in fact, knows the answers to the questions not completed. If student B did not complete the test as a result of a disability that impaired her processing speed, then we have measured her disability (i.e., her slow processing speed) but have not fully measured her mastery of the material. We can compare the speed of students A and B, but we cannot compare their mastery of the material under these testing conditions.

Trade-Off or Separate Strategic Concerns?, 90 Organizational Behavior and Human Decision Processes 148 (2003) (speed/accuracy trade-offs may be influenced by the strategic inclinations of the participants); Deborah L. Schnipke & David J. Scrams, *Exploring Issues of Test-Taker Behavior: Insights Gained from Response-Time Analyses*, Law School Admission Council Computerized Testing Report 98-09 (March 1999).

A typical solution to this problem is to give the individual with a disability additional time to take the examination so that she can demonstrate her ability. The complication is that individuals with disabilities are not the only ones who might better demonstrate their abilities with extra time. In my previous hypothetical, now let us assume that the test was an essay test and the students were asked to write about the material they read in the previous evening. If the testing conditions are timed, student B might not be able to answer all the questions and would certainly benefit from the provision of extra time. Even though student A was able to complete the exam in the standard time, student A might also be able to improve the quality of his answer if provided extra time. In fact, the empirical literature suggests that *most* test takers improve their performance when offered extra time.[6] A further complication is that many tests are given to compare test takers' performances; the results are curved. The LSAT and law school exams share that central feature. If extra time is to be given to some test takers in a comparative, curved context, then it is important for the extra time to be apportioned *fairly*, especially if all test takers are likely to improve performance with extra time. How much extra time is appropriate? How would one make that determination?

This chapter will offer some insight into how to think about some of those questions. It will suggest that our current approach to extra time allocation is haphazard at best. Alternatively, we could seek to lessen the "speededness" component of exams so that these basic issues of fairness arise less starkly. Unfortunately, it is not easy to create a law school exam or standardized testing instrument that is "unspeeded." Creating fair testing instruments for all students is more challenging than others have previously acknowledged. The difficulty of the exercise, however, should not cause us to stop trying to attain fairness. Fairness must be our governing principle even if our practices fall short of that goal.

---

[6]   See infra IB.

Part I of this chapter will examine the literature that supports the provision of extra time for some students with disabilities. It will argue that the "differential boost" theory that is often used to justify extra time for some students with disabilities is more complicated to apply in practice than is often recognized. Part II will apply the literature on timed exams to the LSAT. It will discuss the history of the development of the LSAT and show how it has emerged as a speeded exam that is currently used on a rank-order basis to predict first-year grades. It will argue that the LSAT is not a particularly strong predictor of those grades but that it is probably as good a predictor of such grades for students who receive extra time as for students who do not receive extra time. More importantly, this part will question why the LSAT takes its current form as a highly speeded exam that is scored on a rank-order basis. This type of examination has a disparate impact on students with undiagnosed learning disabilities as well as students who excel in accuracy but not speed (and who might make very good lawyers). Part III discusses law school exams, suggesting that they, too, often include an overemphasis on speed rather than accuracy. Part IV concludes that a focus on students with disabilities can help us see the unfairness of the LSAT and law school exams for many students, including those who do not receive accommodations. Rather than try to make these exams fairer through the accommodation process, this chapter urges the Law School Admission Council and law professors to try to make these exams fairer for all students by decreasing the emphasis on speededness.

I. THE CASE FOR EXTRA TIME

The argument for extra time as an accommodation results from two observations: (1) that certain disabilities cause students to proceed more slowly when taking written examinations and (2) that the provision of extra time "evens the playing field" so that these students can demonstrate their abilities, rather than their disabilities, when taking an exam. The first observation is well established; the second observation is more controversial.

This chapter will focus on requests for extra time by students diagnosed with a learning disability (LD)[7] or attention deficit disorder (ADD)[8] because those are the two categories that present the most requests for extra time as an accommodation, as well as the categories for which the most empirical research is available. Although these results may be generalizable to other kinds of disabilities, this chapter makes no claim for such generalizability. Given the conflicting nature of the research concerning LD and ADD, it seems important to

---

[7] This term *learning disability* (LD) has various definitions. See Kenneth A. Kavale & Steven R. Forness, *What Definitions of Disability Say and Don't Say: A Critical Analysis*, 33 J. Learning Disabilities 239 (2000). These researchers argue that the most frequently used definition of LD is the legal definition found in the Individuals with Disabilities Education Act. Id. at 240. These researchers suggest a more sophisticated, operational definition, which tries to identify more precisely the nature of the student's psychological process deficit. Id. at 251. The diagnosis of a learning disability can be challenging because the tests used to measure aptitude might, themselves, have a component that is problematic to a student with a learning disability. Hence, researchers have extensively debated how to measure the existence of a learning disability. See generally David J. Francis et al., *Defining Learning and Language Disabilities: Conceptual and Psychometric Issues with the Use of IQ Tests*, 27 Language, Speech, and Hearing Services in Schools 132 (1996); David J. Francis et al., *Psychometric Approaches to the Identification of LD: IQ and Achievement Scores Are Not Sufficient*, 38 J. of Learning Disabilities 98 (2005); Briley Proctor & Frances Prevatt, *Agreement Among Four Models Used for Diagnosing Learning Disabilities*, 36 J. of Learning Disabilities 459 (2003); Kenneth A. Kavale et al., *Responsiveness to Intervention and the Identification of Specific Learning Disability: A Critique and Alternative Proposal*, 28 Learning Disability Quarterly 2 (2005). This chapter presumes that certain students have measurable learning disabilities and does not engage the literature on how to determine the existence of a learning disability other than to discuss some problems with the methodology used by LSAC to determine the existence of a learning disability.

[8] See generally Russell A. Barkley, *Attention-Deficit Hyperactivity Disorder: A Handbook for Diagnosis and Treatment* (2006). For a discussion of the relationship between ADHD and learning disabilities, see Laurie E. Cutting & Martha Bridge Denckla, *Attention: Relationships between Attention-Deficit Hyperactivity Disorder and Learning Disabilities* in Handbook of Learning Disabilities (eds. H. Lee Swanson, Karen R. Harris & Steve Graham 2003).

proceed cautiously before making assumptions about the validity or appropriateness of accommodations.

A. Processing Speed Evidence

The educational psychology literature consistently establishes that children with LD[9] in reading have slower processing speeds than other children.[10] A recent study by Michael Weiler and a team of researchers confirmed this finding.[11] Their research documented that children with LD score within the expected range for age "on measures of Oral Language, Motor Speed, and Visual Spatial skill, but less well ... on measures of Written Language, consistent with their well-documented phonological processing problems."[12]

---

[9] See, e.g., M. Kay Runyan, *The Effect of Extra Time on Reading Comprehension Scores for University Students with and without Learning Disabilities*, 24 J. of Learning Disabilities 104 (2001).

[10] This chapter focuses on students who have a learning disability that produces slower processing times in reading. Not all students with learning disabilities, however, have difficulties with reading. Instead, they could have a deficit in language, writing, or math. See Kavale, supra note 7, at 252. There is also some dispute about the difference between a specific learning disability in reading and a reading disability. See Kenneth A. Kavale et al., *Responsiveness to Intervention and the Identification of Specific Learning Disability: A Critique and Alternative Proposal*, 28 Learning Disability Quarterly 2, 4 (2005). This chapter does not engage that dispute. Most requests for accommodations on standardized tests are from students who claim to have a learning disability in reading. See Lawrence J. Lewandowski et al., *Assessment of Reading Rate in Postsecondary Students*, 21 J. of Psychoeducational Assessment 134, 135 (2003).

[11] Michael D. Weiler et al., *Processing Speed in Children with Attention Deficit/Hyperactivity Disorder, Inattentive Type*, 6 Child Neuropsychology 218 (2000).

[12] Id. at 227. One problem with these studies as applied to law students is that they are typically performed on children. There is no consensus on how to assess reading rates of adult populations. See Lawrence J. Lewandowski et al., *Assessment of Reading Rate in Postsecondary Students*, 21 J. of Psychoeducational Assessment 134 (2003) (reporting that the curriculum-based assessment method is a more accurate testing instrument than the Denney Reading Rate measure for adult students even though the Denney is the more commonly used instrument).

The evidence about students with ADD is more complicated. Weiler and his researchers focused their attention on children with attention deficit disorders who were impulsive and inattentive but not hyperactive.[13] They concluded that these students were similar to students with LD. They experienced "diminished speed of processing."[14] From this study, they concluded that educators should consider "reducing the pace at which information is delivered" and "relaxing time constraints" for this group of students because the source of their problems may be "efficiency of cognitive processing."[15]

The Weiler study is one of many to conclude that children with slower processing speeds should be provided extra time as an accommodation for their disability.[16] As the next section will demonstrate, however, the leap from slower processing speed to extra time is more complicated than acknowledged by some researchers.

B. Extra Time as an Accommodation

From the prior discussion, it is clear that a disability makes it difficult for some students to demonstrate their knowledge under speeded circumstances because they may simply not have enough time to demonstrate their understanding. We could give extra time to the student

---

[13] Id. at 219.

[14] Id. at 229.

[15] Id. at 230.

[16] See, e.g., Jennifer Hartwig Lindstrom, *The Role of Extended Time on the SAT for Students with Learning Disabilities and/or Attention-Deficit/Hyperactivity Disorder*, 22 Learning Disabilities Research & Practice 85 (2007) (concluding that SAT results can be interpreted in the same way when students with disabilities have an extended-time administration as compared with the standard-time administration); Nicole Ofiesh et al., *Using Speeded Cognitive, Reading, and Academic Measures to Determine the Need for Extended Test Time among University Students with Learning Disabilities*, 23 Journal of Psychoeducational Assessment 35 (2005) (acknowledging the widespread use of extra time on exams and suggesting which tests are appropriate for determining allocation of extra time).

with a disability, but, then, what do we do with the other students? Should they get extra time as well?

The conventional answer, under the "differential boost" theory, is no.[17] Under this theory, students with disabilities would benefit *more* from a particular accommodation than other students. Nondisabled students are able to demonstrate their knowledge and ability through the regular exam process; their performance is not significantly affected by provision of an accommodation. By contrast, students with a disability would receive a differential boost through the provision of the accommodation. An example would be the provision of a large-typeface exam. A student with normal vision would experience no change in test performance through the use of an exam with large typeface. A student with a visual impairment, however, might have a marked increase in performance through the use of the exam with large typeface.

The differential boost theory becomes more difficult to justify in the context of an accommodation like extra time because that accommodation might benefit both students with and without disabilities. Further, whether extra time produces a "differential boost" might depend on the type of examination. A reading exam might produce different results than a math exam when extra time is allocated.

Although extra time is a frequently provided accommodation for the LSAT and law school exams, few studies have validated that accommodation under the differential boost hypothesis. Studies have been conducted of both math and reading tests.[18] On tests of

---

[17] See Lynn S. Fuchs & Douglas Fuchs, *Helping Teachers Formulate Sound Test Accommodation Decisions for Students with Learning Disabilities*, 16 Learning Disabilities Research & Practice 174, 175 (2001).

[18] For an excellent summary of these tests, see Lynn S. Fuchs & Douglas Fuchs, *Helping Teachers Formulate Sound Test Accommodation Decisions for Students with Learning Disabilities*, 16 Learning Disabilities Research & Practice 174, 175–76 (2001).

basic math skills, studies have not supported the differential boost theory. Students with learning disabilities and students without learning disabilities achieved about the same improvement in performance with extended time. The exception to this pattern was a study in which students were asked to complete complex math problems. Extended time particularly benefited students who had an underlying learning disability in reading but no learning disability with respect to math.[19]

Not all studies of reading comprehension have been able to validate the differential boost theory. A study of 400 students, 200 with and 200 without learning disabilities, was unable to confirm the differential boost theory. Students without learning disabilities benefited at least as much from extended time as students with learning disabilities.[20] By contrast, M. Kay Runyan was able to validate the differential boost theory in her study of university students.[21] She administered a reading test to thirty-one university students, sixteen of whom were identified as having learning disabilities. The students were given twenty minutes to take the test and then allowed to use whatever time was needed to complete the test, if they had not completed it within twenty minutes. For the normally achieving students, the provision of extra time made no significant difference in their performance. For students with learning disabilities, the provision of extra time made a significant difference in performance. Moreover, the extra time "evened the playing field" by causing the students with learning disabilities to have test scores that were not significantly

---

[19] Id. See also Stephen N. Elliott & Ann M. Marquart, *Extended Time as a Testing Accommodation: Its Effects and Perceived Consequences*, 70 Exceptional Children 349 (2004) (reporting that students without disabilities benefited at least as much with extra time as students with disabilities on a math test).

[20] See Fuchs et al., supra note 17, at 175–76.

[21] See M. Kay Runyan, *The Effect of Extra Time on Reading Comprehension Scores for University Students with and without Learning Disabilities*, 24 J. Learning Disabilities 104 (2001).

different from those of the normally achieving students. Without accommodations, however, their scores were significantly different.[22] Studies by Nicole Ofiesh also support the differential boost theory,[23] whereas G. E. Zuriff argues that methodological problems distort the findings from some studies that purport to support the differential boost theory.[24]

A recent study examined the differential boost theory for students with ADHD in the context of a math exam. The researchers concluded that students without ADHD actually benefited more from extra time than students with ADHD.[25] The students with ADHD were typically taking medication for their condition. They examined

---

[22] Id. at 106.

[23] With a sample size of 30 university students with learning disabilities and 30 university students without learning disabilities, Ofiesh found that the LD students, in general, received more benefit from extended time than non-LD students. See Nicole S. Ofiesh, *Using Processing Speed Tests to Predict the Benefit of Extended Test Time for University Students with Learning Disabilities*, 14 J. of Postsecondary Education and Disability 39 (2000). In a more recent study, Nicole Ofiesh, Nancy Mather & Andrea Russell also conducted research that supports the differential boost theory. See Nicole Ofiesh, Nancy Mather & Andrea Russell, *Using Speeded Cognitive, Reading, and Academic Measures to Determine the Need for Extended Test Time Among University Students with Learning Disabilities*, 23 J. of Psychoeducational Assessment 35 (2005).

[24] See G. E. Zuriff, *Extra Time for Students with Learning Disabilities: An Examination of the Maximum Potential Thesis*, 13 Applied Measurement in Education 99 (2000). Zuriff critiques five studies, not including any cited in this chapter, that purport to support the differential boost (or what he calls the maximum potential) thesis. His criticism of small sample size and research design problems would arguably apply to the Runyan and Ofiesh studies cited in this chapter. The Fuchs study, which used a much larger sample, does not support the differential boost theory, as discussed previously. Although it is true that students with learning disabilities have slower processing speeds as a result of their impairment, the Zuriff critique should make us aware that it is challenging to find appropriate responses to recognition of that disability.

[25] See Lawrence J. Lewandowski et al., *Extended Time Accommodations and the Mathematics Performance of Students with and without ADHD*, 25 J. of Psychoeducational Assessment 17, 19–20 (2007).

the number of correct answers on a math test after twelve minutes and after eighteen minutes for a group with ADHD and a control group without ADHD. The students were between ten and thirteen years of age. Although both groups benefited from extended time, the researchers found that the *nondisabled* students benefited *more* from extra time than the students with ADHD. Interestingly, they found that the performance of the two groups did not differ significantly if the students with ADHD were given time and a half, and the control group was given standard time.

What can we learn from these varied results? At a minimum, they reflect how difficult it is to determine the appropriate amount of extra time under a differential boost theory.[26] In the Runyan study, for example, it appears that the normally achieving test takers had ample time to take the test through the provision of twenty minutes. The test already felt "untimed" to them because of the provision of twenty minutes. Hence, the availability of extra time did little to boost their performance. The students with learning disabilities, however, as Runyan reported, did not typically complete the test within twenty minutes. Hence, extra time differentially boosted their performance. In the other studies, discussed previously, the normally achieving students appear to have felt that the test was "speeded" so they benefited from the provision of extra time. To see a differential boost effect, the researchers would probably have had to allow much more time for all study participants to complete the test under regular conditions in order for extra time to have little effect on the normally achieving students.

These results present a quandary for law school test administrators. If normally achieving law students find the LSAT or law school exams

---

[26] For an excellent article discussing the challenges involved in assessing the amount of extra time that is appropriate, see Nicole S. Ofiesh & Charles A. Hughes, *How Much Time? A Review of the Literature on Extended Test Time for Postsecondary Students with Learning Disabilities*, 16 J. on Postsecondary Education and Disability 2 (2002).

to be "speeded," is it fair to give extra time to students with various disabilities? If so, how do we determine how much extra time provides a "speeded" equivalence?

One significant challenge in the law school context is that each professor gives a different exam each test administration. So we cannot use historical data to predict how much extra time would provide a "speeded" equivalence. Further, the number of students who receive accommodations is so small that it is difficult even to conduct an empirical analysis. The Law School Admission Council (LSAC) has a less significant challenge because of the large number of test takers and the comparably large number of students who take the exam under conditions of accommodation. Nonetheless, the amount of extra time probably has to be individualized for each student. It is doubtful that LSAC can make a precise decision for each student irrespective of how many pieces of data it collects from physicians and others about test takers.

None of these caveats means that we should give up trying to provide extra time to some students with disabilities on exams. The empirical evidence is clear – some students do have disabilities that slow their processing speed and these students can only demonstrate mastery of the subject matter with more than the standard time allocated for exams. In the next two sections, I will explore what LSAC and law schools have done to deal with the "speededness" of their exams. In the final section, I will offer recommendations in light of these findings.

II. THE LSAT

A. Development of the LSAT

The first record of testing for admissions purposes was at Columbia Law School in 1921, when Dean Harlan Stone initiated an experimental testing program.[27] Dean Merton Ferson proposed a law school admission test in the 1920s to law school deans with the cooperation of West Publishing Company and the assistance of the psychologist George Stoddard.[28] It was administered to current first-year law students to determine whether it was a reliable predictor of their performance[29]; named the Stoddard-Ferson Aptitude Test, it was used for several years by some law schools.[30] Yale Law School began aptitude testing for admissions purposes in the mid-1920s, the University of California developed an admissions test in 1938, and the University of Iowa developed a legal aptitude test in 1943.[31]

Law school admissions were very different at that time than they are today. Students did not necessarily have to complete a four-year degree before entering law school and the number of applicants was not nearly as large as today. For example, Yale Law School sought to admit a class of 120 students out of about 400 applicants.[32] Some argued that it was better to use an aptitude test to weed out those who would not pass their first year than to use law school grades for the weeding-out process.[33]

These early tests had their critics, including Professor John H. Wigmore.[34] Wigmore was not opposed to the concept of testing, but he claimed that his data from Northwestern Law School suggested that the Stoddard-Ferson Test was not a good predictor of first-quarter

---

[27] Thomas O. White, *LSAC/LSAS: A Brief History*, 34 J. Legal Education 369 (1984).

[28] Merton L. Ferson, *Law Aptitude Examinations*, 5 The American Law School Review 563, 564 (1922–26).

[29] Id. at 564.

[30] White, supra note 27, at 369.

[31] Id. at 369–70.

[32] Albert B. Crawford & Tom Jay Gorham, *The Yale Legal Aptitude Test*, 49 The Yale Law Journal 1237, 1237 (1940).

[33] Id. at 1237.

[34] John H. Wigmore, *Juristic Psychopoyemetrology – or, How to Find Out Whether a Boy Has the Makings of a Lawyer*, 24 Ill. L. Rev. 454 (1929–1930).

grades or grades for the entire law school experience.[35] One of the test developers observed, in reply, that the Stoddard-Ferson Aptitude Test was only to be given to applicants who "have already met various standard criteria of admission to a law school"[36] and was to be only one of many criteria in law school admissions. Henry B. Witham, acting dean, College of Law, University of Tennessee, conducted a study to assess the predictive validity of the Stoddard-Ferson Aptitude Test at his law school and concluded that the test was best at predicting who would be in the bottom one-quarter of the law school class.[37] Wigmore had focused his attention on the validity of the instrument for the top quartile of the class and had done a very rudimentary analysis of only eleven students in a class of sixty-seven.[38] In fact, a fuller study of his entire data set reveals that the aptitude test did provide reasonable predictive validity for grades during law school.[39] Ironically, these early tests offered some of the highest predictive validity of any tests administered to law school applicants.

Yale Law School devised its own aptitude test, which was a ninety-minute exam and consisted of verbal comprehension, logical inference and analogies, and legal material.[40] Initially, the test had a correlation

[35] Id. In fact, an analysis of his data suggests that the test did a decent job of predicting first-year grades – as good or better than the current LSAT. The Pearson Correlation between ABRecord and law school admission test was 0.495, and between ARecord and law school admission test was 0.470. By contrast, as we will see in Part II.C the correlation between law school grades and LSAT scores is around 0.41.

[36] George D. Stoddard, *Correspondence: Legal Aptitude Tests*, 25 Ill. L. Rev. 446, 447 (1930–1931).

[37] Henry B. Witham, *Correspondence*, 25 Illinois L. Rev. 448, 450 (1930–1931) (concluding that 75 percent of those who scored in the bottom one-fourth of the test also placed in the bottom one-fourth of their law school class).

[38] Wigmore, supra note 34.

[39] See supra note 35.

[40] Crawford, supra note 32, at 1238. The content of this test appears similar to that of various modern tests except for one section in which the student is expected to recall the facts of a case five minutes after being given an opportunity to study it. Id. at 1239.

coefficient of 0.64 in predicting first-year grades in law school, which is considered good for that kind of testing instrument.[41] Because of the importance of factors such as hard work, and the variability of grading among professors, one would not expect any factors to be able to predict law school grades with absolute precision. Hence, social scientists typically consider a predictive index above 0.50 as good, and above 0.70 as excellent.[42]

These early ventures into testing caused the Association of American Law Schools to express interest in a general examination to be given to all applicants to law schools.[43] Although this interest was first expressed in 1938, serious efforts did not begin until after World War II. Most "law schools had reduced operations to a

---

[41] Id. at 1241.

[42] Id. at 1241 n. 6. Assessing the validity of such a testing instrument through a predictive validity study of first-year grades poses many difficulties. Two are worth mentioning with respect to these early attempts at validation. First, such a study only examines those who attend law school. We have no way of knowing how candidates who were denied admission would have performed. Second, the range of performance of those who are studied is relatively narrow. At Yale, for example, more than three-fourths of all grades were between 70 and 79. Id. at 1245. Crawford and Gorham use those factors as explanations for why the predictive validity coefficient fell from 0.64 to 0.55 during the course of their study. They said: "Therefore, it follows necessarily that the more any factor (whether college grades or test scores) is actually utilized in selecting students, so as to curtail their distribution by progressively cutting off the lower end, the less likely will that factor correlate with the criterion it purports to predict." Id. at 1241. Nonetheless, even their 0.55 coefficient is good within the standards of the testing community. (It was also better than the 0.46 and 0.38 values found for the Stoddard-Ferson and the Thorndike tests used at the University of Illinois and Columbia Law School, Id. at 1248, and better, we will see, than the LSAT.) They also argue that a primary purpose of the test was to weed out failures and that the failure rate did decline after the use of this test as one part of the admissions process. Id. at 1242.

[43] Thomas O. White, *LSAC/LSAS: A Brief History*, 34 J. Legal Education 369, 370 (1984).

bare minimum"[44] during the war, so interest in testing lay dormant during that period.

The first version of what is now the LSAT was developed in 1947.[45] That year also marked a time when law schools found themselves faced with a growing applicant pool as many World War II veterans sought to apply to college and law school.[46] Initially, law schools hoped to use the LSAT as one factor among many in admitting applicants and, principally, for weeding out unqualified applicants rather than using scores on a rank-order basis.[47] In the early years, it appears that the test did not produce a wide range of scores so that it could not be used on a rank-order basis.[48] Hence, suggestions were made about how to increase the difficulty of the test to produce a wider range of scores.

The LSAT was not initially developed to play the central role that it currently plays in the admissions process and law school rankings. When Yale first began offering an admissions test in 1930, it administered the test at the second stage of a two-step process.[49] When the Law School Admissions Council (LSAC) decided to develop its own LSAT examination, it actually debated whether to allow candidates to know their results on the test.[50] Had the test designers envisioned the importance the test would have in the admissions process, it is hard to imagine that they would have considered not telling the candidates their scores. Today, of course, not only do candidates know their LSAT scores, but law schools themselves know their median LSAT

---

[44] Id. at 370.

[45] William P. La Piana, *Merit and Diversity: The Origins of the Law School Admissions Test*, 48 St. Louis U. L. J. 955, 963 (2004).

[46] Id. at 962.

[47] Id. at 977.

[48] Louis Toepfer of Harvard Law School apparently complained in 1956 that everyone had high scores. Id. at 978.

[49] La Piana, supra note 45, at 956–57.

[50] Id. at 970–71.

score, which plays such a crucial role in the *U.S. News & World Report* ranking system.[51]

The most consistent theme with respect to the content of the LSAT is that it has undergone extensive change over time. The first version of the LSAT was administered in 1948 and consisted of ten sections administered over an entire day.[52] The content of the various subtests changed in nearly every testing administration; the entire test was shortened to a half-day in 1951. The content of the subtests continued to change until 1961, when an afternoon session consisting of a writing ability and a general background section was added.[53] The afternoon session continued until 1971, when it was dropped. The content of the subtests continued to change. From 1947 to 1984, LSAC experimented with forty-one different subtests on the LSAT.[54] Arguments for inclusion or exclusion tended to focus on the predictive validity of the subsection as well as difficulties with grading or scoring a section.

---

[51] LSAT score is one of the two most significant factors in the *U.S. News* ranking system. See La Piana, supra note 46, at 988. The "LSAT scores a weight of 12.5% in calculating each law school's ranking" in *US News & World Report*. David A. Thomas, *Predicting Law School Academic Performance from LSAT Scores and Undergraduate Grade Point Averages: A Comprehensive Study*, 35 Ariz. St. L. J. 1007, 1007 (2003). Further, according to a study commissioned by the Association of American Law Schools, "90% of the overall differences in ranks among schools can be explained solely by the median LSAT score of their entering classes." This factor has caused one commentator to report that there is an "arms race" among law schools for higher LSAT scores. See Williams D. Henderson & Andrew P. Morriss, *Student Quality as Measured by LSAT Scores: Migration Patterns in the U.S. News Rankings Era*, 81 Ind. L. J. 163, 165–55 (2006) (quoting AALS report).

[52] Lynda M. Reese & Ruth Anne Cotter, *A Compendium of LSAT and LSAC-Sponsored Item Types 1948–1994* (Law School Admission Council Research Report 94-01, April 1994) at 5.

[53] Id. at 6.

[54] Id. at 7–9.

In addition to the content of the test changing, the length of the test has also varied. It was a six-hour test from 1948 to 1951.[55] It then became a three-and-a-half-hour test. In 1961, it became a full-day, three-score test with scores on general background, writing, and LSAT.[56] The afternoon session was eliminated in 1971; the test became three hours and fifty minutes. In 1974, the test was reduced to three hours and twenty minutes. Presently, the test is three hours and twenty-five minutes.[57]

Today's law professors would probably be surprised at the content of the current version of the LSAT. It contains three scored sections: Logical Reasoning, Analytical Reasoning, and Reading Comprehension.[58] There is also a nonscored Writing Sample. It would be difficult to do well on this exam without studying for the specific types of questions. In the Logical Reasoning section, the test taker has to be able to identify the type of reasoning used in a section.[59] Test takers who prepare for these questions can learn skimming strategies such as eliminating answers with non-matching conclusions; otherwise, this section can require time-consuming and careful reading, which is hard to muster in the time permitted.

---

[55] Lynda M. Reese & Ruth Anne Cotter, *A Compendium of LSAT & LSAC Sponsored Item Types, 1948–1994*, LSAC Research Report 94-01, 10 (1994).

[56] Id. at 10.

[57] Id. at 11.

[58] *Kaplan Test Prep & Admissions*, Kaplan Premier Program 2008 ed. (Kaplan Publishing 2007).

[59] The hardest part of this section appeared to be the Parallel Reasoning section. The test taker is required to determine which answer choices use similar reasoning to the given argument. This section requires the test taker to analyze six arguments to find the best match. Alternatively, the test taker is asked to answer with the choice that is flawed in the same way as the given argument. Again, the test taker needs to analyze six arguments to find the best match. Finally, some questions in this section asked the test taker to identify which answer choice best describes the *method* of argument used by the author. If the test taker did not know the definition of the methods identified, this question would be very difficult.

The hardest section for a student who has not studied for the exam would probably be the Analytical Reasoning section. It consists of logic games. As various study guides explain, there are shortcuts that one can employ to do logic games such as drawing a sketch of the information provided.[60] This type of "analytical reasoning" section would seem to be easiest for students with strong nonverbal aptitude who can "see" the logic game. Anecdotally, I have been told that these questions are extremely difficult for visually impaired students, who cannot readily draw a picture of the rules from the logic game. The labeling of these sections as "logical reasoning" and "analytical reasoning" gives them apparent facial validity, but closer examination suggests that students could be both analytical and logical yet not sufficiently test-savvy to do well on these questions.[61]

The Reading Comprehension section is most similar to questions that students have probably seen on other standardized exams. They read passages and respond to questions about those passages. Studying can probably improve those skills, but, unlike the other two parts of the exam, the format of the exam questions is probably familiar to most students.

In sum, the LSAT is not an exam that a student might casually take and expect to do well. Two-thirds of the test consists of time-pressured, detailed questions that would warrant preparation.

---

[60] Kaplan, supra note 58, at 59.

[61] I sent some Logical Reasoning questions to my faculty and asked them to tell me what answers they were able to record within four minutes (the time allotted for those questions). Most faculty were able to provide me with the correct answers, but most also reported they had to use more than the allotted time to get these answers. The logic game question took several minutes to answer and caused them to exceed their time allotment. Some of the younger members of my faculty, who had helped teach in LSAT prep courses, were able to answer the questions more quickly because they knew some shortcuts. This was certainly not a scientific sample, but it was interesting to learn that most faculty had little idea what kinds of questions were being asked on the LSAT although we place significant weight on LSAT scores during the admissions process.

B. Scoring of LSAT

The LSAT is a timed testing instrument. At the present time, the LSAT consists of four scored thirty-five-minute sections and one unscored thirty-five-minute section that is used for future norming purposes.[62] These sections average around 25 questions so that students, in total, take between 101 and 103 scored questions in 140 minutes. In addition, there is a thirty-minute unscored writing section. Thus, with the inclusion of the unscored experimental section and the writing section, the total test time is three hours and twenty-five minutes. The results from the multiple choice questions are then reported on a scaled score between 120 and 180. In other words, there are sixty different outcomes that are possible on a test with about one hundred questions. Because there is no penalty for guessing, 99.2 percent of the test takers answer at least twenty questions correctly; that corresponds with a score of 125. Hence, about 80 raw score points are used to divide up students on a 55-point scale.[63]

For example, on the 2005 exam, the test was curved so that 8 scaled score points were used at the top of the scale to distinguish among the top 1 percent of the test takers. In other words, a scaled score of 172 corresponds to a raw score of 88–89, whereas a score of 180 corresponds to a raw score of 98–101.[64] Yet, a 172 is the 99.1th percentile and a 180 is the 99.9th percentile. Because of the curve, the scores are quite bunched around the mean. The mean score (50.5 percent) is 151, which corresponds to a raw score of 55. One more correct answer increases the student's scaled score to 152 and the 54.8th percentile. An equivalent 4.3 percent leap at the top of the scale would require a student to answer as many as

---

[62] Kaplan, supra note 58, at 4.
[63] LSAC, October 2005 Conversion Table, from 5LSNG5, available at www.lsac.org (2005).
[64] Id.

eighteen more answers correctly. In other words, small changes in the number of correct answers around the mean result in large percentage movements up or down the scale; scale changes in the number of correct answers result in little percentile movement at the top (or very bottom) of the scale.[65] The exact results vary from year to year, but, as it is a curved exam, there will be bunching around the mean.

It is important to understand how the LSAT is scored because it gives one a better sense of the importance of each test question. If a student's goal is to receive a perfect score, 180, the student can achieve that score with a raw score ranging from 98 to 101. Or, if a student's goal is to score in the top one percentile, then the student can achieve that result with a raw score ranging from 88 to 101 – a 13-point range. If a student takes the test for the first time and scores at the 50th percentile (151) and has a goal of raising that score to the 60th percentile (153), the student only needs to answer correctly four or five more questions.

These small differences are important because of the way law schools rank-order LSAT scores. In fact, the LSAT has a significant

---

[65] William Kidder makes this point in his article on the gender bias inherent in use of the LSAT:

> The median score on the LSAT is a 151. Starting with an example of two students, suppose that Michelle obtained a 150 on a recent LSAT and Michael scored a 152 on the same test. In practical terms, this means that Michael answered only two more questions correctly out of the 101 scored questions on the test. In the high-stakes contest of law school admissions, these two questions will place Michael at the 54th percentile of applicants and Michelle at the 46th percentile. Because there have been as many as 100,000 law school applicants in recent years, the two additional questions that Michelle missed can rank her several thousand places behind Michael in the national applicant pool.

William C. Kidder, *Portia Denied: Unmasking Gender Bias on the LSAT and Its Relationship to Racial Diversity in Legal Education*, 12 Yale J.L. & Feminism 1, 19 (2000).

error of measurement that is inherent in each score. At a 95 percent confidence interval, the error of measurement is 5.2 points.[66] Hence, a 151 score and a 153 score are statistically indistinguishable, yet the difference between those two scores is likely to have a significant impact on a candidate's ability to be admitted to a law school.[67]

For the average test taker – the candidate who scores around 151 – then small changes in the number of correct answers can have a big impact on his or her score. In turn, whether one has enough time to answer the questions could have a great influence on one's performance. LSAC has not made direct studies of the time-pressured aspect of the exam for all test takers, but its studies of accommodated students give some insight into the time-pressured elements of the test. When students with disabilities take the exam twice – once without accommodations and once with accommodations – their scores typically improve by more than 8 scaled points, which can be equivalent to a 20-percentile improvement.[68] LSAC reports that extra time–accommodated test takers indicate that they had enough time (but not too much time) to complete the multiple choice section of the exam but provides no comparative data for nonaccommodated test takers. Some regular test takers may have ample time to complete the exam, but, for those who do not, their scores may reflect their speed rather than their ability with respect to some of their responses. If accommodated test takers are given an opportunity to take the test with ample time, then it would seem appropriate for all test takers to have the same opportunity.

---

[66] Kidder, supra note 65, at 19.

[67] LSAC does report scores in a "band" to suggest that schools do not give undue weight to small differences in test scores.

[68] Andrea Thornton et al., *Accommodated Test Taker Trends and Performances for the June 1993–February 1998 LSAT Administrations*, LSAC Technical Report 01-04, 13 (2001).

C. Data on Validity

1. General Evidence on Validity

a. Validity of Overall Results   The concept of "validity" is used to explain what inferences are permissible from test results.[69] The LSAT is used as a screening device for law school admissions. There are two general ways that one could validate the LSAT for that purpose: construct or predictive validity.[70]

By *construct validity*, one means that "test responses and score correlates to some quality, attribute, or trait of persons or other objects of measurement."[71] If one used construct validity for the LSAT, one might argue that it directly measures the skills and abilities necessary to be a good lawyer. LSAC has never attempted to validate the LSAT through a construct validity model, presumably because it is nearly impossible to define the skills and abilities necessary to be a good lawyer.[72] And, if one could define those skills, it would certainly be challenging to design a test that could measure them. Skill inventories for lawyers have included such diverse abilities as collecting facts, interviewing clients, legal analysis, oral presentation, written exposition, and law office mechanics.[73]

Predictive validity models, by contrast, do not purport to measure directly the characteristics needed to be successful in law practice.

---

[69] "Broadly speaking, validity is an inductive summary of both the existing evidence for and the actual as well as potential consequences of score interpretation and use. Hence, what is to be validated is not the test or observation device as such but the inferences derived from test scores or other indicators." Samuel Messick, *Validity of Test Interpretation and Use* 2 (1990).

[70] See generally Paul Kline, *A Psychometric Primer* (2000); Samuel Messick, *Validity of Test Interpretation and Use* 7 (1990).

[71] Messick, supra note 69, at 3–4.

[72] See generally H. Russell Cort & Jack L. Sammons, *The Search for "Good Lawyering": A Concept and Model of Lawyering Competencies*, 29 Clev. St. L. Rev. 397 (1980).

[73] Id. at 401 n. 20.

Instead, "predictive validity indicates the extent to which an individual's future level on the criterion is predicted from prior test performance."[74] The criterion could be performance as a lawyer. In that case, we would ask how the LSAT score predicts future performance as a lawyer. But it is virtually impossible to define "performance as a lawyer." So, instead, LSAC seeks to validate the LSAT by saying it can help predict first-year grades in law school.[75] LSAC has never tried to validate the LSAT under the construct model; instead, it asserts that the LSAT can be used to help predict performance during law school.[76]

---

[74] Messick, supra note 69, at 7.

[75] In a predictive validity study, a correlation coefficient is generated that ranges from -1.0 to 1.0, which describes the relationship between the score and the predicted criterion (in this case, performance in law school). If the correlation coefficient were 1.0, then we would say that a perfect relationship existed between the test score and the predicted criterion. In real life, a perfect score of 1.0 is highly unusual. "If we want to know how much explanatory information the test provides, there is a common method to determine that information based on the observed coefficient. The measure of the variance in the criterion that is explained by the predictor is defined by squaring the coefficient. A correlation coefficient of 0.3, for example, means that the test explains only 9% of the variation in predicted performance. In other words, the test leaves unexplained 91% of the variance reflected in the performance measure." Michael Selmi, *Testing for Equality: Merit, Efficiency, and the Affirmative Action Debate*, 42 UCLA L. Rev. 1251, 1264 (1995).

[76] LSAC's registration information for the LSAT states: "The LSAT is designed to measure skills considered essential for success in law school: the reading and comprehension of complex texts with accuracy and insight; the organization and management of information and the ability to draw reasonable inferences from it; the ability to think critically; and the analysis and evaluation of the reasoning and arguments of others." LSAT & LSDAS Information Book at 1 (available at lsat.com). This statement by LSAC actually combines both criterion and predictive validity measures because it asserts what specific skills are needed to perform well during law school. In fact, it does not have any data proving that the test really does test for those skills; it simply knows that the test has some ability to predict performance during the first year of law school. For the purpose of this chapter, it is also interesting to note that LSAC does not assert that speed is one of the qualities needed to perform well during law school, although, as I will discuss, the test is a strong measure of speed.

The fact that LSAC does not seek to validate the LSAT under a construct model can easily be misunderstood by a layperson. Because the content of the LSAT looks a bit like material that a student might see in law school, one might think that LSAC is seeking to measure skills needed in law school directly. In fact, LSAC even claims that the test "is designed to measure skills considered essential for success in law school."[77] But, in reality, that is not an accurate way to understand their attempts to validate the testing instrument. If they were attempting to validate the test through construct validity, they would need to have psychologists closely study those who do particularly well in law school (or even as lawyers) and try to create a test that would measure the skills and abilities of those people. Construct validity is comparatively easy to determine for jobs that require physical skills. If a truck driver needs to be able to safely drive a truck, then we give applicants to be truck drivers a road test in which they demonstrate their skills. Giving an adequate road test might be time consuming so we might prefer to give a paper and pencil test to a roomful of applicants to be truck drivers. We might find, for example, that people who become successful truck drivers do well on a test that examines how to change the oil on an automobile. They may not need that skill as a truck driver, yet the acquisition of that skill correlates well with the skill that they do need.

The problem with a predictive validity model is that all sorts of extraneous or unacceptable factors might predict success in law school. For example, having a family member who is a lawyer might correlate with success in law school, as might socioeconomic status, but we would probably not consider those to be acceptable criteria for admission. One's score on a Sudoku puzzle or a crossword puzzle might also correlate with success, but those criteria might also be considered too arbitrary to be used. So, instead, LSAC administers a test that appears to be valid under a construct validity model but actually validates it under a predictive validity model.

[77] Id.

Predictive validity measures, however, do not offer strong evidence of reliability. A predictive validity coefficient for predicting something like grades is rarely higher than 0.5, which means it predicts no more than 25 percent of the variance in the outcome measure.[78] LSAC uses a predictive validity model to claim that the LSAT is a good predictor of first-year grades in law school. LSAC could probably use a test that was highly weighted toward reading comprehension and get about the same predictive validity as if it chose a test weighted heavily toward mathematics. The first test might select a heavily female population and the second test might select a heavily male population, but both might be equally valid under a predictive validity model. Hence, if several different types of test items produce the same predictive validity, then there is some arbitrariness in which test questions are actually used. LSAC has never been able to develop a testing instrument with higher than a 0.41 predictive validity coefficient, but it has developed *many* different testing instruments that achieve about that outcome. All of these testing instruments do not select the *same* population; they each select populations equally likely to do well in law school. Therefore, the fact that a testing instrument meets a benchmark score as a predictive validity measure does not mean that it could not be modified to be equally valid yet select a different population.[79]

Although LSAC has been historically satisfied with its correlation coefficient of 0.41 for predictive validity, not all educational psychologists would be comfortable with that figure. Professor M. A. Brimer's critique of correlation coefficients of 0.70 underscores the weakness of such claims:

We can assume that we have constructed an examination which has a mean of 50 and a standard deviation of 10. We can then look at the

---

[78] Selmi, supra note 75, at 1263–64.

[79] With respect to this chapter, an interesting question would be whether the LSAT's predictive validity would change if *all* applicants were given 50 percent more time to complete the exam (but it otherwise remained unchanged).

case of a candidate who obtains a mark of 50. The mark of such a candidate would be subject to such a degree of error that we could have only minimal confidence that his true mark would fall somewhere between 15 and 85. In 5% of cases our candidates with an obtained mark of 50 would have true marks outside even those limits. When one remembers the arguments that go on over the difference between as little as 5 marks in an examination, the enormity of our practice in making such discriminations is apparent.[80]

His argument suggests that it is inappropriate to use an exam on a rank-order basis with predictive validity values of 0.41.

Because predictive validity is the dominant strategy used to validate the LSAT, one should be aware of the inherent limitations of such a strategy. In a predictive validity study, one compares LSAT score to first-year grades in law school. The sample only includes those who actually attended law school. Thus, although the average LSAT score for all test takers is 151, the average LSAT score for those whose data are used in a predictive validity study is 156.[81]

From the outset, attempts were made to validate the LSAT in a predictive validity model. In 1945, Frank H. Bowles, admissions director at Columbia Law School, sought to develop an examination to assist law school admissions.[82] He asked the College Board to develop a test that would have a "correlation coefficient of 0.70 or higher."[83] By 1947, it was agreed that a test would be developed to be used by many of the leading law schools, and they would seek to have the results "correlate with first year grades."[84] By this measure, the test was considered to be successful from the outset because it was reported to correlate well with first-year grades, although it is not clear what was the exact correlation.[85]

---

[80] M. A. Brimer, *Professional Examinations*, 10 J. Soc'y Pub. Tchrs. L. 37, 43 (1968–1969).

[81] Thornton II, supra note 134, at 12.

[82] La Piana, supra note 45, at 962.

[83] Id.

[84] Id. at 964.

[85] La Piana, supra note 45, at 976.

A 0.7 correlation would be excellent because it would suggest that the LSAT could predict 49 percent of the variation in law school grades.[86] In fact, the LSAT's validity does not approach the 0.7 benchmark specified when the test was first developed. In a 2002 report, researchers for LSAC reported that the predictive validity of the LSAT, when used alone, to predict first-year grades is 0.41, meaning that it predicts about 16 percent of the variation in first-year grades.[87]

The 0.41 correlation coefficient, which has been static over time, is far worse than the goal set by LSAC when the test was first developed. As LSAC notes, there are at least two measurement reasons for that imprecision. First, there is a certain amount of measurement error inherent in the test. Schools tend to admit students within a relatively small band of LSAT scores. In real terms, there may not be much difference between students at the top and bottom of that range when we consider the 5-point error band associated with each individual score. Second, and related, the selected students within a school tend to be more homogeneous than the entire applicant pool. This is a "restricted pool" problem.[88]

The small correlation coefficient should caution us about using the LSAT on a rank-order basis. The fact that the correlation coefficient is highest for those in the top one-quarter of the pool suggests that the LSAT may be a useful mechanism for predicting who might be the most successful, though, even for that group, the correlation coefficient is only 0.46,[89] suggesting that it accounts for about 21 percent of the variance. By contrast, the LSAT is a poor predictor of law school performance for those in the bottom quartile of the exam. For the

---

[86] "An indication of how much agreement there is between sets of scores may be obtained by squaring the correlation coefficient. Thus a correlation of 0.8 indicates 64% agreement." Paul Kline, *A Psychometrics Primer* 25 (2000).

[87] See Lisa Anthony Stilwell, Susan P. Dalessandro & Lynda M. Reese, *Predictive Validity of the LSAT: A National Summary of the 2001–2002 Correlation Studies*, Law School Admission Council LSAT Technical Report 03-01 (October 2003) at 5–6.

[88] Stilwell et al., supra note 87, at 4.

[89] Id. at 5.

bottom quartile, the correlation coefficient was only 0.36 for 2001 and 0.34 for 2002, suggesting it predicts about 12 percent of the variance for those test takers.[90] Although early studies of law school admissions tests suggested that the test was particularly good at weeding out people who would otherwise have difficulty earning passing marks in law school, the current version of the LSAT does not seem to serve that purpose well.[91]

It is true that the predictive validity of the LSAT improves when used in conjunction with undergraduate grade-point average (GPA).[92] Predictive validity improves to 0.50 when used in conjunction with

[90]   Id. at 5.

[91]   This is a complicated assertion, however, because very few students currently flunk out of law school. The test does serve a "weeding out" function by causing students not to be admitted to various law schools, and we have no way of knowing how students would have performed if they had been admitted. One might argue that the fact that few students flunk out shows that the LSAT is serving its weeding-out function well. But the fact that the LSAT does not do a good job predicting who will be in the bottom quartile of the class should, at least, make us suspect that many factors other than ability as measured on the LSAT predict poor performance in law school.

[92]   Reese & Cotter, supra note 52, at 18. Although LSAC apparently studied the predictive validity of various subtests, items were retained despite poor evidence of reliability. The Practical Judgment test item fell into that category. It was used from 1975 to 1982. Id. at 19. Despite the fact that predictive validity studies showed it had "no predictive value," it was used for eight years. Id. at 19. I still remember taking this test item in 1978. Until I figured out a trick for doing this type of question, it totally baffled me. You had to indicate whether an item was a major objective, major factor, minor factor, major assumption, or unimportant issue. Id. at 74–75. Those terms were poorly defined. The trick to getting the right answer was to construct an outline. A minor factor was a subpoint on the outline. The word *minor* did not mean less important; it meant tertiary. I was not surprised to see that this test item did not correlate at all to first-year grades in law school. It probably correlated with whether someone had studied the test questions in advance. I am sure that I would have done very poorly on this section if I had not looked at the types of questions in advance. The fact that I can remember this one section of the exam nearly 30 years later suggests that it struck me as very arbitrary at the time. LSAC's own data revealed that it was an arbitrary test component, yet they used it for eight years.

undergraduate GPA, meaning that it can predict 25 percent of the variance in first-year grades.[93] That combined measure is commonly called the index and can assist schools in making admissions decisions.

But the best-known national ranking publication, *U.S. News & World Report*, does not rank on the basis of the index.[94] It separately reports schools' median LSAT score and median GPA. It then gives more weight to the LSAT than the GPA in its ranking system. Further, it does not produce a combined score for each student that takes into account both his or her LSAT and GPA. Because women, on average, perform less well than men on the LSAT but perform as well as men in law school, this ranking system disadvantages schools that have admitted women on the basis of their projected law school grades, despite their LSAT score.

One conclusion that can be drawn from this extensive discussion is that the LSAT is not a strong predictor of success in law school. Its validity, however, will depend, in part, on how law school grades themselves are determined. If the LSAT, for example, would be given under conditions of "extreme speed" and law school exams were also given under such conditions, then we would expect to see a strong correlation even if neither instrument were truly a valid measure of what is required to be a competent lawyer. But this relationship is complicated by the overall low predictive reliability of the testing instrument. One problem with an "extreme speed" testing instrument is that there may be an excessive number of students ranked at the bottom because they did not have time to do more than guess the right answer. Those students might be at the bottom of both the LSAT and law school exams, but neither exam does a very good job of distinguishing among them. A testing instrument is more likely to produce a high validity coefficient if everyone has an opportunity to demonstrate his or her knowledge because then there will not be a cluster of "guessers." On the other hand,

---

[93] Stilwell, supra note 87, at 5.

[94] *U.S. News & World Report*, Law Methodology, http://grad-schools.usnews.rankingsandreviews.com/usnews/edu/grad/rankings/about/08law_meth_brief.php (2008).

if a testing instrument is quite easy, the untimed version might produce an undifferentiated cluster at the top. The challenge is to find a testing instrument that has little or no speededness component and produces a range of responses under nonspeeded circumstances.

b. Validity of Discrete Test Items LSAC studies have also examined the characteristics of discrete test items rather than merely overall predictive validity of the examination taken as a whole. Some test items were dropped because they were hard to construct or expensive to grade. For example, the Debate test item produced relatively high predictive validity scores (between 0.44 and 0.75) but was abandoned because it "was difficult to construct."[95]

Because LSAC is constantly experimenting with the LSAT, its content has varied considerably over time. From 1976 to 1982, for example, it was mathematical in orientation because it included a section called Quantitative Comparison in which "the test taker was required to compare two quantities and state which is greater, state if they are equal, or state that there is insufficient information to make a judgment."[96] Sample test questions required the test taker to use principles of geometry to calculate angles or lengths of sides.[97] Not surprisingly, some studies showed that this section favored white males.[98] Nonetheless, this test item was as "valid" as other test items that favored reading skills because validity was defined in terms of predicting first-year grades, not using the skills necessary to be a lawyer.

LSAC has often experimented with using writing sections on the LSAT even though those sections have never been found to correlate well with success in the first year of law school. The use of these items reflects the tension between a test that is assessed on the basis of predictive validity and a test that is assessed on the basis of construct validity. Writing skills are considered important to lawyers yet do not

---

[95] Stilwell, supra note 87, at 14.
[96] Reese & Cooter, supra note 52, at 20.
[97] Id. at 79.
[98] Id. at 20.

appear to predict success in law school. A test of writing ability was used from 1961 to 1970 with a separate score being given for that part of the test.[99] "Validity studies showed that the writing measures pretested did not contribute to the prediction of writing ability and did not improve the prediction power of the LSAT."[100] A predictive validity perspective allows LSAC to justify instruments that emphasize quantitative skills because such skills will help predict first-year grades in law school. If the first year of law school, however, were transformed to look more like the practice of law, with an emphasis on polished writing, one must wonder what kind of content would have to be contained in the LSAT for it to predict first-year grades.

LSAC's conclusion that a writing test did not predict first-year grades is consistent with a finding by William Henderson that LSAT scores do a poor job of predicting grades on writing projects during law school.[101] At a highly selective national law school, where students frequently wrote papers and had high incoming LSAT scores, he found that the predictive correlation coefficient from the LSAT to in-class exams was 0.265 but dropped to 0.057 for assigned papers.[102] At a regional law school, where there were fewer assigned papers but a broader range of LSAT scores, he found that the validity coefficient dropped from 0.453 for in-class exams to 0.285 for assigned papers.[103] Those differences were statistically significant.[104] It is interesting that most, if not all, law schools require students to write papers during law school, presumably because they think that the skills developed are important to the practice of law, yet they use a testing instrument for admission to law school that does not predict whether students will

---

[99] Id. at 26.

[100] Id. at 26.

[101] William D. Henderson, *Speed as a Variable on the LSAT and Law School Exams*, Law School Admission Council Research Report 03-03 (February 2004).

[102] Id. at 12.

[103] Id. at 12.

[104] Id. at 13.

perform well on untimed written exercises like papers. Although not perfect, undergraduate GPA was a better predictor of performance on assigned papers than LSAT scores in Henderson's study.[105]

Henderson's data have some inherent limitations because he does not control for whether the paper courses use the same curve as the exam courses.[106] At most law schools, courses with papers have smaller enrollment than courses with exams and tend to have a higher overall grade distribution. The restriction in grade range makes it more difficult to have a correlation between LSAT score and grade in a writing course. Henderson did find that the LSAT score correlated better with the grade in a paper course when the paper course was a first-year legal writing course.[107] It is common for first-year legal writing courses to be graded on an established curve that models the other first-year courses, and that may help explain the higher correlation with LSAT score. Nonetheless, the correlation coefficient between grades in a first-year required legal writing course at a regional law school and LSAT was lower than between grades in courses with in-class exams and LSAT,[108] suggesting that the LSAT does a comparatively poor job of evaluating whether students can engage in high-quality legal writing.

In sum, the LSAT does a decent, but not great, job of predicting performance in law school, particularly when law school exams are timed essay exams. The type of test items that are particularly valid

[105] For the national law school sample, the correlation coefficient for Undergraduate Grade Point Average (UPGA) was 0.192 for assigned papers as compared with a correlation coefficient of 0.057 for LSAT. For the regional law school sample, the correlation coefficient for UGPA was 0.333 for assigned papers as compared with 0.285 for LSAT. Henderson does not report whether those differences are statistically significant.

[106] Henderson's data reflect that paper courses have an overall higher GPA and more restricted grade range. See William D. Henderson, *The LSAT, Law School Exams, and Meritocracy: The Surprising and Undertheorized Role of Test-Taking Speed*, 82 Tex. L. Rev. 975, 1005 (Table 7) (2003–2004).

[107] Id. at 1014.

[108] The correlation coefficients were 0.347 for first-year required legal writing and 0.480 for in-class exams. Id. at 1014.

may have little bearing on our sense of the skills actually needed to practice law. A predictive validity model, however, does not claim to be valid as a direct measure of those skills themselves.

c. Speededness The LSAT is commonly viewed as a speeded exam, with test preparation services offering coaching on how to improve performance by improving one's ability to do well in a limited time frame.[109] It is difficult to measure the speededness aspect of the LSAT directly because there is no penalty for guessing; hence, most students will mark an entry for each question. In the only rigorous study to date of a test comparable to the LSAT, the researchers concluded that the test score "was largely affected by the time limits."[110] More than half of the test takers (53 percent) found it necessary to engage in "rapid-guessing behavior" in order to complete the exam.[111]

LSAC has kept track of the "speededness" of the various subcomponents of the exam, but, as their researchers recognize, this assessment is limited, because there is no penalty for guessing.[112] The Analytical Reasoning section, for example, has been a mainstay of the exam since 1982. LSAC researchers conclude that it is not speeded because between 83 and 94 percent completed this section of the test, and more than 80 percent of all test takers reached the last item of this section.[113] Because there is no penalty for guessing on the LSAT, however, one would expect that test takers would record an answer to every question even if they did not have time to answer the questions carefully. LSAC researchers also seem inclined to conclude that a test item does not contain a speededness

---

[109] Henderson, LSAC Study, supra note 101, at 7.

[110] Id. at 5 (reporting results of study by Scrams and Schnipke).

[111] Id.

[112] "It should be noted, however, that since LSAT scores are based on the number of questions a test taker answers correctly, many test takers realize that they are unwise to leave unanswered questions at the end of the test and should guess at items they do not have time to thoughtfully answer." Reese, infra note 113, at 12.

[113] Lynda M. Reese & Ruth Ann Cotter, *A Compendium of LSAT and LSAC-Sponsored Item Types 1948–1994*, Law School Admission Council: Research Report 94-01 (April 1994) at 13.

component even when the evidence appears to suggest otherwise. For example, the Reading Comprehension section "has appeared on more forms of the LSAT than any other item type."[114] LSAC researchers concluded that "for the most part" this section was not speeded even though only 66 percent of the test takers completed this section of the exam during some administrations of the LSAT.[115]

It is unclear whether LSAC abandoned test items because of strong evidence of speededness. The Best Argument item type, for example, was used from 1949 to 1951.[116] It appeared as thirty, thirty-five, or thirty-six questions and, in some testing situations, candidates were given only one minute per test item. In that version, only 52.4 percent completed the section and 80 percent reached only twenty-two of thirty items. It was dropped after a few years of use. An "Opposite" test item was added in 1950[117]; it was apparently designed to have a speededness component. Eighty percent of the test takers reached 63 of 130 test items, and only 9.6 percent finished the section. The Data Interpretation item type, however, was used from 1949 to 1976 despite strong evidence of speededness in some versions of this test item.[118] In its most speeded version, only 49.2 percent of test takers completed the section.

In a very thoughtful study[119] and article,[120] William Henderson points out that examinations with a strong speededness component test for different abilities than untimed examinations. In other words, rank-order scores are likely to differ significantly depending on whether a test has a significant speededness component. "Within the field of psychometrics, test-taking speed and reasoning ability are

[114] Id. at 21.
[115] Id. at 21.
[116] Id. at 13.
[117] Id. at 18.
[118] Id. at 14.
[119] William D. Henderson, *Speed as a Variable on the LSAT and Law School Exams*, Law School Admission Council Research Report 03-03 (February 2004).
[120] William D. Henderson, *The LSAT, Law School Exams, and Meritocracy: The Surprising and Undertheorized Role of Test-Taking Speed*, 82 Tex. L. Rev. 975 (2003–2004).

viewed as distinct, separate abilities with little or no correlation."[121] The speededness component of the LSAT, however, does not undermine its validity within the predictive validity model used by LSAC to validate the LSAT. Because speed is also an element of performance on in-class, timed law school exams, the validity of the LSAT is actually enhanced by having a speededness component.[122]

The larger question, which will be discussed in Part II, is whether it is valid for law school exams to have a significant speededness component. LSAC is simply trying to create an exam that will predict law school performance. So long as law school performance is determined, in part, by the ability to do well on timed testing instruments, LSAC will be compelled to include a speededness component in its testing instrument to improve its predictive validity coefficient. If LSAC, by contrast, defined the validity of its testing instrument with respect to untimed papers written during law school, then it would have to redesign the test to achieve an acceptable validity coefficient.

One might argue that it does not really matter whether the LSAT has a speededness component because the content of the LSAT is largely arbitrary. Any combination of items, one might argue, is acceptable so long as those test items do a decent job of predicting who will do well in law school. That arbitrariness might be acceptable if it did not result in disparate impact on certain subgroups of law school candidates. In this chapter, I argue that timed testing instruments are particularly difficult for students with certain learning disabilities as well as various psychological disabilities such as ADHD or anxiety disorders. Some students with these disabilities request accommodations; others do not. If the test did not have a significant speededness component, then these requests for accommodation would become less necessary.

If the evidence were strong that speededness is an important component of success as a lawyer, then this disparate impact might be

---

[121] William D. Henderson, *The LSAT, Law School Exams, and Meritocracy: The Surprising and Undertheorized Role of Test-Taking Speed*, 82 Tex. L. Rev. 975, 979 (2003–2004).

[122] See generally Henderson, supra notes 119 and 121.

acceptable. But, as will be discussed later, there is no evidence that the type of speededness measured on the LSAT is important to the practice of law.

The speededness emphasis also causes another problem, which will be discussed later – it causes some students to ask for extra time when taking the LSAT so that they can have an equal opportunity to demonstrate their skills and abilities. That accommodation, in turn, raises the question of whether their test score, with extra time, is a "valid" score. Does it predict first-year grades as well for that subgroup as for all test takers? If the LSAT were not an instrument with a significant speed component, many individuals with disabilities would not have to make the request for extra time, and the question of the validity of their scores under conditions of extra time would not arise.

2. Students with Disabilities

LSAC takes the position that the LSAT is not a "valid" measuring instrument for individuals who take the exam under conditions of accommodation even though it is "valid" for all other test takers. As discussed previously, LSAC considers the 0.41 predictive validity coefficient sufficient to establish the exam's validity for all test takers.[123] To understand its rationale for the conclusion that test scores are not "valid" for extra-time test takers, one must understand how accommodations take place and what data exist on students who receive extra time as an accommodation.

a. The Accommodation Application Process Students with disabilities may request accommodations from the Law School Data Assembly Service (LSDAS) as part of the LSAT registration process. LSAC began offering accommodations for the LSAT in 1982.[124] Although no formal studies have been done of the accommodation request process, data

---

[123] See supra notes 78–80 and supporting text.

[124] Laura F. Rothstein, *Bar Admissions and the Americans with Disabilities Act*, 32 Hous. Law. 34, 36 (Oct. 1994).

collected by LSAC suggest that that process has become more rigorous over the years. A technical report prepared in October 2001 reported the frequency of accommodation requests from 1993 to 1998. Those data reflect that the number of requests for accommodations peaked in 1996–97 while the number of approved requests dropped from previous years. Subsequent to 1996, there has been a decline in the number of accommodation requests, which LSAC attributes to "administrative changes that led to more uniform guidelines for granting the approval of testing accommodations."[125] In other words, the approval process became more rigorous and the number of accommodation requests declined.

Further, the amount of time extension provided also declined during this period. In June 1993, LSAC provided double time to nearly all of the students who received time extensions. In October 1993, LSAC began to offer time and a half rather than double time to some students. Starting with October 1996, LSAC began to offer time and a half to more students than double time. Thus, LSAC became more rigorous in its selection criteria and more stringent in the amount of extra time provided, beginning in 1996.

Today, a student who desires to take the LSAT under conditions of accommodation must undergo a rigorous application process. For the purposes of this discussion, I will focus on students who seek extra time because of a cognitive impairment. The LSAC guidelines require that such students meet the following guidelines:

- the student must submit test results that are no more than three years old and reflect testing based on adult norms
- the evaluator must be someone who has comprehensive training and direct experience in working with adult populations
- the student must submit test scores from a comprehensive battery of exams and include a diagnostic interview, aptitude testing,

---

[125] Andrea E. Thornton, Susan P. Dalessandro & Lynda M. Reese, *Accommodated Test Takers Trends and Performance for the June 1993 through February 1998 LSAT Administrations* 8 (Law School Admission Council Technical Report 01-04, May 2002).

achievement testing, information processing testing, and person-
ality testing; all actual test scores and subscores must be submitted;
the report of assessment must include a specific diagnosis and the
report of assessment must recommend specific accommodations

- the evaluator may *not* recommend that the LSAT be given as an
  untimed instrument.[126]

In addition to those medical requirements, the applicant is required to
complete a lengthy report about his or her accommodation history. If a
candidate, for example, ever had an Individualized Education Plan (IEP)
under the IDEA, then the candidate is expected to provide copies of past
IEPs. Because the IEP process is a yearly one, and IEP reports can be
dozens of pages in length, a candidate could be required to provide more
than 100 pages of IEP documentation alone. The instructions also
require a candidate to disclose when he or she ever received accommodations for prior tests and what score the student received on such tests.
If the candidate received accommodations in college, then the candidate
must provide a letter from the Office of Disabilities on its official letter-
head detailing all the accommodations the candidate ever received.

In order to request an accommodation, a candidate is also advised
to provide this documentation well in advance of the registration dead-
line. LSAC promises to reply to the candidate within two weeks of
receiving the request and, if an accommodation is denied, allows a
candidate to submit further documentation. LSAC recommends that
candidates start the accommodation request process six months in
advance of the exam in case LSAC requires further documentation.

---

[126] See http://www.lsat.com (last viewed 4/26/07). Presumably, an expert cannot also *not*
recommend that an individual receive a waiver from taking the LSAT altogether.
Some blind students have asserted that even under conditions of accommodation,
their score is not predictive of their ability to perform well in law school because the
logic games require the construction of charts, diagrams, and graphs. Such skills are
not necessary to performing well in law school, but the lack of such skills could
preclude admission to law school through a low LSAT score. See Naseem Stecker,
What's the Score: The LSAT and the Blind, 80 Mi. Bar. J. 46 (January 2001).

These requirements make the accommodation process an expensive one. Students often receive a diagnosis of a disability at a young age and do not continue to have expensive diagnostic testing done to confirm the existence of the disability. Most students would only have had testing done as a child because they only recently reached the age of adulthood. But these rules require them to have a complete battery of tests completed after entering college. Few health insurance plans would cover such testing, which could easily cost $2,000 with the required extensive reporting requirements. If the student's parents had not kept the IEP reports, I do not know how a student would be able to collect such information.[127]

The LSAC requirements, also, do not closely conform to the opinions of many educational experts about the diagnosis of a specific learning disability in reading. For example, LSAC requires that students provide results of a timed reading comprehension measure, which has been normed on adults, and recommends the Nelson-Denney Reading Skills Test (NDRT).[128] The NDRT, however, was designed to "quickly capture adult students' reading levels and screen for those who may benefit from remedial as well as accelerated services. It is not validated for purposes of individual diagnosis."[129] Researchers have found that the NDRT is not a good diagnostic tool; the Curriculum Based Measure (CBM) is a more reliable diagnostic instrument. The LSAC requirements also do not appear to conform to current standards for administering and using other diagnostic instruments.[130]

---

[127] It seems ironic that LSAC requires adult test taking and adult norms yet also wants to see IEP reports from elementary school. If those data do not confirm the existence of a disability, then it is hard to know why they are relevant for this process.

[128] *LSAC Guidelines for Documentation of Cognitive Impairments*, at 2.

[129] Lewandowski et al., supra note 25, at 135.

[130] See, e.g., Earl S. Hishinuma, *Issues Related to WAIS-R Testing Modifications for Individuals with Learning Disabilities or Attention-Deficit/Hyperactivity Disorder*, 21 Learning Disability Quarterly 228 (1998) (suggesting ways that the WAIS-R should be modified to accommodate students with learning disabilities).

These extensive application procedures did not exist prior to 1997. Hence, it is not surprising that there was a dramatic drop in applications for accommodations after these practices were instituted.[131] The application process itself would seem to be a significant safeguard against fraud.

Despite the extensive documentation necessary to attain accommodations, LSAC takes the position that it cannot "validate" the accuracy of test results taken under conditions of extended time. Hence, their background material clearly states:

Candidates who seek additional test time on scored sections of the test should pay particular attention to the following:

- If you receive additional test time as an accommodation for your disability, LSAC will send a statement with your LSDAS Law School Report advising that your score(s) should be interpreted with great sensitivity and flexibility.
- Scores earned with additional test time are reported individually and will not be averaged with standard-time scores or other non-standard-time scores.
- Percentile ranks of nonstandard-time scores are not available and will not be reported.
- All information related to your request for accommodations will remain confidential unless you authorize its release.

In other words, candidates who take the LSAT with extra time and have submitted extensive documentation to validate the appropriateness of extra time receive a score that is sent to law schools. Their LSAC reports, however, include no percentile rank or index score.

[131] LSAC reports the following data from Thornton et al., supra note 124, at 8:

Year	1993–94	1994–95	1995–96	1996–97	1997–98
Requests for accommodation	No data available	1,489	1,560	1,645	1,425
Approved requests	1,195	1,348	1,255	1,087	822
Administered requests	970	1,113	951	798	630

Table 5.1. *LSAC Data*

	1993–94	1994–95	1995–96	1996–97	1997–98
Approved requests	1,195	1,348	1,255	1,087	822
Administered requests	970 (81.2%)	1,113 (82.6%)	951 (75.8%)	798 (73.4%)	630 (76.7%)

The difference between test takers who are admitted to law school and others may be particularly important in understanding the scores of accommodated test takers. Those who take the LSAT under conditions of accommodation may not be reflective of all individuals with disabilities who seek to be admitted to law schools. The very existence of the LSAT may have a significant screening effect on this population. This becomes clear by examining LSAC's own data. LSAC reports the data in Table 5.1 for individuals whose requests for accommodation were approved.

As discussed, these individuals who received accommodations submitted extensive paperwork well in advance of the test in order to have these requests for accommodation approved. Nonetheless, in recent years, nearly one-quarter of them do not bother to take the LSAT under conditions of accommodations (and presumably do not take the test at all). Why is that? One can only speculate, since LSAC offers no explanation for that trend, but there are some grounds for speculation. Quite possibly, such individuals concluded that, even with accommodations, they were unlikely to be able to attain a score that reflected their ability to do well in law school. Hence, they decided not to take the LSAT at all. What is my basis for such speculation? It is that the dropoff in accepting accommodations (from 82 to 75 percent) coincided with LSAC's typically offering candidates one and a half time rather than double time. When LSAC reports that such individuals had their requests "approved," it is failing to note that, most likely, the full amount of accommodation they requested was not approved.

The difference between double time and time and a half is substantial. The LSAT lasts three hours and twenty-five minutes. Double time results in six hours and fifty minutes. Time and a half results in five hours and seven and a half minutes. One can well imagine that some test takers might believe they cannot perform adequately unless they receive the additional one hour and forty-three minutes that is available to double time test takers. In any event, we have no way of knowing the predictive validity of the scores of the nearly one-fourth of individuals who sought accommodations, were granted some accommodations, but chose not to take the exam. Not including such a large portion of all students with disabilities in the predictive validity study would appear to skew the results.

b. Validity for Accommodated Test Takers   LSAC has reported the average LSAT score for nonaccommodated test takers compared with test takers who received extra time as an accommodation. LSAC reported the data in graph form, without reporting the precise score that corresponds to each data point, but, nonetheless, it appears that the nonaccommodated test takers, on average, scored 151 on the LSAT from January 1993 to February 1998.[132] From January 1993 to February 1995, accommodated, extra time test takers, on average, seemed to score one to two points higher than nonaccommodated test takers. Beginning in January 1995, when LSAC started to require additional documentation for accommodations and began offering less extra time, this difference diminished. In fact, beginning in January 1996, this difference may have disappeared altogether. Unfortunately, LSAC groups all the data together to report that "Accommodated/Extra time test takers tended to have higher LSAT scores than the standard LSAT-taking population, on average" without noting the changes over time.[133] But it does appear, at least for the period in which double time was the standard extra time accommodation, that accommodated test

---

[132] Thornton I, supra note 124, at 16–17.
[133] Id. at 16.

takers scored a point or two higher on the LSAT's scaled score than nonaccommodated test takers.

LSAC commissioned a study in 2002 to assess the "predictive validity" of accommodated LSAT scores.[134] Despite the evidence that the LSAT only has a predictive correlation coefficient of 0.41 for all test takers, they presumed the general validity of the test and only assessed its differential validity – whether it was less valid for accommodated test takers. Did the LSAT scores of accommodated test takers predict their scores as well as those of nonaccommodated test takers? And, in particular, were the scores predictively valid for those test takers who received extra time as an accommodation?

To answer this question, the researchers examined data from students entering law school in 1995 through 1999 because first-year grades would be available for those students. The LSAC investigators focused their attention on the students who received extra time accommodations and for whom complete data were available to assess predictive validity. Although the researchers do not report how many students received extra time accommodations during the years of their study, it is possible to estimate that that number was around 3,000 for the years under investigation.[135] The study, however, was limited to those students who enrolled in law school and for whom an undergraduate GPA and first-year average from law school were available. That reduced the sample to 1,249 students. No attempt was made to examine the LSAT scores of the 1,700 or so law school candidates who were not in the study. Not surprisingly, this group – who actually enrolled in law school and completed the first year – had a stronger profile than the typical

---

[134] Andrea E. Thornton, Lynda M. Reese, Peter J. Pashley & Susan P. Dalessandro, *Predictive Validity of Accommodated LSAT Scores*, Law School Admission Council Technical Report 01-01 (May 2002).

[135] This estimate comes from the authors' statement that the number of students receiving the accommodation of extra test time varied from 1,104 in 1994–95 to 610 in 1997–98. Thornton I, supra note 124, at 10.

LSAT exam taker. Their average LSAT was 157.57[136] as compared with 151 for the entire population. But, as was found in a study of the entire population that takes the LSAT, the average scores of the students who received the accommodation of extra time were slightly higher than for the population as a whole – 157.57 compared with 156.23.[137]

For the sample of 1,249 students, the researchers then created a matched sample, which consisted of students who did not receive accommodations but were otherwise matched for LSAT, undergraduate GPA, gender, ethnicity, and year of entering class. Because two-thirds of the extra time test takers were male, the matched sample was also about two-thirds male. For some reason, though, the matched sample consisted of more Caucasians than the extra time group. Whereas 78 percent of the candidates who received extra time were Caucasian, the matched sample was 96 percent Caucasian.[138] No explanation was offered for this discrepancy.

The researchers concluded that LSAT when used alone, or in combination with undergraduate GPA, overpredicted first-year grades in law school for the students receiving accommodations.[139] This conclusion is very important for students who receive extra time accommodations on the LSAT because it justifies LSAC's not providing an index score or percentile score for them in their LSAT report that is sent to law schools. If the purpose of the "index" is to project first-year grades, LSAC takes the methodological position that it cannot provide an accurate index for students who took the LSAT with extra time accommodations because the correlation between their index score and first-year grades is far weaker than it is for nonaccommodated students.

[136] Thornton II, supra note 134, at 12.
[137] Id. at 12.
[138] Id. at 10.
[139] Id.

There are two problems with this conclusion. First, it is premised on the assumption that the index score is a good predictor for nonaccommodated students. In fact, it is not a strong predictor for any group of students although it is somewhat less accurate for students who receive extra time accommodations. Assuming the LSAT is valid for nonaccommodated test takers, how much worse does it have to be in order for it not to be a "valid" predictor for accommodated students? For all students, the LSAT score correlation coefficient is 0.41; for students who receive extra time accommodation it is 0.34.[140] In other words, the LSAT accounts for about 16 percent of the variance in first-year grades for nonaccommodated students and accounts for about 11.6 percent of the variance for students who receive extra time accommodation.

In a similar study conducted of the SAT I exam, the authors discovered similar discrepancies between scores of accommodated and nonaccommodated test takers but did not conclude that those results demonstrated the invalidity of test results for accommodated test takers.[141] They found that SAT I score had a 0.35 correlation coefficient for students with a learning disability who received extra time as compared with 0.40 for students without disabilities. On the basis of these results, they concluded that "SAT scores were fairly accurate predictors of [first-year grade-point average]."[142] (When High School Grade-Point Average [HSGPA] was also considered as a factor, they found that the correlation coefficient for both groups was 0.49.)[143] And they concluded: "This study provides evidence that the SAT I: Reasoning Test is a valid tool for helping admissions officers select students with learning disabilities (who receive extended time

[140] Id. at 12.
[141] See Cara Cahalan et al., *Predictive Validity of SAT I: Reasoning Test for Test-Takers with Learning Disabilities and Extended Time Accommodations*, Research Report No. 2002-5 (2002).
[142] Id. at 9.
[143] Id. at 9.

accommodations) for college admission."[144] The College Board no longer "flags" the scores of students who receive extended time on the SATs.

LSAC's treatment of its validity study with respect to students with disabilities leads to the general problem of how it deals with validity evidence. LSAC knows, through other validity studies that it has conducted, that LSAT scores also underpredict the first-year grades of female law students.[145] Yet, LSAC uses one percentile index for both men and women, suggesting that the scores are equally meaningful for both groups. Further, as *U.S. News & World Report* has given increased weight to LSAT scores in its ranking, many law schools have also moved to placing greater emphasis on LSAT scores. The differential validity of the LSAT score, therefore, harms female law school candidates. Nonetheless, LSAC feels no need to delete LSAT percentiles for men out of the fear that their results overpredict their performance. Why not? Further, their studies confirm that for students who take the LSAT more than once, the average of their LSAT test scores is a better predictor of first-year grades than either score standing alone.[146] Yet, LSAC provides students with a predictive index based on *each* of their LSAT scores while knowing methodologically that *neither* of those results is the most accurate predictor. Again, one must wonder why LSAC allows individuals who have taken the test twice (and typically improved on the second test taking) receive an index based on their higher test score even if that result overpredicts their first-year grades. Index scores are only withheld for students who receive extra time

---

[144] Id. at 10.

[145] Jennifer R. Duffy & Peter J. Pashley, *Analysis of Differential Prediction of Law School Performance by Gender Subgroups Based on 1999–2001 Entering Law School Classes*, Law School Admission Council LSAT Technical Report 03-04 (January 2006).

[146] See Susan P. Dalessandro & Lore D. McLeod, *Law School Admission Council, The Validity of Law School Admission Test Scores for Repeaters: A Replication*, Law School Admission Council LSAT Technical Report 98-05 (September 1998).

accommodations based on a methodologically flawed study. Over-prediction is apparently acceptable for male candidates and for students who can afford to take the LSAT twice but is not acceptable for students with disabilities.

In any event, the conclusion that the LSAT overpredicts first-year grades for candidates who receive extra time accommodations is not surprising because first-year exams are frequently time pressured. The researchers did not control for whether students received extra time accommodations during their first year of law school. If they did not receive such accommodations, then one would expect the LSAT score to overpredict first-year grades. This result is also not surprising because the researchers included data from the years in which the standard accommodation was double time as well as years in which the standard accommodation was time and a half. Beginning in October 1996, there was a sharp dropoff in the number of students who received an accommodation of double time as compared with time and a half.[147] Other data reveal that the average scores of accommodated test takers declined slightly after those changes were instituted. Whereas accommodated test takers had been scoring a point or two higher, on average, than nonaccommodated test takers until February 1996, those differences virtually disappeared after June 1996.[148] Thus, it would be useful to know whether the predictive validity of the LSAT score for accommodated test takers improved after February 1996.[149]

The more surprising result from the LSAC data is that GPA is *also* an unreliable predictor of first-year grades for students who receive accommodations on the LSAT. And this is true even though students who received extra time accommodations on the LSAT, on average,

---

[147] The numbers are reported on a graph so it is hard to determine the exact raw numbers that correspond with each point on the graph.

[148] Thornton I, supra note 124, at 17.

[149] Put differently, are there differential validity problems after 1996?

had *lower* undergraduate grade-point averages than unaccommodated students (3.1 compared with 3.23).[150] Even more surprisingly, undergraduate grade-point average overpredicted first-year grades both for students who received extra time accommodations on the LSAT and for students who received accommodations other than extra time on the LSAT.[151]

Obviously, these are correlation, not causation, data. Receiving accommodations on the LSAT does not *cause* a student to get grades that do not accurately predict law school performance. But remember the documentation that LSAC requires a student to complete in order to receive accommodations on the LSAT. The documentation requirements imply that students are more likely to attain accommodations on the LSAT if they had been receiving accommodations during college for a documented disability. Thus, the undergraduate grade-point average was also likely to have been attained under conditions of accommodation that would presumably have the effect of raising the undergraduate grade-point average. When LSAC reports undergraduate grade-point average, however, it does not indicate that those grades were received under conditions of accommodation even though its own data reflect that those grades are as weak a predictor of first-year grades in law school as LSAT scores. For the group that receives accommodations other than time accommodations, their data indicate that the undergraduate grade-point average "provides the largest overprediction results."[152] It is interesting that LSAC does not emphasize this fact in any of its literature. It is careful to emphasize that the LSAT scores for this group are not an accurate predictor of first-year grades, but it neglects to note that undergraduate grade-point average has its own set of problems as an accurate predictor. Ironically, the failure to provide a percentile to a student's LSAT score may actually cause admissions offices to place undue weight

---

[150] Thornton II, supra note 134, at 12.
[151] Id. at 14.
[152] Id. at 13.

on undergraduate GPAs for these students when, in fact, the LSAT is a better predictor of their first-year grades.

What is going on here? Why all this "overprediction"?

It is easy to blame LSAC – that it generates an exam that has too much time pressure and therefore depresses the scores of students with learning disabilities unless they are able to receive accommodations. And there is certainly evidence to support that hypothesis. When a student with a disability takes the LSAT twice – once without accommodations and once with accommodations – his or her score, on average, improves dramatically. Whereas the typical test taker improves by 2.7 points when retaking the exam, the improvement increases to 8.49 scaled score points when an individual changes from an unaccommodated to an accommodated/extra time exam format. In other words, a failure to receive an extra time accommodation results, on average, in a decline in test score of 5 scaled points. For students at the middle of the testing range, a change from a 151 to a 156 is a jump in percentile terms from 50.5th percentile to 70.4th percentile. Similarly, a jump from 146 to 151 corresponds to a jump from 29.4th percentile to 50.5th percentile. Because a small change in the number of right answers has an enormous effect on a student's percentile ranking, if the student is in the middle of the pack, the decision whether to provide extra time has a correspondingly large effect on a student's LSAT score. The crude on/off nature of the accommodation decision with an equally crude decision to give one and a half or double time, without a precise scientific calculation as to how much time is truly warranted, leads to very imprecise LSAT test results, which are used as if they are precise measures.

But another aspect of the overprediction problem is that first-year teachers overly emphasize time-pressured testing instruments. The fact that undergraduate GPA overpredicts first-year grades for students who receive accommodations on the LSAT suggests that these students were able to attain accommodations during college to demonstrate better their understanding of the material. Further, they were probably able to demonstrate their knowledge through a greater variety of testing instruments, many of which were probably not time pressured. Law school, by contrast, especially in the first year, has a rigid uniformity that results in most students' being tested with similar testing instruments. Hence, the students who do well during the first year of law school tend to be the students who do well on an LSAT-type testing instrument – time-pressured exams.

As discussed, the LSAT is a weaker predictor of grades when professors administer take-home exams or require papers. If the first-year curriculum were radically modified to emphasize take-home exams and papers, then the overall predictive validity of the LSAT would likely decline although its validity for students who receive accommodations might improve.

III. LAW SCHOOL EXAMS

A. The Development of the Law School Exam

The essay-style examination that is common in law schools today appears to have a long history of use and of critique. The *Columbia Law Review* published a series of articles on law school examinations in the mid-1920s. These articles focused on the subjective elements of essay exams and suggested that professors seek to move to more objective exam questions.

Professor Ben D. Wood wrote the first of several articles on the measurement of law school work in 1924.[153] He was very critical of the subjectivity and inconsistency of the grading of law school essay exams. He observed that prior studies had demonstrated a

---

[153] Ben D. Wood, *The Measurement of Law School Work*, 24 Colum. L. Rev. 224 (1924).

correlation of 0.60 between grades in French and trigonometry, yet he found correlations between various law school courses to be around 0.40.[154] He also examined the predictability of class standing in the second year of law school on the basis of performance during the first year. The reliability coefficient was 0.70, which he considered to be a poor measure of reliability.[155] Correlation with grades earned as undergraduates at Columbia University or with intelligence test scores was also low.[156] Professor Wood, however, did locate one factor that seemed to improve the reliability of law school examinations. He found that the reliability of the testing instrument improved as the number of questions increased. No law school exam had more than eight questions, and reliability for an exam of that length was 0.71.[157]

On the basis of his investigation, Professor Wood concluded that professors should use some true-false questions rather than rely entirely on essay examinations. He found that the reliability of true-false tests was higher than the reliability of essay exams. Further, he found that the results from true-false tests correlated much more strongly with the results from intelligence tests than the results of the essay-style exams.[158] But he also found that students need to be given 200 true-false questions to answer in a two-hour period for the test to be highly reliable.[159] His study gave brief consideration to whether "speededness" was affecting

---

[154] Id. at 243, Table 6.

[155] Id. at 244. He said: "The error of estimate is over 70% of what the error would be if the estimates were made on the basis of tossing a coin or some other pure chance basis."

[156] The correlation with grades received at the undergraduate level was higher in the first year (0.47) and lower in the third year (0.30). Id. at 244. The correlation with intelligence test scores ranged from 0.42 to 0.57. Id. at 245. He considered those correlations to be low although they are higher than the correlation today found between LSAT and first-year grades in law school.

[157] Id. at 246.

[158] Id. at 249–50.

[159] Id. at 252.

these test scores. He noted that fewer than a dozen students failed to answer all 200 questions and those students were typically students who also received a D or F on the essay part of the final examination.[160] He therefore suggested that their inability to complete the questions was reflective of their inability to master the material.

Professor Wood's findings were very provocative because he was suggesting that more than half of the traditional law school exam be replaced with 200 true-false questions. He demonstrated that such an exam would correlate better with intelligence tests and undergraduate grades than traditional essay exams. Moreover, such exams would be more reliable in terms of providing more consistent grades from professor to professor. His mode of analysis, in some ways, is the reverse of the mode of analysis used for thinking about the LSAT. He was concerned that law school exams did not correlate strongly with intelligence instruments. Therefore, he suggested that the exams be modified to offer a better correlation with such testing instruments. He also encouraged law schools to administer intelligence tests to all incoming law students so that the reliability of law school exams could be measured in light of those testing instruments. He therefore presumed the validity of intelligence instruments as predictors of good performance as a lawyer and sought law school exams that replicated performance on such instruments. But, of course, that line of reasoning raises the larger question of whether the intelligence instruments are valid and, if so, whether we should expect law school grades to correlate with such testing instruments. If we are convinced that good lawyers are those who perform well on intelligence tests, then we could dispense with law school grades and merely rank-order students on the basis of such instruments. The fact that true-false test results correlate better with intelligence tests than essay exams does not tell us which instrument better measures who would succeed more at

---

[160] Id. at 252.

the practice of law. Professor Wood criticizes law school essay exams because they judge "knowledge and ability from hastily-written prose. . . . The impromptu essay is, psychologically, hardly more a mirror of a student's knowledge and ability to think in the law of trusts than an impromptu speech would be. The case of the impromptu essay is aggravated by the slender samplings of material and of performance which the time limits and its necessary brevity entail."[161] Objective questions were considered more reliable.

Professor Wood's essay, however, makes an important observation. He notes that essay exams are more reliable to the extent that they can cover more material. But the need to confine such tests to a few hours and restrict the amount of time that a professor will spend grading such exams apparently precludes extending the scope of the exam to create more comprehensiveness. In the foreword to Wood's essay, Dean Harlan Stone observes: "When I reflect that in the past dozen years I have devoted at least a solid year of working time, probably much more, to the painstaking reading of the thousands of examination books which have come to my desk in that period, I have reason to realize the sacrifice which law teachers are making to maintain the existing standards of measurement of law school work."[162] With Dean Stone already suggesting that law professors spend too much time grading exams, it does not seem plausible for Professor Wood to propose a solution that would lengthen the exam process. Nonetheless, lengthening the standard three- to four-hour essay exam so that students responded to more

---

[161] Id. at 230.

[162] Harlan F. Stone, *Foreword to the Measurement of Law School Work*, 24 Colum. L. Rev. 221, 222 (1924). The desire to find ways of testing that save the time of law professors was also highlighted in the foreword written by Dean Huger W. Jervey introducing Professor Wood's second contribution to this study of the use of true-false questions. Huger W. Jervey, *The Measurement of Law School Work*, 25 Colum. L. Rev. 316, 316 (1925).

questions could certainly have also increased the reliability of the testing instrument by increasing coverage without changing its basic structure to a true-false exam.

Professor Wood's study also raises the larger question of how much consistency we should expect among aptitude tests, undergraduate grade-point average or scores on other law school exams, and the grade on a particular exam. Is a high correlation evidence of a better testing instrument? If the practice of law requires a variety of skills and abilities, then possibly we should not expect high correlation figures among these various measures of ability or learning. We require students to take a wide variety of courses presumably because we think these courses teach different content and skills that would be useful to lawyers. Hence, one could say that the measure of a well rounded curriculum is that students obtain a variety of grades in different courses as they learn a variety of skills and content. If there is high inter-course reliability, then we might wonder whether the tests are simply measuring a student's inherent ability rather than whether the student mastered the material taught in a specific course.

In his second installment of the measurement of law school work, Professor Wood refines his suggestions somewhat. He concludes that true-false exams should be used in conjunction with essay exams, and that essay exams should provide students with a choice of essay topics.

By giving the student a choice of two problems out of four or five alternatives, we increase the chances that he really knows the facts necessary for the solution of his chosen problems. If the student knows the pertinent facts and fails to present a cogent and convincing solution, the teacher may with much greater assurance lay his failure to lack of reasoning ability. If, on the other hand, the student is compelled to write on three out of three questions, he may fail on one or even two, not for lack of reasoning ability, but because he chanced not to know the particular rule or rules pertinent to a particular feature of the problem. Reducing the number of questions on an Essay examination without giving the student a choice of problems will inevitably weaken the essay examination as a measure of reasoning ability unless the problems are so carefully selected by the Professor as to insure that every student who deserves to pass knows the facts and rules pertinent to a satisfactory solution. Otherwise, the Essay examination of two or three required problems is merely a more unreliable test of information than one of eight or ten problems.[163]

Professor Wood's recommendation about the essay exam derives from his assumption that the entire testing instrument must be confined to three or four hours. Because the true-false questions take two or so hours to answer, that leaves only about one and a half hours for essay questions. In that brief period, it is not possible for students to answer more than two questions. But Professor Wood had previously discovered that essay exams are more reliable if they contain more questions. Hence, his suggestion that professors use two hours of true-false questions negatively implicates the way essay questions can be used. By giving students an element of choice, he concludes that the true-false questions can test breadth of knowledge and the essay exam can test reasoning ability. There is no need to use eight essay questions to test breadth of knowledge if the true-false questions had already tested that element.

In essence, Wood is suggesting that the true-false questions and the essay questions could serve different purposes. His data in support of that assertion, however, do not entirely fit his hypothesis. Wood demonstrates the reliability of the true-false questions by noting that they have a much better correlation with the scores on essay questions on other exams than do essay questions themselves.[164] If the true-false questions test a different type of knowledge than essay tests, then we might expect the true-false questions to be correlated with each other but not with the results

[163] Id. at 320.
[164] Id. at 324.

of the essay tests.[165] Wood is also excited to report that the results of the true-false tests correlate better with the Thorndike Intelligence Test than do the essay tests.[166] But it is not clear why that fact makes the true-false questions a particularly reliable measure of law school performance. It may simply reflect that there is more of an IQ component to performing well on true-false questions than essay questions. If the purpose of law school exams is to measure knowledge learned in law school, rather than preexisting knowledge, then one could argue that the essay exams are at least as valid a measure of performance in law school as the true-false questions.

Professor Michael Zander examined much of the evidence that Wood studied but reached different conclusions. Writing in 1968, he concluded that one disadvantage of the traditional essay exam is that it gives the "candidate little time to think."[167] He observes that "our form of examination system handicaps the student who is confused or overwrought by the strain and anxiety of exams. It gives inadequate or no credit for work done during the year. It does not test ability to do research even of the most superficial kind."[168] He concludes that a more appropriate testing instrument would be the "48 hour, 3,000 word answer" because it "can be an extremely valuable test of the capacity to think and write with some modicum of

---

[165] In his third installment, Wood appears to recognize the problem with the suggestion that true-false and essay exams measure different abilities. He notes the strong correlation between scores on true-false questions and scores on essay questions and states, "The conclusion seems inescapable that the new-type examination is consistently more reliable and more valid than the old-type, as to both knowledge and reasoning ability." Ben D. Wood, *Measurement of Law School Work: III*, 27 Colum. L. Rev. 784, 790 (1927). It is not clear why Wood recommends the use of both the essay exam and the true-false exam if the true-false exam offers a more reliable indication of the same skills and abilities tested on the essay exam.

[166] Id. at 325.

[167] Michael Zander, *Examinations in Law*, 10 J. Soc'y Pub. Tchrs. L. 24 (1968–1969).

[168] Id. at 32.

style in a lawyerlike manner."[169] He also recommends giving students "credit towards the exams for work done during the course of the year."[170] Finally, he recommends that examinations break down the traditional barriers between subjects by requiring "students to take at least one paper which would cover a variety of fields and would test their diagnostic skills."[171] Although these suggestions were made about forty years ago, few of them, as we will see, have been implemented in law schools today.

B. Today's Exams

1. Literature on Law School Exams

Professor Phillip Kissam argues that the grading of law school examinations has evolved from an Aristotelian model to an objective model.[172] Under the Aristotelian model, exams were graded "under a general or holistic approach that gave considerable emphasis to a professor's practical judgment about the professional promise indicated by different student answers" and were generally accorded an A, B, or C although D and F grades were also available.[173] He describes this model as Aristotelian "because of its capacity to take account of the skills of interpretation, conventional and creative imagination, practical reason, and practical judgment, all of which are associated with Aristotle's philosophy of ethical or normative decisionmaking."[174]

---

[169] Id. at 33.
[170] Id. at 33.
[171] Id. at 34.
[172] See generally Phillip C. Kissam, *Law School Examinations*, 42 Vand. L. Rev. 433 (1989).
[173] Id. at 445.
[174] Id. at 446.

With the modern pressures to rank-order students on the basis of their examination answers, law school grading has gone to a more objective model, which Kissam describes as "piecemeal and fragmented," because the professor searches for "the many specific elements to a 'right answer'" and reads the exam "in a negative state of mind in order to produce the many quantitative distinctions that are inherent in objective grading practices."[175] He argues that this objective methodology rewards "a student's abilities to perform the basic functions of issue spotting, rule specification, and rule application quickly and productively."[176] He criticizes these quantitative methods as giving "little if any consideration to the broader, more practical, and professionally oriented skills that can be recognized by the Aristotelian method."[177]

The need to move to a rank-order system of grading has, in turn, caused law professors to turn to time-pressured examination instruments. Such testing instruments can easily yield a wide range of student answers, allowing a professor to comply with a curving requirement. But such examinations only test a limited range of abilities. "The principle of speed rewards students for answers that merely identify a maximum number of issues and specify precisely many different rules. This principle tends to de-emphasize, discourage, and penalize student writing that involves coherence, depth, contextual richness, and imagination."[178]

Various justifications are offered for the timed nature of law school exams, and the "speededness" that they frequently require. When I gave a faculty workshop on the topic, these are some of the justifications that I heard:

- That it reflects the real-world time pressures of being a lawyer
- That clients pay lawyers by the hour so "quick" lawyers are more valuable lawyers

---

[175] Id. at 446–47.
[176] Id. at 447.
[177] Id. at 447.
[178] Id. at 453.

- That a timed testing instrument forces students to synthesize the material in advance of the exam and keep up with the material which, together, would enhance learning

Clinical professors, however, dispute that law school exams reflect the way time pressures operate in practice. For example, Professor Janet Motley, who is a clinical professor, observes that "there is rarely an occasion in practice when [speed] is required."[179] Further, she argues that asking students "to speedily answer a complex legal problem" implies that that is the way they should practice law. "The enticement to take on an overly burdensome caseload is unchecked by regard for professional excellence when hasty problem-solving is the training norm."[180] Professors, themselves, she observes, would never work under the kind of time constraints that they impose on students during the exam process.[181]

Admittedly, there are times in practice when it is an advantage to be quick. During depositions, or oral arguments, one often has to think of a sequence of questions or arguments fairly quickly. But those are examples of verbal quickness, not quickness in writing. Further, many other factors rather than pure speed are involved in those contexts. Because of the verbal context, one may be reading interpersonal cues to assess what direction is appropriate. Or, one might need to be quick when making objections in the courtroom. That quickness requires certain listening skills that are not tested on law school exams. Law school exams best reflect memos that one might write to another lawyer or briefs that one might write to a judge. It is hard to think of many circumstances where one would want to complete those documents in a few hours rather than devote at least eight hours to them. Even if one *could* complete a draft in a few hours, one would most likely want to turn in a more polished

---

[179] Janet Motley, *A Foolish Consistency: The Law School Exam*, 10 Nova L.J. 723, 736 (1985–1986).

[180] Id. at 736.

[181] Id. at 736.

product. We teach students the importance of care and precision in law and then test them on their ability to turn in very unpolished drafts.

The better case for timed exams is that they force students to synthesize the material in advance of the exam. It is probably easier to procrastinate with respect to studying material if one knows that the exam will be a forty-eight-hour take-home exam. But would a student be more likely to procrastinate if the exam were eight hours rather than four hours? Or what about five or six hours instead of three hours? Is the time limit a mere administrative convenience rather than pedagogically appropriate?

Even if one accepts the assertion that a shorter exam causes students to synthesize the material in advance, one might ask whether other processes – other than three- to four-hour essay exams – could produce the same result. One underlying assumption with respect to law school grading is that one exam at the end of the semester is an appropriate way to construct nearly the entire grading profile. That choice of measuring instrument puts enormous pressure on students irrespective of whether it is four hours or four days in length. In college, students are accustomed to quizzes and midyear exams, along with finals. Yet, law school has always emphasized the single exam at the end of the year. A major justification for this examination process is efficiency. Unlike undergraduate professors who teach large courses, law professors do not get teaching assistants who assist in grading exams. Given the hours that it takes to grade essay exams, it is simply not realistic to expect law professors to engage in that exercise more than once during the semester. The lack of evaluation during the semester makes it more important for the final exam to be in a format that encourages students to be prepared throughout the semester. Increased use of multiple-choice competency quizzes or reading checks might be able to solve that problem without the use of time-pressured final exams. Or maybe law professors could even hire teaching assistants to help them grade quizzes that involve some writing. It is even possible that law professors *could* read short essays throughout the semester and give the students some feedback, in advance of the exam, to encourage them to synthesize in advance.[182]

The durability of the three- to four-hour essay exam as the primary determinant of one's grade is rather surprising given the changes that have occurred in legal education in the last twenty years. We have changed the first-year curriculum many times, added lots of clinical courses, started to teach alternative dispute resolution, and admitted a much more diverse class of students. Despite all these changes, the law school exam has remained relatively static. It is time to reexamine our devotion to this testing instrument.

2. A Modest Survey and Empirical Study of Exams

Today's law students are accustomed to a particular type of examination, especially in the first year. The exam is typically a three- to four-hour exam primarily consisting of essays but possibly including some multiple-choice or short objective questions. In some cases, the student may take a longer version of this exam for anywhere between six and twenty-four hours. Irrespective of the length of the examination period, the exam is likely to test them on their ability to spot issues, state doctrine, discuss the law in "gray" areas, evaluate the strength of arguments, and see both sides of an argument. Sometimes, students

---

[182] One option I have tried is to make practice questions available on Westlaw through a service called "TWEN" in advance of the final. Students are encouraged to answer the questions anonymously and send me their answers to evaluate. I limit the word count on these practice questions to 1,000 words and find that it takes me no more than ten minutes to read a student response and offer some constructive suggestions. Not all students take advantage of this opportunity to get feedback. The availability of this opportunity encourages students to synthesize the material in advance of the final and also gives them a way to get quick feedback on how they approach exams. I usually can provide them with an assessment on the same day that I get the sample answer. Less than half of the class takes advantage of this opportunity. Because the exam answers are submitted anonymously, I have no way of knowing whether those students perform better on the final.

are also asked to make policy arguments or assess what is the best argument.

I conducted a brief survey of one faculty's grading practices to assess the variety of exams given in law schools. For the purpose of this survey, I only considered courses in which the professor assessed most, if not all, of the grade through an examination. I used the file that the law school maintained for the American Bar Association accreditation committee on all exams administered in the law. During fall 2006, there were forty-seven courses offered in which professors gave final examinations. Every exam administered to first-year students was an in-class examination. The exams varied in length from three hours to three hours and forty-five minutes. First-year students were divided into three sections and had final examinations in three subjects. They had one class with smaller enrollment. Of the exams that students took during their first semester of law school, one or two of those exams contained some multiple choice or true-false questions; they each contained essay questions. With respect to essays, most exams contained three essay questions, although one exam contained as many as eleven essay questions.[183]

In the first semester, the use of objective questions in upper-class courses was comparable to their use in the first-year classes. Twelve of the thirty-two (37.5 percent) upper-class courses (with exams) included objective questions. The number of objective questions was also lower than in the first year with the range being from six to fifty. In the first-year courses, the range was from 15 to 200. Take-homes were also more prevalent among upper-class courses with nine of the thirty-two (28.1 percent) upper-class courses offering exams from seven hours to the entire length of the exam period. The enrollment in classes with

---

[183] It is hard to compare or describe the essay questions because some professors asked single questions with many parts; other professors asked a series of short questions. Although it would be interesting to compare grades on the basis of the type of essay questions administered, I have not done so for the purpose of this chapter because of the difficulty of labeling the types of essay questions used.

take-homes tended to be smaller than that of the other classes. No class with enrollment over forty offered a take-home exam. Because take-home exams were limited to comparatively small-enrollment classes, most students would take courses in which the exams were timed in-class exams.[184]

The pattern for the second semester was similar. The faculty offered forty courses with exams. The smaller number of courses with exams can be explained, in part, by the fact that all first-year students were required to take legal writing during the spring semester. Hence, there were more writing courses offered in the spring semester than in the fall semester. Of those forty courses with exams, twelve were first-year courses. (Each first-year student had four exams during the second semester.) Nine of the first-year courses were graded with a timed in-class exam, one had a twenty-eight-hour exam, and two had an eight-hour exam. Only two of the twelve (16.7 percent) courses used any multiple-choice questions; the other ten graded entirely on the basis of essays. The examination procedures varied considerably by section. One section had two take-home exams, one section had one take-home exam, and one section had no take-home exams. The section with two take-home exams also had no examinations that used objective questions (multiple-choice or true-false) in the second semester. Table 5.2 reflects the variety of exams used for first-year students throughout the year.

Overall, there was a nice balance throughout the year with respect to the use of objective questions. Each student had one or two classes that used some objective questions on the final examination. Less consistency existed with respect to the use of take-home exams. Students were exposed to zero, one, or two courses with take-home exams. If

[184] The difference in enrollment between courses with in-class and take-home exams therefore makes it difficult to compare the grades from these kinds of measuring instruments. Although no systematic data are kept on this subject, it is common knowledge that the grades in small-enrollment courses tend to be higher than the grades in classes with higher enrollment.

Table 5.2. *Exams for First-Year Law Students*

	First semester: Use of objective questions	First semester: Use of take-home exams	Second semester: Use of objective questions	Second semester: Use of take-home exams
Section One	One small section had objective questions; otherwise, no objective questions	No take-home exams	Objective questions in one class	No take-home exams
Section Two	Two classes used objective questions	No take-home exams	No objective questions	Two take-home exams
Section Three	No objective questions	No take-home exams	Objective questions in one class	One take-home exam

student performance varies depending on the type of examination instrument, it would seem to be particularly important to offer consistency in the first year since first-year grades are a factor in the selection of law review and play an important role in employment opportunities. Although many students score consistently irrespective of the type of examination instrument, the type of instrument is important for some students, as will be discussed later.

With respect to the upper-class curriculum, twenty-eight courses were offered with exams. Nine of twenty-eight (32.1 percent) offered some objective questions on their final; that was consistent with the figure for the fall (37.5 percent). Take-home exams were less prevalent in the spring than in the fall. Only five of twenty-eight (17.8 percent) offered take-home exams in the spring compared with 28.1 percent in the fall. Except for one course with forty-two students, all of the classes with take-home exams had enrollment below forty. Hence, the pattern of take-home exams' being more prevalent in small enrollment courses continued.

Table 5.3. *Distribution of Take-Home and In-Class Exams for Courses with Exams*

	Fall 2006	Spring 2007
Take-home exams	9 (19%)	8 (20%)
In-class exams	38 (81%)	32 (80%)

Table 5.3 summarizes the general distribution of take-home and in-class exams at the law school under study. As the previous table suggests, students at this law school are graded overwhelmingly on the basis of in-class, timed exams for courses in which exams are given. That table would not include clinical courses or seminars or other courses evaluated primarily by written work. Nonetheless, the table probably underestimates the prevalence of timed, in-class exams for law students because it does not control for the size of the class. For classes with more than forty students, in-class exams appear to be nearly the universal method of examination after the first year. The class rank is determined predominantly by these in-class, timed instruments.

It is difficult to estimate the time-pressured dimensions of these exams merely on the basis of a description of their format, but it was apparent to me in reviewing the exams that some would be very time pressured. The most time-pressured exams were longer than ten pages, had many subparts to their questions, and offered the students no more than three hours or three and half hours to complete them. Many professors offered what they described as "extra" time beyond the amount specified in a question. That extra time ranged from five to forty minutes, but it was hard to see how that extra time decreased the time-pressured aspects, especially for professors who insisted that students not begin writing until the "extra time" had expired. A review of the exams also suggests that the time pressure varies enormously on in-class exams. One professor gave the students four hours to answer two relatively short questions; another professor gave the students three hours to answer two relatively short questions; by contrast, one professor asked students to answer thirteen questions in three and a half hours. In another course, the three-hour exam was thirty-one pages in length. The take-home exams were probably less time pressured than the in-class exams but the time pressures among the in-class exams did vary.

None of this variation in exams really matters unless the variation affects the resulting rank order among students. Data that I have collected suggest this variation does affect the rank ordering. To reach that conclusion, I examined test scores collected by a professor at a law school. She had her students for an entire year and gave them two examinations – one at the end of the fall semester and one at the end of the spring semester. The students were told that each exam was 50 percent of their grade. For various reasons, a few students each year did not take both exams, and they were not included in this study. Enrollment in the classes was about sixty students.

I examined four years of data. In year one of the study, the professor gave what she self-identifies as a "very speeded" exam in the fall semester. She then gave a take-home exam in the spring semester. In year two, she gave an in-class exam in the fall semester, but she adjusted the exam to make it less speeded than in the previous year. She again gave a take-home exam in the spring semester. In year three, she gave an in-class exam in both semesters; these exams were similar to the in-class exam she gave in year two. In year four, she gave an in-class exam in the fall semester and a take-home in the spring semester. Once again, her in-class exam was the less speeded version that she had begun to use in year two.

I calculated the correlation coefficient in each year between the student scores on the fall semester exam and the student scores on the spring semester exam. As predicted by the educational psychology literature, the correlation coefficient was highest when she used comparable testing instruments in the fall and spring (year three) and lowest

Table 5.4. *Correlation Coefficients between Fall and Spring Exams*

	Types of exams compared	Pearson correlation coefficient
Year One	Very speeded in-class exam and take-home exam	0.467 (22% variance)
Year Two	Less speeded in-class exam and take-home exam	0.626 (39% variance)
Year Three	Less speeded in-class exam and less speeded in-class exam	0.753 (57% variance)
Year Four	Less speeded in-class exam and take-home exam	0.638 (41% variance)

when she used a highly speeded exam in the fall and a less speeded exam in the spring (year one). Table 5.4 shows the results.

These data offer two key insights. First, they support the hypothesis that the type of examination instrument does affect the rank order. The lower correlation coefficient when two different types of exams are used suggests that different kinds of exams do test for different skills and abilities. Specifically, timed and untimed instruments may test for different skills and abilities. Further, these data suggest that professors can modify in-class instruments to make them less timed and more like take-home exams. Finally, we should remember that these data are for *all* students. There are too few students in any class who are identified as having learning disabilities for me to consider their test scores separately. For students with learning disabilities who are not receiving extra time accommodations, one would expect the correlation between in-class and take-home instruments to be even lower than that reported for all students. And for students with learning disabilities who do receive extra time, there is the difficult question of how much

211

extra time is appropriate. If interviewed by the office of disability services, this professor might have indicated that her in-class exam in year one had a significant time pressure for students without disabilities but contained little time pressure in year three. Would it be possible to individualize the allocation of extra time so that all students are taking the exam under comparable conditions? If time-pressured, in-class exams were not the overwhelmingly common type of exam administered in law school, obtaining the correct answer to that question would not be so important.

One last way to view the data of this professor, which also gives insight into the meaning of the LSAT's low correlation coefficient, is to compare the ranking of students in year one of the data. In year one, the correlation coefficient that sought to predict the score on the spring semester exam from the score on the fall semester exam was similar to the correlation coefficient that predicts the grades during the first year of law school from the LSAT score. The LSAT correlation coefficient is 0.41; the correlation coefficient for this professor's students was 0.47 (a modest improvement).

In Table 5.5, I report how the ranking of students would change depending on which exam was used for ranking purposes. I have deliberately only listed those students for whom the ranking would change considerably. My reporting includes about one-fourth of the fifty-three students for whom I have complete data.

For some students, the change in performance was quite dramatic. The significant improvement on the untimed instrument compared with the timed instrument for student numbers 2, 4, 6, 7, 8, 11, and 12 would cause me to wonder whether those students might have an undiagnosed learning disability. Students 2 and 4, in particular, had wide swings in performance – more than two standard deviations. Of course, there are always some students who take a while to "catch on" during law school, and those results deserve further investigation to see whether they are otherwise replicated in these students' performances. Did these students generally have improvements from the fall to spring

Table 5.5. *Student Percentile Ranking Based on Take-Home or In-Class Exam*

Student number	Take-home exam ranking	In-class exam ranking
1	66%	4%[185]
2	15%	83%
3	19%	36%
4	17%	74%
5	96%	55%
6	2%	23%
7	13%	62%
8	77%	98%
9	36%	4%
10	92%	43%
11	60%	98%
12	55%	96%
13	2%	19%

semester, or was this improvement isolated to a class in which the examination instrument changed from in-class exam to take-home exam? I would recommend that associate deans monitor student performance on the basis of the type of exam to see whether testing for a learning disability is warranted.[186] Unfortunately, there is so little variation at most law schools in examination instruments that such comparisons are not possible. If the performance of students 2 and 4 on this professor's in-class timed instrument is consistent with their general performance on in-class timed instruments, then we can see how

[185] In other words, 65% of the students performed better than this student on the take-home exam but only 4% of students performed better than this student on an in-class exam.

[186] On two occasions, on the basis of such data for individual students, I have suggested testing for a learning disability. In both cases, the students easily met the criteria for a learning disability upon being tested. Both students had less privileged backgrounds where testing would have been unlikely.

the type of examination is very much affecting their employment prospects upon graduation. Whether they are in the top quartile or bottom quartile of their class may depend on the examination instruments used to evaluate their performance.

Returning to the subject of the LSAT, let us again consider student numbers 2, 4, 6, 7, 11, and 12. How might their performance on the LSAT have improved had it been a less time-pressured instrument? Might they have been able to attend a more prestigious law school if the LSAT had been not such a significantly timed instrument? Should some of them have requested extra time on the LSAT but were unaware of a learning disability?

IV. CONCLUSION

The standard response to the observation that some students' disabilities cause them to have slower processing speeds is to suggest that these students be given extra time to take examinations. On exams for which the standard amount of time does not cause a "speededness" component for nondisabled test takers, that solution may be the appropriate solution. The law school setting, however, poses special challenges because exams are graded on a rank-order basis and typically have a speededness component. Similarly, the LSAT is graded on a scaled score and has a speededness component. If students with disabilities are graded on the basis of an essentially "unspeeded" instrument, then we might expect their test scores to be comparatively higher than those for students who learned the material equally well but who took the exam under speeded conditions. It is possible to adjust the allocation of extra time to simulate the same degree of speededness for all test takers, and LSAC may have achieved that result in recent years on the LSAT. But such precision is challenging to accomplish.

Other solutions are also possible, although none is free of problems. The standard amount of time that is allocated for all test takers could be lengthened to lessen the speededness component. Then, when students with disabilities are given extra time, both sets of students are taking an essentially unspeeded exam. Three problems exist with this solution. First, it is not clear that extending time from four hours to eight hours or even twenty-eight hours truly eliminates the speeded element for nondisabled test takers on law school exams. Second, there are administrative challenges in allowing more than eight hours per exam because the exam period might have to extend over several weeks. Self-scheduling of exams could solve that problem, but that solution raises security concerns. Finally, some students might not study as effectively throughout the semester if they thought they had a lot of time to complete the exam.

Another solution would be for law schools (and LSAC) to stop grading exams on a rank-order basis to lessen the challenges of making comparisons between law students. Employers and others, however, might object to law schools' changing their grading system. And, again, students might study less effectively if grades on exams were considered less important.

Finally, law schools could change their examination system overall so that it gives less weight to a timed end-of-semester exam. Students could take untimed multiple-choice competency exams throughout the semester, write short papers throughout the semester, and be graded more significantly on the basis of class participation or oral projects. One of the key advantages to the current system is convenience for law faculty – grading one exam at the end of the semester is far easier than grading numerous instruments throughout the semester. That convenience, however, may not serve a pedagogically sound method of grading. The end-of-semester exam would not have to be as comprehensive if other testing mechanisms had been used throughout the semester. Nonetheless, with class sizes often hovering around seventy to eighty for first-year classes, it would probably be difficult to persuade law faculty to change their grading systems.

Although no solution is perfect, my research does strongly suggest that there is a fairness problem when all faculty members give comparable speeded exams during law school, especially in the first year, when grades typically also serve the purpose of determining law review standing. Processing speed clearly affects the performance of some students, and not all those students receive accommodations during law school. Thus, at a minimum it seems important to grade students within a section on the basis of more than one type of examination instrument. Ideally, half of their exams would be take-home exams and half would be in-class exams.

Adopting a variety of law school exam formats is not simply fair to students with disabilities. It is good exam procedure for all law students. The practice of law involves a wide variety of skills. If all law school exams have a strong speededness component, then we are not measuring that variety of skills – we are testing speededness over and over again.

Because we allow law faculty substantial discretion in the construction of exams, it is difficult to implement the recommendations made in this chapter. Associate deans and others involved in curriculum matters, however, can examine their law school's testing practices as a whole and see whether they have struck the right balance, particularly in the first year. Subtle changes could produce better results for everyone by allocating faculty to first-year classes, in part, on the basis of their testing practices. This chapter suggests that law schools have an obligation to examine their testing practices and to see how they could be improved to attain greater fairness in the allocation of grades. We teach our students the importance of the principle of fairness; we can set a good example by implementing that principle ourselves.

6

Voting

IN RECENT YEARS, FEDERAL LAW HAS MADE IMPORTANT inroads for individuals with disabilities by seeking to make polling places more accessible. While that change has been important, this chapter argues that an integration presumption has caused disability rights advocates to ignore another aspect of voting that must become more accessible – absentee voting. This chapter argues that absentee voting needs to undergo some fundamental changes so it can become a vehicle for improving voting participation by individuals with disabilities. By focusing on the goal of increasing participation, rather than merely integration, we can make voting more accessible to individuals with disabilities. From an anti-subordination perspective, we should be seeking to enhance the basic citizenship rights of individuals with disabilities by improving the voting process.

In recent decades, absentee voting has become a central feature of our electoral landscape as a result of the liberalization of many states' laws and individual voters' decisions to vote in the comfort of their homes.[1]

Daniel Tokaji was the coauthor of a longer version of this chapter that was included in an ABA-sponsored McGeorge Law Review Symposium. For that complete version, see Daniel P. Tokaji & Ruth Colker, *Absentee Voting by People with Disabilities: Promoting Access and Integrity,* 38 McGeorge Law Review 1015 (2007).

[1] Terry Christensen, *Absentee Balloting Has Changed Voting – and That's Good,* S. J. Mercury News, Oct. 10, 2006, at A1 (noting an increase in the use of absentee ballots in California, from 3 percent in 1970 to 47 percent in June 2006).

All states now allow at least some categories of voters to cast their votes before Election Day, most commonly by mail. Most states permit "no excuse" absentee voting, under which ballots may be cast by mail regardless of whether the voter provides an excuse for not going to the polls on Election Day. Several states allow some classes of voters to obtain permanent absentee status, obviating the need to apply for an absentee ballot before every election. And one state, Oregon, has eliminated precinct-based voting entirely, going to an all-mail voting system in which everyone casts the functional equivalent of an absentee ballot.

The trend toward expanded absentee voting coincides with greater attention to accessible voting for people with disabilities.[2] Individuals with disabilities have long been excluded from voting, some by laws expressly disenfranchising them and others by persistent barriers at the polls. In recent decades, Congress has made some efforts to promote accessibility, most notably through the Voting Accessibility for the Elderly and Handicapped Act of 1984,[3] the Americans with Disabilities Act of 1990 (ADA),[4] and the Help America Vote Act of 2002 (HAVA).[5] The implementation of these statutes has emphasized the elimination of barriers to in-precinct voting by people with visual or mobility impairments. The paths to polling places are supposed to be accessible, and the available machinery is supposed to allow voters with visual impairments to vote privately and independently. While these laws have helped improve the accessibility of polling places, they have not fulfilled their promise of ensuring accessible voting for all persons with disabilities.[6]

---

[2] This chapter uses the terms *individuals with disabilities*, *people with disabilities*, and *voters with disabilities* to include elderly people who have physical or mental disabilities.

[3] 42 U.S.C. § 1973ee to 1973ee6 (West 2000).

[4] 42 U.S.C. § 12131-12134 (West 2007).

[5] 42 U.S.C. §§ 15301-15545 (West 2005).

[6] See generally U.S. Gen. Accounting Office, Voters with Disabilities: Access to Polling Places and Alternative Voting Methods (2001), available at http://www.gao.gov/new.items/d02107.pdf [hereinafter GAO, Access to Polling] (on file with the *McGeorge Law Review*); U.S. Election Assistance Comm'n, A Summary of the 2004 Election Day Survey, Access to Voting for the Disabled 20 (2005).

Unfortunately, the nexus between these two areas – absentee voting and accessible voting – has received far too little attention. Absentee voting is critical to many people with disabilities because it facilitates their participation in elections even if they cannot secure transportation, enter the polling place, or use voting equipment without assistance. Disability advocates estimate that 40 percent of voters with disabilities use absentee ballots.[7] Although some have pushed for greater access to the polls as a way of promoting integration, almost everyone recognizes that absentee voting is essential in allowing many individuals with disabilities to exercise the franchise. Thus, even those states that require an "excuse" to vote absentee allow those who are too severely disabled to vote at the regular polling places to obtain and cast a paper ballot by mail. Absentee voting may also allow people with disabilities to receive help from a trusted third party – such as a relative or caregiver – in the privacy of their homes, without the embarrassment or difficulty entailed in getting help from a stranger at the polls.

States have greatly increased their use of absentee voting in recent years[8] – not necessarily to improve voting opportunities for individuals with disabilities but, instead, as a way to make voting more convenient for *everyone*. Ironically, this recent focus on absentee voting has largely ignored the problems faced by people with disabilities who want or need to vote absentee.

The purpose of this chapter is to discuss how to promote accessible absentee voting. An accessible system would allow voters with disabilities to obtain and cast absentee ballots privately, independently, and accurately. To be clear, increasing the accessibility of absentee voting should not excuse policymakers or election officials from their responsibility to make polling places more accessible.

---

[7] Interview with Jim Dickson, vice-president of governmental affairs, American Association of People with Disabilities (Feb. 10, 2007) (notes on file with the *McGeorge Law Review*).

[8] See supra note 2.

Voters with disabilities should have the same right as other voters to choose whether to vote on Election Day at a polling place *or* in advance of the election through some form of absentee voting. By the same token, policymakers or election officials should not impose unnecessary obstacles to participation by people with disabilities in the name of promoting integrity. Integrity need not be sacrificed for accessibility; those are false dichotomies.

Rather than proposing "best practices," something that is premature at this juncture, this chapter puts forward a menu of accessibility improvements, public education, and affirmative outreach that election officials and policymakers should consider. Most significant among these suggested improvements is a different model of absentee voting. Under the present model, the burden lies with individuals with disabilities to obtain and cast an absentee ballot by mail. The proposed model would place the burden on state and local authorities to ensure that voters have accessible technology where they live, allowing them to vote in person – secretly and independently – with assurance that the choices made are their own, rather than those of a third party. These changes would be especially feasible, and could be particularly important, in institutional settings such as nursing homes. Many people likely to have problems voting independently reside in such facilities. Moreover, these are the settings where voters are most vulnerable to fraud and coercion. This reform has the possibility of immediately improving accessibility while reducing the risk of fraud. It reaches people who live in segregated settings and therefore doesn't fall prey to the integration paradigm.

Part I of this chapter discusses the obstacles to participation by people with disabilities and recent legislative efforts to eliminate those obstacles. Part II focuses on the barriers that people with disabilities face in obtaining and casting absentee ballots and considers what should be done to make absentee voting compliant with federal disability access requirements. Part III concludes by suggesting how the accessibility of absentee voting might be enhanced while managing its risks.

I. THE STRUGGLE FOR ACCESSIBLE VOTING

People with disabilities have long faced impediments to the full exercise of their voting rights, both through laws that expressly disenfranchise them and through other persistent barriers to voting. In a September 2004 Harris Poll, approximately 20 percent of voters with disabilities reported that they were unable to vote in federal elections as a result of barriers in getting to or voting at the polls.[9] This part discusses state laws barring some people with disabilities from voting, many of which remain on the books today. It then moves to a discussion of barriers that people with various disabilities face in voting at the polls and Congress's efforts to deal with those problems.

A. Formal and Informal Disenfranchisement

There is a long history of excluding certain classes of people with disabilities from voting.[10] In 1793, Vermont required voters to have "quiet and peaceable behavior,"[11] and, in 1819, Maine's Constitution excluded "persons under guardianship" from voting.[12] Similar exclusions exist under many states' laws even today. Delaware excluded those who were "idiots" or "insane" from voting in 1831.[13] The practice of disenfranchising people with certain disabilities expanded substantially in the mid-nineteenth century,[14] and many states still have

---

[9] Noel Runyan, *Improving Voter Access: A Report on the Technology for Accessible Voting Systems* 6 (Dēmos 2007).

[10] Kay Schriner et al., *Democratic Dilemmas: Notes on the ADA and Voting Rights of People with Cognitive and Emotional Impairments*, 21 Berkeley J. Emp. & Lab. L. 437, 440-43 (2000).

[11] Vt. Const. of 1793, ch. II, § 42.

[12] Me. Const. of 1819, art. II, § 1.

[13] Del. Const. of 1831, art. V, § 2.

[14] Schriner, supra note 11, at 441–42.

these provisions today. In fact, people with certain cognitive impairments are, along with felons and minors, currently among the only citizens still disenfranchised as a matter of law.[15] In various states, those restrictions apply to people who are "mentally incompetent," "non compos mentis," "of unsound mind," "incapacitated," "idiotic," or "insane." Several states automatically disenfranchise those who are under guardianship without any specific assessment of their capacity to vote.[16]

Although the express disenfranchisement of people with disabilities is not my main focus, many of these state laws raise serious questions under the U.S. Constitution and federal disability rights statutes. In fact, one federal district court struck down a state law prohibiting people under guardianship from voting.[17] The court in *Doe v. Rowe* considered a Maine procedure under which mentally ill citizens under guardianship could be disenfranchised without any specific consideration of whether the individuals lacked the capacity to vote.[18] The court found that Maine's law violated due process by failing to give "uniformly adequate notice regarding the potential disenfranchising effect of being placed under guardianship for a mental illness."[19] The court also concluded that the law violated the Equal Protection Clause, both on its face and as applied. Finally, the court held that

---

[15] All but nine of the states (Connecticut, Illinois, Indiana, Kansas, New Hampshire, North Carolina, Pennsylvania, Tennessee, and Vermont) have constitutional or statutory provisions disqualifying some categories of persons with disabilities from voting. See also Notes, *Mental Disability and the Right to Vote*, 88 Yale L.J. 1644, 1645–47 (1979) ("Only ten states permit citizens to vote irrespective of mental disability. Twenty-six states proscribe voting by persons labeled idiotic, insane, or non compos mentis. . . . Twenty-four states and the District of Columbia disfranchise persons adjudicated incompetent or placed under guardianship. . . . Four states disqualify from voting persons committed to mental institutions, . . . but other laws in three of those states provide that commitment alone does not justify disfranchisement.").

[16] Kingshuk K. Roy, *Sleeping Watchdogs of Personal Liberty: State Laws Disenfranchising the Elderly*, 11 Elder L.J. 109, 115–16 (2003).

[17] *Doe v. Rowe*, 156 F. Supp. 2d 35, 59 (D. Me. 2001).

[18] Id. at 43.

[19] Id. at 50.

Maine's restriction on voting violated both the ADA and Section 504 of the Rehabilitation Act by disenfranchising some people who have the capacity to vote.

Critical to the court's ruling in *Doe v. Rowe* was that Maine's law would deny the right to vote to people who had the capacity to "understand the nature and effect of voting such that they can make an individual choice."[20] To the extent that other states similarly allow people who meet this standard to be disenfranchised, those states' laws arguably violate federal law.[21]

Practices that effectively impede people from participating in elections, despite their ability to "understand the nature and effect of voting," may also violate the Constitution or ADA. These practices may include complex requirements that have the effect of making it difficult for people with cognitive impairments to register or cast their ballots. Also problematic are informal "gatekeeping" decisions – such as relatives' or caregivers' decisions not to assist a person with a disability who needs help in registering or voting, based on the belief that the person lacks the capacity to vote. Like formal legal exclusions, such informal gatekeeping is "likely incompatible with well-developed principles of contemporary mental health law and ethics."[22] Only those people found to lack the capacity to understand the nature and effect of voting after a constitutionally adequate process should be prevented from voting.

---

[20] Id. at 51 n.31. See also Jason H. Karlawish et al., *Addressing the Ethical, Legal, and Social Issues Raised by Voting by Persons with Dementia*, 292 JAMA 1345, 1346 (2004). Under *Doe*, "a person has the capacity to vote if he or she understands the nature and effect of voting and has the capacity to choose among the candidates and questions on the ballot." Id.

[21] See Karlawish et al., supra note 21, at 1346 (recommending that states revise their voting capacity statutes to conform to the *Doe* standard); Paul S. Appelbaum et al., *The Capacity to Vote of Persons with Alzheimer's Disease*, 162 Am. J. Psychiatry 2094 (2005) (suggesting a means by which to determine whether citizens lack the capacity to understand the nature and effect of voting).

[22] Karlawish et al., supra note 21, at 1346.

B. Barriers to Voting at the Polls

Laws that formally exclude people with disabilities are just one type of barrier to equal participation. The American Association of People with Disabilities estimates that more than 14 million people with disabilities voted in the 2000 election but that more than 21 million people of voting age with disabilities did not vote.[23] The issues faced by people with disabilities include difficulties in entering the building where voting takes place, reaching controls or reading ballots or displays, marking ballots because of lack of fine motor skills, communicating orally with poll workers, obtaining auditory feedback, and reading printed ballots or visual displays. They may also find the act of voting at a polling place to be so physically exhausting that they decide not to expend their energy in that particular activity.

Of course, the broad category of voters with disabilities encompasses individuals with many different types of physical and mental impairments. Although it is common to refer to people with disabilities collectively, the types of accommodations required vary, depending upon their disability. Individuals who have the following impairments are among the voters who might require assistance in voting:

- People with mobility impairments that prevent them from walking independently, who rely upon a wheelchair, walker, or other device to ambulate
- People with visual impairments that make it difficult or impossible for them to read a printed ballot
- People with auditory impairments, who are unable to hear instructions from poll workers

[23] DREDF, *Guide to Voting Equipment Usability and Accessibility for People with Disabilities* 2 (2003). This amounts to a turnout rate of 40% compared with more than 50% among all voters in the 2000 election. Stephen E. Finkel & Paul Freedman, *The Half-Hearted Rise: Voter Turnout in the 2000 Election*, in Models of Voting in Presidential Elections: The 2000 U.S. Election 187–89 (2004).

- People with cognitive impairments that prevent them from reading the ballot without assistance
- People with long-term illnesses or impairments that make routine travel exhausting
- People with manual dexterity impairments that prevent them from marking certain types of ballots without assistance

Historically, the courts did not consider barriers to participation legally significant. When Connecticut required that all voting take place in person and prohibited absentee voting, Judge Newman ruled that an accommodation to permit absentee voting for individuals with mobility impairments was not required: "A physically incapacitated voter has no more basis to challenge a voting requirement of personal appearance than a blind voter can complain that the ballot is not printed in Braille."[24] It was unthinkable in the 1970s that voters with physical impairments would seek equal access to the polls.

Prior to 2000, Congress passed some measures designed to improve accessibility to the polls for individuals with disabilities. Among them are (1) the Voting Rights Act of 1965, which gives people with disabilities a right to receive assistance in voting from someone of their choice;[25] (2) Section 504 of the Rehabilitation Act of 1973, which generally prohibits the exclusion of people with disabilities from activities receiving federal financial assistance;[26] (3) the Voting Accessibility for Elderly and Handicapped Act of 1984, which requires that polling places and registration facilities be accessible;[27] (4) Title II of

---

[24] *Whalen v. Heimann*, 373 F. Supp. 353, 357 (D. Conn. 1974) (adding that it is not "the province of courts to weigh the relative ease or difficulty with which the state could accommodate its voting procedures to meet the needs of various handicapped voters"). See also *Selph v. Council of L. A.*, 390 F. Supp. 58, 61 (C.D. Cal. 1975) (holding that the Equal Protection Clause does not require a city to make polling places accessible to individuals with disabilities when absentee voting is available).

[25] 42 U.S.C. § 1973aa-6 (West 2000).

[26] 29 U.S.C. § 794 (West 2000).

[27] 42 U.S.C. § 1973ee (West 2000 & Supp. 2005).

the ADA, which forbids public entities to exclude people with disabilities from services, programs, and activities;[28] and (5) the National Voter Registration Act of 1993, which requires that state offices providing services to people with disabilities provide voter registration.[29]

Despite these laws, voting participation rates among people with disabilities have remained low, and accessibility remains inadequate.[30] A variety of barriers face people with various disabilities. The most thorough study of voting access to date is a report published in 2001 by the General Accounting Office (GAO).[31] As a part of its study, the GAO randomly selected 100 counties and visited polling places in those counties on Election Day in 2000. The GAO examined those polling places from the parking lot to the voting booth, looking primarily at whether they provided access to people with mobility impairments. Overall, the GAO found that 84 percent had at least one impediment, while only 16 percent of all polling places had no potential impediments.[32] "Curbside voting," in which the voting mechanism is taken outside the polling location to the voter when he or she cannot physically enter the polling place, provided the most common means of dealing with such impediments. Still, 28 percent of polling places nationwide had at least one impediment and did *not* offer curbside voting.[33]

---

[28] 42 U.S.C. § 12132 (West 2000).

[29] 42 U.S.C. § 1973gg-5(2)(B) (West 2006).

[30] See Michael E. Waterstone, Lane, *Fundamental Rights, and Voting*, 56 Ala. L. Rev. 793, 827 (2005) ("Social science research demonstrates that the cumulative effect of these problems is decreased voting levels for people with disabilities. The 2000 National Organization on Disability/Harris Survey found that voter registration is lower for people with disabilities than for people without disabilities (62% versus 78%, respectively. A different survey in 1999 found that people with disabilities were on average about twenty percentage points less likely than those without disabilities to vote and ten points less likely to be registered to vote, even after adjusting for differences in demographic characteristics (age, sex, race, education, and marital status).").

[31] GAO, *Access to Polling*, supra note 7.

[32] Id. at 7.

[33] Id.

Some voters are able to enter the polling place but have impairments that make it difficult to vote independently once inside without some form of accommodation. The 2001 GAO Report noted that "the types and arrangement of voting equipment used may . . . pose challenges for people with mobility, vision, or dexterity impairments."[34] People with manual dexterity impairments may have difficulty using voting technology that requires them to mark a paper ballot with a pen or other writing device. People with cognitive impairments, as well as those with visual impairments, may have difficulty reading certain ballot formats. Although polling places sometimes make alternative formats available, those formats are not always effective or readily available. *None* of the polling places that the GAO visited had special ballots or voting equipment for voters with visual impairments, such as audio or Braille ballots. However, "although [the GAO] did not observe such aids on Election Day, some county officials told [the GAO] that, upon request, they try to provide specials aids so that blind individuals can vote independently."[35] The National Organization on Disability reported in 2001 that less than 10 percent of polling places had technology with an audio output that would allow voters with visual impairments to vote privately and independently.[36] Jim Dickson of the American Association of People with Disabilities, who is blind, describes his own experience in a way that captures the practical difficulties that some voters with visual impairments face:

> Once, after my wife cast my ballot, she said to me, "Jim I know you love me. Now I know that you trust me, because you think I'm marking this ballot for that idiot." Twice in Massachusetts and once

[34] Id.
[35] Id. at 7 n. 15.
[36] Nat'l Org. on Disability, *Alert: Most Voting Systems Are Inaccessible for People with Disabilities* (Aug. 2, 2001), http://www.nod.org/index.cfm?fuseaction=page. viewPage&pageID=1430&nodeID=1&FeatureID=225&redirected=1&CFID= 12258791&CFTOKEN=86030427 (on file with the *McGeorge Law Review*).

in California, while relying on a poll worker to cast my ballot, the poll worker attempted to change my mind about whom I was voting for. I held firm, but to this day I really do not know if they cast my ballot according to my wishes. To voters with disabilities, there is always some level of uncertainty when another person marks your ballot for you.[37]

In 2002, stories like this one prompted Congress to expand the requirements for accessible voting technology as part of HAVA.[38] In particular, HAVA requires that people with disabilities be provided "the same opportunity for access and participation (including privacy and independence)" as other voters.[39] Specifically included among those who must be accommodated are voters who are blind or visually impaired.[40] This requirement may be satisfied by providing at least "one direct recording electronic voting system or other voting system equipped for individuals with disabilities at each polling place."[41] Pursuant to HAVA, the Election Assistance Commission (EAC) has issued Voluntary Voting System Guidelines that include specifications regarding accessibility, among other things.[42] HAVA also requires research to be conducted on accessible voting technology. It calls for the EAC to conduct periodic studies of accessible voting for people with disabilities, including those who are blind

---

[37] James C. Dickson, Testimony Before the N.Y. City Council Comm. on Mental Health, Mental Retardation, Alcoholism, Drug Abuse & Disability Services (July 22, 2002), *quoted in* Michael Waterstone, *Civil Rights and the Administration of Elections – toward Secret Ballots and Polling Place Access*, 8 J. Gender Race & Just. 101, 107 (2004).

[38] 42 U.S.C. §§ 15301–15545 (West 2005).

[39] Id. § 15481.

[40] Id. § 15481(a)(3)(A).

[41] Id. § 15481(a)(3)(B).

[42] U.S. Election Assistance Comm'n, Voluntary Voting System Guidelines 54–57 (2005), available at http://www.eac.gov/VVSG Volume_I.pdf (on file with the *McGeorge Law Review*). These guidelines cover such criteria as font size, user interfaces, and audio capacity for technology provided at polling places. Id.

or visually impaired. In addition, HAVA requires the EAC and the National Institute of Standards and Technology (NIST) to report to Congress on "human factor research," including the usability of different types of voting equipment for individuals with disabilities and others.

HAVA has undoubtedly resulted in some significant improvements, at least for those who are able to go to the polls. Still, evidence exists that our election system falls far short of the ideal of secret and independent voting for all citizens with disabilities.[43] A post-2004 survey commissioned by the EAC found that, fourteen years after enactment of the ADA, only 70.9 percent of precincts from reporting states were wheelchair-accessible.[44] It also found many places did not have accessible voting technology in place. Only half of American precincts were reported to have accessible voting systems in 2004, and fewer than a quarter of precincts allowed voters with visual impairments to cast a secret ballot.[45] Moreover, even where polling places and voting equipment are accessible, traveling to the polls on Election Day poses a major obstacle for many people with disabilities. For these people, some form of absentee voting may well present the least burdensome option. Yet HAVA does little or nothing to enhance the accessibility of absentee voting, at least in its most common forms.

---

[43] Michael Waterstone, *Constitutional and Statutory Voting Rights for People with Disabilities*, 14 Stan. L. & Pol'y Rev. 353, 360 (2003) (arguing that disability rights statutes should be interpreted to require "accessible polling places and secret and independent ballots").

[44] U.S. Election Assistance Comm'n, *A Summary of the 2004 Election Day Survey: Access to Voting for the Disabled* 20 (2005). The report noted that more than half of the states failed even to respond to the survey questions on accessibility. Id. While one cannot know for sure, it is certainly possible that nonreporting states' accessibility was even poorer than that of the states that did report.

[45] Kimball W. Brace & Michael P. McDonald, *Final Report of the 2004 Election Day Survey* 14-4 (2005), available at http://www.eac.gov/election_survey_2004/pdf/ EDS-Full_Report_wTables.pdf (on file with the *McGeorge Law Review*).

II. TOWARD ACCESSIBLE ABSENTEE VOTING

Absentee voting is no panacea. It does not substitute for accessible polling places and voting technology. Absentee voting typically occurs in one's home. In a jurisdiction where most voters go to the polls on Election Day, absentee voting effectively segregates voters with disabilities from the rest of the polity. Moreover, absentee voting often requires additional steps beyond going to a polling place on Election Day. A voter has to request the absentee ballot and then comply with various antifraud rules as part of casting the ballot. These directions can be more complicated than Election Day voting and therefore dissuade someone from voting who otherwise cannot readily travel to the polling place on Election Day. Perhaps most important, it may be difficult or impossible for some people with disabilities to vote independently with an absentee ballot. HAVA requires that accessible technology be made available at the polls but does not require that it be provided to those people voting in their homes.

Absentee voting is nevertheless essential to many members of the disability community. To the extent that states rely on absentee voting, voters with disabilities should have the same opportunities as others to vote by this mechanism. In this part, I consider the accessibility issues raised by current absentee voting practices against the backdrop of the ADA, which requires states to make all their programs and activities accessible to the maximal extent possible.

A. Absentee Voting and the ADA

Although HAVA focused on having accessible voting technology at the polling place, other federal civil rights laws require that accessible voting be provided to a wide range of people with disabilities. Of particular note are Title II of the ADA, which covers "public entities,"[46]

[46] 42 U.S.C. § 12131(1)(a) (West 2005).

and Section 504 of the Rehabilitation Act,[47] which imposes similar obligations on federally funded programs and activities. Because states create the rules governing both federal and state elections, state election officials are covered by ADA Title II. In fact, when Congress enacted the ADA, it listed voting as one of the areas in which individuals with disabilities had historically faced discrimination.[48] Congress also noted that individuals with disabilities have been "relegated to a position of political powerlessness in our society."[49]

Title II is largely interpreted through regulations. Among those regulations are those governing new or altered facilities, which provide that

> each facility or part of a facility altered by, on behalf of, or for the use of a public entity in a manner that affects or could affect the usability of the facility or part of the facility shall, to the maximum extent feasible, be altered in such manner that the altered portion of the facility is readily accessible to and usable by individuals with disabilities, if the alteration was commenced after January 26, 1992.[50]

At least one court has held that the technology used for voting falls within the regulation's broad definition of *facility*.[51] Absentee ballots are not technically a facility, but the subject matter of this regulation should apply to absentee voting procedures because absentee ballots are akin to a facility. Absentee balloting effectively replaces what would otherwise be a public facility for the purpose of voting. Rather than enter a polling place, a person opens an envelope and follows

---

[47] 29 U.S.C. § 794 (West 2007).
[48] 42 U.S.C. § 12101(a)(3) (West 2005).
[49] Id. § 12101(a)(7).
[50] 28 C.F.R. § 35.151(b) (2006).
[51] *Am. Ass'n of People with Disabilities v. Hood*, 310 F. Supp. 2d 1226, 1235 (S.D. Fla. 2004). But see *Am. Ass'n of People with Disabilities v. Shelley*, 324 F. Supp. 2d 1120, 1126 (C.D. Cal. 2004) (applying ADA regulation regarding services, programs, and activities, 28 C.F.R. § 35.150, in a case involving voting technology).

instructions that are intended to mimic what would happen at the polling place. In other words, absentee ballots are functionally a substitute for a physical facility.

This regulation is particularly useful in that it focuses attention on a state's obligations when it changes its practices. In 2006, dozens of states changed their absentee voting mechanisms, and more are likely to do so in the future. This regulation reminds states that they need to make these new or altered mechanisms accessible *to the maximal extent feasible*.

Even if a court did not consider absentee voting to be a "facility," the ADA Title II regulations also require that "services" be offered on a nondiscriminatory basis. The general rule against discrimination states that "no qualified individual with a disability shall, on the basis of disability, be excluded from participation in or be denied the benefits of the services . . . of a public entity."[52] The opportunity to vote by absentee ballot is a "service" offered as part of its operation of elections. States cannot offer absentee voting in an inaccessible format and then insist that all voters with disabilities vote only at public polling places. If they choose to offer the "service" of absentee voting, then they need to offer it in an accessible manner. As I shall explain, however, not all states have taken adequate steps to ensure that absentee voting is available in an accessible format.

B. Current Practices

With this legal backdrop in mind, this section considers how well current absentee voting practices comply with the letter and the spirit of the ADA's accessibility mandate. Making such an assessment is necessarily impressionistic, given the impracticability of knowing the

---

[52] 28 C.F.R. § 35.130(a) (2006).

accessibility practices of thousands of local electoral jurisdictions throughout the country. Moreover, people have numerous types of disabilities – and many people have a combination of disabilities – that will require different types of accommodations in the voting process. These disabilities include cognitive impairments that preclude understanding complicated directions, fine motor and cognitive impairments that impede an individual's ability to record his or her desired vote, and visual problems that make it difficult to read regular print. Hence, current absentee voting practices are likely to fall short of meeting the goal of secret and independent voting for all voters.

Successfully casting an absentee ballot typically requires the voter to do three things: (1) request an absentee ballot, (2) mark his or her choices on the ballot, and (3) comply with the electoral jurisdiction's rules regarding the return of the absentee ballot. Completing these three steps may pose a significant challenge for many voters with disabilities.

The state of Ohio's election process provides an example of the difficulties that people with different disabilities are likely to encounter when voting by mail-in absentee ballot. Ohio recently became a "no excuse" absentee voting state and, at the same time, imposed certain identification requirements on those individuals who vote by absentee ballot.[53] Under this law, absentee voters are required to provide certain identifying information, both when they request an absentee ballot and when they return their completed absentee ballot.[54]

In the November 2006 election, voters who requested an absentee ballot by mail or telephone received two pages of instructions on different-colored paper, containing many paragraphs of instructions on each page. Some of these instructions related to compliance

[53] *See* Ohio Rev. Code Ann. §§ 3509.03, 3509.04, 3509.05 (West 2006) (codifying the subcommittee on House Bill 234).
[54] Ohio Rev. Code Ann. §§ 3509.03, 3509.04, 3509.05 (West 2006).

with Ohio's voter identification rules[55] and could be confusing for individuals with cognitive impairments. For example, voters were instructed that they could comply with the voter identification requirement by including their driver's license number, the last four digits of their social security number, or a copy of various documents, such as a utility bill, that showed their name and current address.[56] One complication is that an Ohio driver's license includes two numbers. In the 2006 general election, many voters did not know which number should be recorded – something that proved especially tricky because the "correct" number, in the state's view, was not the one appearing at the top of the license, but instead the one appearing in a less prominent position beneath the driver's address. In fact, this requirement was so confusing that the secretary of state agreed to a consent order on the eve of the election governing those who used an incorrect form of identification.[57] Further, voters had to include identifying information in two places – one on a sheet of paper that accompanied the ballot and another on the outside of the sealed envelope.

Even if voters succeed in applying for an absentee ballot, completing and returning that ballot could pose serious challenges for some

---

[55] Ohio's rules regarding identification for absentee voters were challenged before the 2006 general election *Ne. Ohio Coal. for the Homeless v. Blackwell*, 467 F.3d 999 (6th Cir. 2006) (staying Temporary Restraining Order (TRO) against identification requirements for absentee voters). A few days before the election, parties ultimately agreed to and the district court entered a consent order clarifying the rules for that election. Consent Order, available at http://moritzlaw.osu.edu/electionlaw/litigation/documents/NEOCHConsentOrd.pdf. Additional filings in this case are available at http://moritzlaw.osu.edu/electionlaw/litigation/NEOCHv.Blackwell.php

[56] See Ohio Sec'y of State, 2006 Voter Information Guide, available at http://www.sos.-state.oh.us/sos/PublicAffairs/VoterInfoGuide.aspx?Section=16 (on file with the *McGeorge Law Review*). J. Kenneth Blackwell, Ohio Sec'y of State, Directive 2006-78 3 (Oct. 26, 2006), available at http://moritzlaw.

[57] See Consent Order, *Ne. Ohio Coal. for the Homeless v. Blackwell*, 467 F.3d 999 (6th Cir. 2006) (No. C206-896), available at http://moritzlaw.osu.edu/electionlaw/litigation/documents/NEOCHConsentOrd.pdf (on file with the *McGeorge Law Review*).

voters with disabilities. Ohio's 2006 absentee voting materials included an insert regarding a ballot measure that was included in the absentee ballot but not on the official ballot used by voters at the polling place. The absentee ballots had been printed before the secretary of state ruled that one ballot measure could not properly be on the ballot. Additionally, the absentee ballot contained so many inserts that it required more than standard postage. Rather than clearly indicate the amount of required postage, or provide a postage-free envelope, the instructions simply instructed the voter to realize that more than standard postage *might* be required. This statement added to the confusion of the already-confusing ballot. (Ohio has recently announced that it will provide a postage-paid return envelope for absentee voting in the 2008 election.) Election officials tried to enhance the readability of the 2006 instructions by using a large typeface on different-colored paper. In the end, however, there was little that election officials could do to enhance the ease of voting because the underlying rules and instructions were quite complicated, especially with regard to voter identification.

Absent a showing of compelling need, states should not implement requirements that voters produce identification in order to vote, particularly because many voters with disabilities are likely to lack a driver's license, the most common form of state-issued photo identification.[58] Alternatively, electoral jurisdictions might waive identification requirements as an accommodation for voters who mark a box indicating that they have a disability and do not have a driver's license.

Voters with visual impairments may also have difficulty obtaining and casting an absentee ballot without assistance. Although Ohio voters could request an application for an absentee ballot by telephone, Ohio law requires that the absentee ballot application itself must be

---

[58] See John Pawasarat, *The Driver License Status of the Voting Age Population in Wisconsin* (2005) (unpublished paper, available at http://www.uwm.edu/Dept/ETI/barriers/DriversLicense.pdf) (on file with the *McGeorge Law Review*).

completed in writing.[59] For voters with visual impairments, as well as those with cognitive impairments, the absentee ballot application process could be a severe barrier to access.

Marking a paper ballot may also pose a significant challenge for voters with visual impairments. Recall that under HAVA, every polling place must have at least one unit accessible to voters with disabilities, including voters with visual impairments.[60] States have met this requirement through voting equipment, such as direct record electronic (DRE) machines that have an audio capacity for voters with visual impairments.[61] (DRE machines are also helpful to voters with learning disabilities who may have trouble reading or lining up printed material.) This technology allows these voters to vote secretly and independently. Because an electronic voting machine cannot be sent through the mail to all voters, they are required to use paper-based systems such as optical-scan ballots, which have inherent limitations for voters with visual impairments.[62] "Tactile ballots" have been created to help voters with visual impairments read and mark their ballots. These ballots utilize raised surfaces that a voter may feel with his or her hands, but many people with visual impairments still cannot review and verify their choices.[63] Large-print absentee ballots might accommodate a subset of voters with visual impairments but may create problems of their own. The optical-scan ballots used for mail voting must typically be of a standard size to be fed through optical-scan machines that "read" the ballot. Because a large-print ballot would necessarily have to be configured differently from the ballots used by other voters, it would likely be necessary for election officials to take

[59] Ohio Rev. Code Ann. §§ 3509.03, 3509.08 (West 2006).

[60] 42 U.S.C. § 15481(a)(3) (West 2005).

[61] Daniel P. Tokaji, *The Paperless Chase: Electronic Voting and Democratic Values*, 73 Fordham L. Rev. 1711, 1723–24 (2005).

[62] See Brennan Center for Justice, *The Machinery of Democracy: Voting System Security, Accessibility, Usability, and Cost* 76 (2006), http://ceimn.org/files/BrennanCenter VotingTechnologyAssessmentReport.pdf (on file with the *McGeorge Law Review*).

[63] Id.

the large-print ballots marked by the voters and then re-record their choices on standard-sized substitute ballots in order for them to be counted.

Voters with fine motor skill impairments may also have difficulty with mail-in ballots. Ohio's 2006 absentee ballot again serves as a good example. The instructions indicated that voters should fill in the "bubble" on the ballot, which would be read by an optical scanner once received by election officials. This requirement could prove difficult for many voters with limited use of their hands. By contrast, those voting at the polls might be provided with electronic voting systems with "sip and puff" technology, allowing voters to cast their ballots even if they cannot use their hands at all.[64]

It might be possible to develop accommodations that would allow individuals with some of these impairments to cast absentee ballots by mail. For example, some voters with dexterity impairments might be able to use a stamp beside their desired choice if it is too difficult to use a pen or pencil. To the extent that these voters are not able to mark their ballots in a conventional way, it might be necessary for election officials to ensure that they have been fully completed. For example, in a system where voters must darken a bubble, election workers should inspect those bubbles to make sure they are filled in properly. If a voter circles the bubble rather than filling it in, then election officials should be permitted to create a substitute ballot that can be read by the optical scanner while preserving the original. Similarly, if a voter does not fill the bubble in darkly enough for the scanner to read the mark, then the election official should be permitted to create a substitute ballot with the appropriate circles darkened. These procedures will help ensure that all voters' ballots are counted. Although they may well involve considerable time and expense for election officials, they are especially important for people with manual dexterity impairments that prevent them from exerting sufficient pressure to make a machine-readable mark on

---

[64] See Tokaji, supra note 62, at 1769–70.

the ballot. They are also important for people with cognitive impairments that may impede their ability to read complex instructions.

The preceding descriptions are meant to provide a sampling of the types of problems that voters with various disabilities are likely to experience in requesting, marking, and returning absentee ballots. Accessible voting technology now available at polling places has the potential to allow some of these voters to cast secret and independent ballots in a way that is difficult, if not impossible, with mail-in absentee ballots. As a practical matter, however, many voters with disabilities will find it less burdensome to vote from their homes than to go to the polls on Election Day. For these voters, it is necessary to consider other means to facilitate absentee voting.

C. Alternative Absentee Voting Methods

States could take several steps to make absentee voting more accessible for people with disabilities. At a minimum, state and local electoral jurisdictions' Web sites should meet all recommended guidelines for Web site design so that individuals with visual impairments can easily navigate the system and learn how to register to vote or request an absentee ballot. Some other modest changes to mail voting that could improve its accessibility include providing Braille or large-print ballots for voters with visual impairments. More fundamentally, state and local election officials should consider providing methods for people with disabilities to vote absentee, other than traditional mail voting.

One possibility is to expand the ways in which voters can obtain and return absentee ballot applications. All states allow voters to accomplish these tasks in person or by mail, but, as of 2004, there were ten states that did not allow voters to obtain absentee ballot applications via telephone.[65] Allowing voters to file absentee voter applications by telephone would

---

[65] GAO, *Evolving Election System*, supra note 13, at 106.

eliminate problems that can occur when these applications may only be made by mail. States might also allow voters to apply for absentee ballots by e-mail, Web sites, or facsimile even though some voters with disabilities will not be able to use these methods. From an accessibility standpoint, an even better option would be to provide voters with disabilities the option of attaining permanent absentee voter status, so that they would not need to apply for an absentee ballot in every election.

State and local election officials should also consider expanding the ways in which absentee ballots may be cast, including phone and Internet-based methods.[66] The state of Oregon has experimented with two alternative methods to accommodate voters with disabilities in that state's otherwise all-mail system.[67]

The first method, the Accessible Ballot Marking System (ABMS), is a form of phone voting. Although phone voting has some serious limitations in its present incarnation, it has the potential to enhance access for some voters with disabilities.[68] In Oregon's phone voting system, voters may use a special accessible telephone system, which is located at county offices. The system has a standard phone pad marked with a raised dot on the 5 key for easy navigation by people with visual impairments. Voters make their choices using a phone key-pad and the results are then faxed from a remote location to the county

---

[66] The United Kingdom has used telephone voting to accommodate some people with disabilities. See AT Network, Issue Brief on Accessible Voting Machines, available at http://www.atnet.org/index.php?page=accessible-voting-machines (last visited Aug. 29, 2007) (on file with the *McGeorge Law Review*).

[67] See e-mail from Chad Eggspuehler to Professor Daniel Tokaji (Nov. 14, 2006; 09:49 EST) (on file with the *McGeorge Law Review*) (recounting a conversation with Oregon's HAVA director, Gene Newton); e-mail from Gene A. Newton, HAVA Director, to Chad Eggspuehler (Nov. 15, 2006; 08:53 EST) (on file with the *McGeorge Law Review*). The descriptions of the Oregon system in the following paragraphs were derived from these e-mails.

[68] See Brennan Center for Justice, supra note 63, at 77 (describing limitations of phone voting systems for people with auditory and fine motor skill impairments).

office (face down, to protect voter privacy). Voters who are not able to read the ballot themselves may obtain assistance from a bipartisan team of election workers. Of course, voters who obtain such assistance must forfeit the privacy that is secured by polling place, accessible voting technology. This system also requires the voter to travel to the election office, so it is not a perfect substitute for regular absentee voting. Nonetheless, this technology might be adapted to allow phone voting from voters' homes. Because voters who use this system likely lack the ability to drive their own automobile or readily obtain transportation, the requirement to travel to a county office eliminates the convenience that other voters are able to obtain by voting from the privacy of their homes. Hence, it is not surprising that few voters took advantage of this alternative in Oregon. It is an example of what might be called technical rather than meaningful accessibility compliance. But if this system could be expanded to allow voters with visual impairments to vote from their homes, then it could provide both technical and meaningful accessibility.

The other alternative method used in Oregon is for voters to receive a HyperText Markup Language (HTML) ballot by e-mail. To use an HTML ballot, voters must have a computer with e-mail, a Web browser, and a printer. And they must own whatever software is necessary for them to "read" computer text. Voters may "mark" their HTML ballot using their Web browser and, when they have finished doing so, print it out and mail it. This option works with voice-activated software and text-enlargement programs, allowing voting in the privacy of one's home. But it can only be used if the voter has adequate assistive technology at home. Further, some voters may not be able to verify their choices independently or may need assistance in mailing the ballot through the regular mail system, undermining the privacy of the system.

Despite these apparent advantages to alternative methods of casting an absentee ballot, Oregon's alternative voting methods have been lightly used. Only eighteen voters used the ABMS system in Oregon's

2006 elections, while only eighty-three voters used the HTML system. Moreover, not all of these voters were individuals with disabilities. For example, in Washington County – the Oregon county that had the heaviest use of the HTML system – a total of thirty-two people voted through this method, only five of whom were people with disabilities.[69] Still, the ABMS and HTML systems provide useful examples of ways in which absentee voting could be made more accessible for at least some voters with disabilities.

Another possibility that state and local election officials should consider is to take the polling place to the voter. Rather than making these voters go to a central location before Election Day, election officials could go to voters where they live. This option is especially promising for voters with disabilities who live in institutional settings like nursing homes, where large numbers of voters reside. In fact, some other countries actually have special stations set up in institutional settings through an election procedure sometimes referred to as "mobile polling."[70] In addition, there are twenty-three states with absentee voting procedures specifically directed to people in nursing homes, senior citizen housing, mental health facilities, VA hospitals, or like facilities.[71] State procedures typically require election officials to take absentee ballots to facilities, where they may supervise and provide assistance to voters.[72] Even where the law does not require it, election officials may engage in outreach to facilitate voting by individuals who reside at institutions with a significant number of residents who have

---

[69] The others using the HTML system were fifteen military voters, five people voting from out of state, and seven people voting from out of county. E-mail from Gene A. Newton to Chad Eggspuehler (Dec. 11, 2006) (on file with the *McGeorge Law Review*).

[70] See Jason Karlawish & Richard Bonnie, *Voting by Elderly Persons with Cognitive Impairments: Lessons from Other Democratic Nations*, 38 McGeorge L. Rev. (2007) [draft at 6, 11–13, 22].

[71] Amy Smith & Charles P. Sabatino, *Voting by Residents of Nursing Homes and Assisted Living Facilities: State Law Accommodations*, 26 BIFOCAL 1, 1 (2004).

[72] Id. at 4.

disabilities. If that option is adopted, it is very important for election officials to provide special training to the workers at those facilities because they are likely to have many requests from voters who need assistance or desire to use assistive technology. For example, in Franklin County, Ohio, officials have established relationships with nursing homes and group homes and travel to these locations in order to help people with disabilities apply for and cast absentee ballots.[73] The Board of Elections works with the state's association of nursing homes to identify institutions in the county and sends them a letter offering assistance with absentee voting applications and ballots.[74] Poll workers at these facilities should receive special training to prepare them to assist a population that may face challenges in casting their ballots.

A variant on this alternative that electoral jurisdictions should consider is taking accessible technology to voters. People voting at the polling place now have access to technology that can accommodate many voters with visual, manual, and cognitive impairments. Yet some of these voters may find it difficult or tiring to go to the polls on Election Day and thus would be unable to use this technology. A potential means of dealing with this problem is to have election officials take accessible voting technology to nursing homes and other locations with significant numbers of voters.[75] This would combine the stay-at-home advantages of absentee voting with the accessibility advantages of current technology that is now available only at public polling places.

---

[73] Interview by Daniel Tokaji with Matt Damschroder, Board of Elections, Franklin Co., Ohio (Dec. 19, 2006) (notes on file with the *McGeorge Law Review*).

[74] Id.

[75] In order for this option to provide meaningful accessibility, it would be very important for poll workers stationed at a nursing home to have special training in working with individuals with disabilities and for a high percentage of the machines at such places to be accessible to people with a wide range of disabilities. Anecdotally, we have heard that nursing homes are sometimes chosen as polling places, but inexperienced poll workers can be overwhelmed with the challenges presented by the large number of voters needing assistance or extra time at such polling places.

Making absentee voting more accessible to people with disabilities demands thinking beyond the mail voting paradigm. While some people with disabilities will be able to vote through this method, there is a high risk of incomplete applications, improperly marked ballots, and other mistakes that can prevent one's vote from being counted. Just as important, paper ballots do not allow some voters with disabilities to vote secretly and independently, as is possible with technology available at the public polling place. Phone and Internet-based methods of voting may offer a partial solution to these barriers, although their present incarnations have some significant limitations that prevent many voters with disabilities from using them. Election officials need to engage in outreach by making contact with facilities in which significant numbers of voters with disabilities reside.[76] Taking accessible technology to voters in their homes appears to be a promising solution.

III. CONCLUSION

It is tempting to advocate a set of "best practices," but the existing research on the problem is not sufficiently well developed at this stage to provide a basis for recommendations of this sort. Instead, this part suggests a menu of choices for policymakers and election officials to consider. Some combination of the following possible reforms should make it easier to obtain and cast an accurate ballot while safeguarding the absentee voting process from ballot manipulation:

- *Better Outreach.* The prevalent model requires voters to take the first step, by initiating contact with election officials to request and then return an application for absentee voter status. As a practical matter, this is likely to prove difficult for many voters with physical and

---

[76] See Smith & Sabatino, supra note 72, at 4 (noting that procedures that require local election authorities to "initiate contact with covered facilities" may help eliminate barriers to effective participation).

cognitive disabilities, some of whom may not be aware of a forth-coming election.[77] Election officials should take affirmative steps to make contact with nursing homes, group homes, and similar facilities well in advance of Election Day to make sure that residents can comply with deadlines for applying for absentee voter status. Such outreach is particularly vital for voters of lower socioeconomic status, who are already among the least likely to participate.

- *Easing the Application Process.* Existing processes for obtaining an absentee ballot can be confusing for many voters, especially those with cognitive disabilities. Relatively simple steps that could be taken include broadening the means through which absentee ballots can be requested. Applications should be permitted by phone and Internet-based means, as well as through the mail and in person. It is also critical to simplify the requirements for obtaining an absentee ballot. Ohio provides a prime example, where a highly complex voter identification law effectively imposed a barrier to access. To the extent that people with cognitive impairments have trouble complying with such rules, resulting in their being denied an absentee ballot, there is a strong argument that these rules violate the ADA. This author strongly encourage states with similar requirements for obtaining an absentee ballot to consider simplifying their laws.
- *Permanent Absentee Voter Status.* One way of easing the burden on voters with disabilities is to allow those with long-term disabilities to secure permanent absentee voter status, thus obviating the need for them to apply for an absentee ballot in every election. There are, of course, risks that are associated with allowing permanent absentee voter status, because it might make it easier for unscrupulous individuals to take advantage of people in their care and engage in fraud. For example, a nursing home provider could conceivably induce people with cognitive impairments to sign

[77] See Smith & Sabatino, *supra* note 72, at 4.

applications for permanent absentee voter status, enabling him or her to intercept, vote, and return all of their absentee ballots in subsequent elections. Such risks can be mitigated through procedural mechanisms, like sending election officials to locations where a significant number of people vote absentee.

- *More Accessible Ballots.* Easing the application process is only part of the battle. If voters cannot actually vote their absentee ballots secretly and independently, then their right to vote is compromised. While mail-in absentee ballots have some inherent limitations, there are steps that could make this means of voting more accessible to people with physical and cognitive disabilities. Tactile and large-print ballots could assist some voters with visual impairments. HTML ballots, which can be marked and printed with a home computer, may help others vote independently. The obvious limitation of such technology, however, is that it may exclude a significant segment of the polity – especially those of limited means who do not have ready access to such technology. Still, these mechanisms hold some promise for some voters, for whom traveling to the polls poses a significant burden. Policymakers and electoral jurisdictions should give consideration to alternative methods of voting. One possibility is phone voting. In its present form, phone voting requires voters to go to a central location, thus limiting its accessibility for those who have difficulty traveling outside their homes. Possibly, phone voting could be expanded in the future to allow more people with disabilities to vote independently.

- *Guidance for Caregivers.* Even with the best imaginable accommodations, some voters with disabilities are likely to require third-party assistance in applying for and voting an absentee ballot. For individuals assisting such voters, the line between providing appropriate assistance and engaging in impermissible coercion or proxy voting may be unclear.[78] These problems may be particularly

---

[78] See Karlawish et al., supra note 21, at 1347–48.

significant for voters with cognitive impairments like dementia, who depend upon spouses, children, or institutional caregivers for support. There is a danger that such people, well-meaning though they may be, will "inject[] their own preferences into interactions with voters, such as suggesting how the ballot should be cast."[79] Another problem is that such caregivers may provide an inappropriate "gatekeeping" role by failing to help someone obtain an absentee ballot – even though they still have the ability to understand the nature and effect of voting.[80] Such caregivers need to receive specific instructions on the legal requirements for voting and on the degree of assistance that is permissible. Caregivers should also be encouraged to seek assistance and advice from election officials if they are uncertain about whether they may be crossing an impermissible line.

- *Mobile Polling.* A final possibility is to take the polling place to the voter by having election officials go to nursing homes and similar facilities prior to Election Day and assist people in casting their votes. If accompanied by appropriate procedures, this method of voting could enhance both the accessibility and the integrity of absentee voting. A related possibility is that accessible technology – which HAVA requires only at polling places – could be taken to voters where they live. This option would be most feasible at facilities like nursing homes, where large numbers of people with disabilities live, but it is also possible that election officials could take accessible voting equipment to voters in group homes or even private homes on request. This option could be especially important for the many voters with disabilities who live in poverty, for whom it is especially difficult to obtain transportation to a polling place where accessible equipment may be found. To the extent that local jurisdictions lack the resources to accomplish this option,

[79] Id. at 1348.
[80] Id. at 1346.

Congress or state legislatures should consider making funds available, as a means of ensuring that no person with a disability is left out of the democratic process.

This list is undoubtedly incomplete. Other means can certainly be developed to promote the accessibility and integrity of absentee voting. Accordingly, policymakers and election officials must devote greater attention to the needs of people with a wide range of disabilities who choose to vote absentee. Despite the intense scrutiny that has been given to election administration in the past several years, there remains a large and scarcely examined crack at the intersection between absentee voting and accessible voting. Absent further reform, many people with disabilities will continue to fall through that crack.

7

Reflections on Race: The Limits of Formal Equality

In THIS BOOK, I HAVE ARGUED THAT THE FORMAL equality model has not been well equipped to help attain substantive equality for individuals with disabilities, because it does not correctly target who is deserving of assistance and has not been effective in developing appropriate remedies. Chapter 3 argued that the courts have undermined Congress's attempts to legislate an anti-subordination model in the employment context under the Americans with Disabilities Act by failing to protect the 43 million Americans whom Congress identified as being entitled to assistance. Chapter 4 demonstrated that Congress presumed under the Individuals with Disabilities Education Act that an integrated educational environment is better than a more segregated educational environment in the K–12 context even though the available empirical data do not support that presumption. I argued that the integration presumption was reflexively borrowed from the racial context without consideration of whether it was effective in the disability context. While Chapter 4 suggested that we have overused integration tools in the K–12 context, Chapter 5 argued that we should be seeking *more* integrated methods of testing in the higher education context. Once again, empirical data, rather than unwarranted presumptions, should guide policy so that we can help individuals with disabilities attain substantive equality. Chapter 6 applied an anti-subordination perspective to the area of voting to argue that we could do a better job of improving the availability of voting to individuals with disabilities if we moved beyond the integration paradigm to consider how to make in-home voting more accessible to individuals with disabilities. Throughout this book, I have been agnostic about the remedy of integration and have insisted that integration be chosen as a remedy only when it can be shown to be likely to produce substantive equality.

Because my anti-subordination framework was initially developed in the race context, it is appropriate to end this book by asking what I may have learned about how the anti-subordination framework could better fit that context. I argued that the integration presumption, for example, may have made sense in the disability context when first developed in the mid-1970s at a time when disability-only settings were often inhumane warehouses. But I argued that current empirical data and a changing society make that presumption outdated. It is not that we have "solved" the problem of disability discrimination and can abandon the search for remedies. It is that the nature of disability discrimination has changed over the past thirty years and it is time to be flexible to consider a new array of remedies based on contemporary empirical data. What might we see if we applied the same perspective to race discrimination and allowed empirical data to guide our quest for remedies?[1]

I should note at the outset that I enter this discussion with much trepidation because I do *not* want to be associated with the perspective that we no longer need race-conscious remedies to solve the problem of race discrimination. I consider Justice O'Connor's statement "We expect that 25 years from now, the use of racial preferences will no longer be necessary to further the interest approved today"[2] to be the result of a creative imagination or wishful thinking rather than empirical data. I have seen no data that suggest that the problem of racial discrimination and educational inequality is behind us.

---

[1] I have also read extensively about how this perspective might be applied to the gender educational context but found the empirical literature too inconclusive to offer any observations at this time.

[2] *Grutter v. Bollinger*, 539 U.S. 306, 343 (2003).

My anti-subordination perspective can provide two useful insights in this area. First, this perspective can help us understand why race-conscious tools must continue to be necessary to attain substantive equality. An equality perspective that is not constrained by principles of formal equality will select race-conscious tools in the education area when those tools are likely to improve the educational performance of historically subordinated groups such as African-American children. Second, the remedies that are selected under an anti-subordination perspective will be driven by the empirical data rather than unwarranted presumptions. These data can help us identify that certain types of integrated educational environments are likely to attain positive outcomes for African-American children. The law should support school districts' choosing the tools needed to attain those educational environments even if race-conscious means need to be part of that tool chest. In fact, this chapter will argue that a failure to use race-conscious tools is likely to lead to unacceptable educational results for many African-American children. The Supreme Court's formal equality model has caused it to leap to various conclusions about appropriate educational programs without examining any empirical literature in depth.

This chapter will examine the litigation involving Seattle, Washington, and Jefferson County, Kentucky, to make those arguments. These school districts were the target of extensive litigation, as resolved by the Supreme Court in *Parents Involved in Community Schools v. Seattle School District No. 1*.[3] In both cases, the school districts used race-conscious measures to help attain racial integration in their public schools, and, in both cases, the Supreme Court used a formal equality model to resolve the dispute. Chief Justice Roberts authored the opinion for the Court striking down those plans, in which he made the classic formal equality statement "The way to stop discrimination on the basis of race is to stop discriminating on the basis

---

[3] 127 S. Ct. 2738 (2007).

of race."[4] That approach, I will argue, is simplistic and simply wrong.

In Part I of this chapter, I will discuss the evolution of the specific plans adopted by both school districts so the reader can see the modest nature of the use of race in both cities. Further, I will show that this modest use of race was not a result of data or literature suggesting that such limited uses of race are most likely to attain the best possible educational gains for minority children. In fact, as I will argue in Part II, the empirical literature suggests that more educational gains would have been likely to have been made through increased use of racial factors in school assignments. The modest use of race was in response to community pressure (by white parents) *not* to use race at all in school assignment and in response to an awareness of the restrictions imposed by constitutional law. Formal equality has become a political and litigation tool for some white parents to derail an attempt by school districts to create an educational program that is likely to be more successful for minority children.

From an anti-subordination perspective, the courts have the racial equality model exactly backward. The empirical literature, which I will discuss in Part II, suggests that the only way to end race discrimination is to take race into account in school assignments from kindergarten onward. If the school plans were to be struck down in Seattle or Jefferson County, they should have been struck down for *not using race enough*. School districts, and courts, are caught in the limitations of the formal equality model and therefore try to create school assignment plans to use race as little as possible to achieve token integration. Such token integration is not likely to attain substantive equality for minority children and, ironically, is likely to be struck down by the courts as being too race-conscious. In this chapter, I will argue that we should abandon a formal equality model and replace it with an anti-subordination model that measures equality by virtue of the

---

[4] Id. at 2768. This statement was also contained in the Ninth Circuit's dissenting opinion. See 426 F.3d at 1191 n.34.

substantive educational results attained by school districts, not whether they used race-conscious means to attain those results.

I. SEATTLE AND JEFFERSON COUNTY

A. Seattle

The record in the Seattle case shows how difficult it is to get the community to cooperate with attempts to integrate schools at the youngest grades, and to accept efforts that have a mandatory school assignment component. In 1977, Seattle adopted a plan that "divided the district into zones, within which majority-dominated elementary schools were paired with minority-dominated elementary schools to achieve desegregation. Mandatory high school assignments were linked to elementary school assignments, although various voluntary transfer options were available."[5] A state initiative soon attempted to stop this plan although the United States Supreme Court ultimately declared the initiative unconstitutional.[6] Seattle modified its desegregation plan in 1988 to decrease its reliance on mandatory busing, which, under the prior plan, had required the mandatory busing of nonwhite students in disproportionate numbers. Community dissatisfaction, rather than educational outcomes, seems to have caused these changes. In 1998, Seattle made further modifications. This time, it limited its diversity efforts to the high schools, and 90 percent of the students in the district were assigned to their first-choice school. "Of the approximately 3,000 incoming students entering Seattle high schools in the 2000–01 school year, approximately 300 were assigned to an oversubscribed high school based on the race-based tie breaker."[7]

---

[5] *Seattle School District No. 1 v. Parents Involved in Community Schools*, 426 F.3d 1162, 1168 (9th Cir. 2005).

[6] *Washington v. Seattle School District No. 1*, 458 U.S. 457, 470 (1982).

[7] 426 F.3d at 1170.

The Seattle School Board decided to make race a factor in assignment to public high schools in 1998 in order to create more equal educational opportunities in the city. The school district acknowledged that despite its best efforts, "it remains a stark reality that disproportionately, the schools located in the northern end of the city continue to be the most popular and prestigious, and competition for assignment to those schools is keen."[8] Because of housing patterns segregated on the basis of both race and socioeconomic factors, it also remained true that minority students tended to live in south Seattle and would not be assigned to schools in north Seattle if neighborhood housing patterns exclusively determined school choice. Hence, the Seattle School Board created what it called a "tie breaker" mechanism for schools that were not racially balanced, which it defined as schools in which the racial composition deviated by more than 15 percent from the overall population of the students attending Seattle's public schools. It limited application of the tie breaker to students entering the ninth grade and did not use it for students in the higher grades.[9] Although it experimented with using mandatory busing to achieve racial balance, it abandoned it in light of parental complaints and, instead, moved to a system whereby parents would request their "choice." The racial balancing plan affected who was given his or her first choice from those who chose one of the five most popular schools as their first choice but did not result in anyone's being bussed to those schools who had not selected that school as first choice.

Litigation ensued after the adoption of the 1998 plan.[10] Two of the lead plaintiffs alleged that they were assigned to Ingraham High School rather than one of the three premier high schools in Seattle. They alleged that school buses were not available to transport them to Ingraham so that they would have had to spend over four hours commuting

---

[8] Id. at 1225.
[9] Id. at 1239.
[10] See *Parents Involved in Community Schools v. Seattle School District No. 1*, 137 F. Supp.2d 1224 (W.D. Wash. 2001).

to high school each day. Because of the unacceptability of that option, the parents chose to send them to private schools that were presumably closer to their homes.[11] (The Washington Supreme Court later noted when it heard the case that the long commute occurred because the students refused to list the names of any local schools on their school choice form. The Court concluded, "It is impossible to determine what their commute would have been had they participated in the selection process."[12]) The district court upheld the plan as meeting various constitutional requirements. Its primary focus was on whether the program used a racial preference as little as possible to attain racial diversity. The court's opinion focused little attention on two factors that I have suggested should be important: (1) whether there was evidence that the academic performance of minority students who benefited from this racial "tie breaker" appeared to improve as a result of their ability to be educated at one of the excellent schools in predominantly white neighborhoods and (2) whether this program was effective given that it did not begin until ninth grade and was only mandatory for one year of school. Given the greater educational resources that the court acknowledged existed at the most popular schools, it is highly likely that students saw an improvement in educational performance upon being admitted to one of those schools. Nonetheless, the opinion contains no discussion of that fact. Although the educational benefits from integration may have been higher if adopted in earlier grades, it appears that Seattle abandoned using race as a factor in the lower grades for political rather than educational reasons.

On appeal, the Ninth Circuit concluded that the plan violated Washington State law and did not reach the federal constitutional issues.[13] It did not discuss the effectiveness of the education offered

---

[11] See *Parents Involved in Community Schools v. Seattle School District No. 1*, 285 F.3d 1236, 1241 (9th Cir. 2001).

[12] 72 P.3d at 156.

[13] 285 F.3d at 1253.

under the plan; it focused entirely on whether the plan could be considered an impermissible race-conscious plan. Several months later, a petition for rehearing was granted by a three-judge panel and the first appellate opinion was vacated.[14] The Ninth Circuit requested that the Washington Supreme Court agree to hear the novel state constitutional law issues raised by the case, because the prior decision had rested entirely on state law. Although the earlier Ninth Circuit injunction was lifted, the Seattle School District chose to suspend using race as a factor in school assignments.[15]

The Washington Supreme Court agreed to hear the case and concluded that the plan did not violate Washington's statutory or constitutional law. Although the opinion did not note any specific evidence about the academic success of Washington's integration program, it did note, "There is strong empirical evidence that a racially diverse school population provides educational benefits for all students. Most students educated in racially diverse schools demonstrated improved critical thinking skills – the ability to both understand and challenge views which are different from their own. . . . Research has also shown that a diverse educational experience improves race relations, reduces prejudicial attitudes, and achieves a more democratic and inclusive experience for all citizens."[16] The Court, however, does not discuss whether those generalities have been shown to be true in Seattle.

After the decision of the Washington Supreme Court, the case returned to the Ninth Circuit.[17] Once again, the Ninth Circuit invalidated the plan. This time it did so under the Fourteenth Amendment to the United States Constitution. The Ninth Circuit's opinion made brief mention of the academic achievement of the students at Seattle's various

---

[14] *Parents Involved in Community Schools v. Seattle School District No. 1*, 294 F.3d 1084 (9th Cir. 2002).

[15] 377 F.3d at 958.

[16] Id. at 162.

[17] *Parents Involved in Community Schools v. Seattle School District No. 1*, 377 F.3d 949 (9th Cir. 2004).

schools, noting that students at the more elite schools had significantly higher standardized test scores than students at the less desirable high schools.[18] But the opinion contained no discussion of how those test scores might have been influenced by students' transferring from one high school to another. The Ninth Circuit concluded that the Seattle plan was unconstitutional because its use of race was not sufficiently narrowly tailored. The use of race was too mechanical and other race-neutral mechanisms were not sufficiently explored to attain diversity.

This decision was not the end of the story in the Ninth Circuit. The Ninth Circuit voted to hear the case en banc.[19] More than a year later, the en banc panel issued its decision affirming the injunction issued nearly four years earlier in favor of the school district. The Ninth Circuit en banc opinion summarized the educational and social benefits that can result from increased diversity such as improved critical thinking skills, socialization and citizenship advantages, and networking advantages.[20] But the court did not examine any evidence as to whether the specific plan adopted in Seattle succeeded in achieving those benefits in that section of its opinion. The only evidence specific to the benefits attained in Seattle was brief testimony by the principal of one high school, who stated that "students of different races and backgrounds tend to have significant interactions both in class and outside of class. When I came to [the high school], there were racial tensions in the school, reflected in fighting and disciplinary problems. These kinds of problems have, to a large extent, disappeared."[21] The dissent notes that the majority only cited the studies that described the benefits that flow from integration and observed that other studies have reached different conclusions.[22] Like the majority, the dissent

---

[18] Id. at 954 n. 1.

[19] *Parents Involved in Community Schools v. Seattle School District No. 1*, 426 F.3d 1162 (2005).

[20] 426 F.3d at 1174–75.

[21] Id. at 1182 (quoting Eric Benson, the principal of Nathan Hale High School).

[22] 426 F.3d at 1205–7.

does not point to any evidence to suggest which results – positive or negative – are likely to result in the Seattle context.

The primary focus of both the majority and dissent is whether racial diversity could be attained through means that were not overtly racial. Everyone seemed to agree that racial diversity was a good, in itself, but everyone also seemed to agree that race-conscious means to achieve racial diversity are, themselves, a harm to be avoided. Hence, if Seattle could attain racial diversity through entirely race-neutral means such as a lottery or even the use of socioeconomic status, then the result of racial diversity would be permissible. The only reason that Seattle found itself the subject of protracted litigation was that it used an overt racial factor to attain racial diversity.

The presence or absence of race as a factor is the primary focus of the courts' opinions. The lead plaintiffs alleged that their first-choice schools were oversubscribed and that they were assigned to a school far from their home that would require four hours for a roundtrip commute on public transportation. Although many students of their race were able to attend those first-choice schools, their odds of being able to attend would have greatly increased if they were nonwhite because, apparently, every nonwhite applicant was admitted to those first-choice schools. The harm they describe is a long commute, which they may have been able to avoid if race had not been a factor in school selection.

The problem with this logic and focus of the various opinions is that the plaintiffs' first-choice high school would still have been oversubscribed under open admissions if race had not been a factor and Seattle had a system of student choice in admissions. Some kind of tie breaker would still have been necessary, and they could have found themselves not admitted to their first-choice schools and assigned to less convenient options. Their "harm" would have been lessened if they knew they got an inferior school assignment because of the operation of a race-neutral lottery? I would suggest that they have learned to "game" the legal system by describing their harm in racial terms when, in fact, they simply wanted access to the best education offered by the public school system in Seattle. They, of course, had no reason to complain for a decade when the operation of the status quo gave them access to white-dominated neighborhood schools. It was only when they lost access to their white enclave that they thought to complain. When they no longer could get free access to their local white-dominated public school, they left the public system and paid to have access to a presumably white-dominated private school. They were only "harmed" when the rules of the game no longer benefited whites who lived in middle-class neighborhoods.

On the basis of the empirical literature discussed in Part II, I would suggest that to the extent there is a problem with the Seattle plan, it is that it is *too narrowly tailored*. Afraid to step on the toes of the public and courts, the city of Seattle came up with a plan that would help a small percentage of the minority students in Seattle who happened to win the lottery to attend one of the predominantly white schools. The formal equality framework under which Seattle had to defend its plan made it virtually impossible to develop an effective, broad-ranging plan. The fact that the Supreme Court could strike down even this extremely narrowly tailored plan suggests that no *effective* plan is likely to pass constitutional muster because, in terms of the empirical literature, an *effective* plan would have to start in kindergarten, be widespread, and be mandatory. Such a race-conscious plan might achieve integration *and* high-quality education, but its use of race would not permit it even to attain serious political or judicial consideration.

The quandary faced by the City of Seattle is caused by the illogical state of equal protection jurisprudence, which has been dominated by the principles of formal equality. The law has developed from the statement from *Brown* that "separate can never be equal" to mean that race can virtually never be an overt factor in trying to attain high-quality education for minority children. Racial diversity is only a permissible objective if it can be achieved through awkward, race-neutral means that, at best, attain incomplete diversity and leave the overwhelming majority of minority students still being educated in substandard educational environments.

What if our lens would change and, instead, we would ask what mechanisms are most likely to attain high-quality education for as many minority students as possible, when a school district has a history of substandard education for those students? Then, we might strike down the Seattle plan *for not going far enough* by still relegating the majority of minority students to a substandard educational environment, especially in the pivotal early grades. Embracing notions of formal equality, the Supreme Court, by contrast, has said that Seattle has *gone too far* in devising a very modest plan that only seeks to attain racial diversity for less than half of the students attending ninth grade in their school system.

The school system's desire to attain racial diversity in terms that might be acceptable to the public and the courts caused it to select means that were not even consistent with the empirical literature on the educational benefits of diversity. Their diversity plan did not begin until ninth grade, it only included one year of education (because transferring could occur the following year), and it was only mandatory if the deviation from random diversity was more than 15 percent. Because the overall nonwhite population in the school system was 60 percent nonwhite, a school would not be subject to the plan if its nonwhite population was as high as 74 percent. It did not apply in seven of the ten Seattle public high schools, and the courts do not provide data for those seven schools. Because schools covered by the plan ranged from 40 to 60 percent nonwhite, though, it is clear that each of the other seven schools is more than 60 percent nonwhite. Of the four "popular" schools covered by the plan, in only three did a shift of nonwhites to the school result. Thus, at most, nonwhites at three of the eleven public high schools operated by the city of Seattle benefited from the integration plan and only at the senior high school grades. Did the plan produce any appreciable improvement in the overall education offered to nonwhites in Seattle? There is no way to know because the various decisions contain no useful data about educational outcomes.

Seattle published an extensive report in December 2006 that tracked student performance over time but contained no data on how the setting for education might affect outcome.[23] Did African-American students who attended schools in which their representation was nearly 10 percent more or less than their expected representation in the population benefit from the so-called advantages of integration? The important point is that a several-hundred-page report that was filled with empirical data *does not even ask any questions about how racial composition of schools correlates with educational outcomes.* The failure to collect data about the results from different learning environments makes it difficult for school officials to structure better learning environments.

B. Kentucky

The litigation in Jefferson County, Kentucky, provides a less complete record to discuss. The outcome, though, was the same – the Court struck down the explicit use of race to attain integrated schools. As in Seattle, the plan for Jefferson County, Kentucky, developed over many years. The Kentucky plan, however, is much more comprehensive and complicated. Kentucky's integration efforts began in 1975 as a result of court-ordered desegregation. In June 2000, the district court dissolved the desegregation decree and ordered the school district to stop using racial quotas at Central High School, and to reevaluate and redesign the admissions procedures in other magnet schools. In response to that court order and community feedback, the school district ended its use of race in assignments to Central High School and

---

[23] See Steven F. Wright, *Seattle Public Schools, Date Profile: District Summary* (December 2006).

three other magnet high schools. But it decided to continue to use race as a factor in what are called "magnet traditional schools."

As did the Seattle plan, the Kentucky plan sought minority school enrollment within 15 percent of their representation in the student population. For the Jefferson County area, that meant a range between 15 and 50 percent African American. (There were no other minorities well represented in the population so the court simply considered race in black/white terms.) The Kentucky plan sought to attain racial integration at all grades, not merely ninth grade.

The racial guidelines did not apply to kindergarten. For the rest of elementary school, children were assigned a school within a "cluster." The clusters were defined, in part, on the basis of racial guidelines in order to attain racial balance. Students were able to request their first- and second-choice schools within the cluster, and nearly all children received one of their two first choices. In middle school and high school, students could attend their neighborhood school or apply for a nontraditional magnet school. Racial guidelines were a factor in admission to some of the magnet and optional programs.

The focus of the litigation was on what were described as "traditional magnet schools." These schools included four elementary, three middle, and two high schools. The traditional program was also offered within two schools and was open to students on a districtwide basis. The traditional schools emphasized basic skills in a highly structured environment and parent participation. Race was used in a more overt way at the traditional schools than at the other schools in the district. Applicants were placed on four lists: black male, black female, white male, and white female. Applicants were chosen from those lists in a way that guaranteed a racial balance (although race was not a factor in selection into kindergarten). Because fewer black than white students tended to apply to traditional schools, black applicants had a higher chance of acceptance to traditional schools than white applicants.[24]

---

[24] 330 F.2d at 848 n. 25.

As in the Seattle litigation, the focus of attention was on whether the program used race as little as possible. The effectiveness of the plan in achieving high-quality education was, at most, a footnote in the courts' opinions. The district court recited the general observation that "racial integration benefits Black students substantially in terms of academic achievement" but offered no evidence as to whether that generalization held true for that school system.[25] In one footnote, the district court commented that students reported in a survey that they thought that going to school in an integrated environment would make them more comfortable working within an integrated workplace.[26] The district court struck down the plan for allocating students to the traditional magnet schools because the means used looked too much like a quota. The court disapproved of the use of separate lists for blacks and whites and concluded that the school district could have attained diversity through less race-conscious means. For students who were not admitted to their first choice because it was oversubscribed, the court concluded that the harm to those students was greater through the use of two separate lists of students rather than a general lottery. No one asked whether the Kentucky plan was successful in improving the academic performance of minority students. The Sixth Circuit affirmed the district court's opinion without further reasoning. As with the district court, the focus of the Supreme Court's reasoning was on whether the plan was sufficiently "narrowly tailored" – whether it used race as little as possible to achieve integration.

The Supreme Court concluded that the Kentucky plan was unconstitutional because its race-conscious measures seemed unnecessary to the attainment of diversity. In Young Elementary, for example, the Court criticized the school district for not being willing to tolerate an enrollment that was 46.8 percent black. Citing Jefferson County's

[25] Id. at 853.
[26] Id. at 854 n. 41.

claim that it needed to have its schools constitute "at least 20 percent" minority group representation "to be visible enough to make a difference," the Court noted that 46 percent is far greater than 20 percent and therefore should be not problematic.[27] But the Court's analysis is overly simplistic and overlooks data that suggest that schools with such high concentrations of African Americans are likely to offer poor educational programs for racial minorities. While it may *also* be true that racial minorities need a critical mass of 20 percent participation to attain positive results in predominantly white educational environments, it is *also* true that schools like Young Elementary are also likely to attain poor results for African-American children.

In theory, Chief Justice Roberts is open to considering evidence about how racial diversity provides educational benefits. He says, "This working backward to achieve a particular type of racial balance, rather than working forward from some demonstration of the level of diversity that provides the purported benefits, is a fatal flaw under our existing precedent."[28] But it is hard to know whether he sincerely means that such evidence could be allowed to support race-conscious measures given his adamant language about the inappropriateness of using race as a criterion in school admissions. Although the studies submitted to the Court might have been able to answer some of those questions, the Roberts opinion makes no attempt to analyze the studies to answer that question. The Court merely asserts that using race-specific means to help "students see fellow students as individuals rather than solely as members of a racial group ... is fundamentally at cross-purposes with that end" without examining any data about students' educational experiences in various educational environments. An examination of our actual educational experiences, rather than platitudes, might help us shape effective educational strategies.

---

[27] 127 S. Ct. at 2756.
[28] Id. at 2757.

C. Conclusion

If one steps back and looks at the legal reasoning that has developed in the race context, it makes little sense. School districts are allowed to try to achieve racial integration so long as they do not use race to achieve that goal. In other words, if they are devious and find race-neutral ways to achieve integration, then they are all right. But, if they are explicit about trying to attain integration by using race-specific means, then their programs are unlikely to pass constitutional muster.

But why do we care so much about integration? I have argued that an important reason that we value integration is a conviction that it helps attain the best possible education for minority children who have historically languished in substandard single-race schools. If the explicit use of race is shown not only to attain integration but to attain high-quality education for minority children, then I have argued that such use of race should certainly be permissible. Given our history of subordination on the basis of race, it is hard to see how race-conscious, integrated education that attains positive outcomes can be unconstitutional. Ironically, the courts' disfavor of the use of racial categories has *hampered* the ability of school systems to attain high-quality education for racial minorities. They are forced to use indirect (race-neutral) means or, if they use race at all, to use it in a very limited manner that is unlikely to be effective. Hence, the city of Seattle has been put in the uncomfortable position of defending its use of race in *only ninth grade for less than 10 percent of the students,* and it abandoned even that modest use of race in the face of litigation. Jefferson County, Kentucky, has sought to defend a broader use of race, but the litigation's fifteen-year history provides little evidence of how the use of race was connected to improved academic performance for minority students.

As the next section will demonstrate, it is very likely that minority students who attend racially integrated schools do perform better academically than their peers who attend single-race schools. That success, however, is likely to depend on the *explicit* use of race to attain

264

meaningful integration. Unfortunately, Supreme Court jurisprudence will make it difficult for school districts to attain those kinds of educational benefits.

II. THE EMPIRICAL DATA

In this section, I will discuss the empirical data cited by the Court in the *Seattle* litigation to argue that the Court did not examine those data adequately or fairly. Then, I am going to examine empirical data that were available but *not* cited by the Court that could provide us with more evidence on what kinds of educational programs are likely to be effective. The data suggest that Seattle's modest approach of integrating a few high schools is not likely to be effective and that Kentucky needed to set a higher threshold for what it considered an adequate racial balance to attain strong results. But, of course, from the Court's perspective, such modifications would have made the programs more rather than less unconstitutional.

A. Empirical Data Cited by the Court

In 1978, Robert Crain and Rita Mahard authored a very thoughtful study in which they examined seventy-three studies that sought to examine the effects of school desegregation on black children. Rather than simply conclude whether desegregation raised the achievement scores of black students, they sought to identify which factors were most closely correlated with positive outcomes for black students.

Their research revealed that the following factors had a positive association with academic achievement for black children. First, they found that desegregation was most effective when it occurred at an early age. They concluded that the "critical point" for desegregation to be effective was grade three or four, a finding that is consistent with other research that has concluded that that age range is a "vulnerable age."[29] They suggested that desegregation efforts are similar to geographic migration: "The elementary school years are an important period for establishing social relationships, so that social relationship should not be disrupted during that time."[30] Their research therefore suggests that school districts should do their utmost to create an integrated educational environment during the early years of elementary school.

Second, they concluded that the curriculum available at the desegregated school has an important effect on educational gains. They note that some researchers have suggested that one is more likely to see gains in math than reading as a result of desegregation, but they account for that difference by observing that it is simply often easier to make major changes in a math curriculum. Because of the role of curriculum in creating educational effects, they note that some segregated schools with strong curriculums have managed to compare favorably with desegregated schools in their community in some subject areas.[31] In terms of their research, one would expect that modern "magnet" schools that highlight strong curriculums in certain subject areas would particularly benefit from accompanying desegregation effects.

Third, their research resulted in the somewhat surprising conclusion that mandatory desegregation plans are more likely to achieve positive academic results for black children than voluntary plans. They examined each of the mandatory or voluntary desegregation studies very carefully and concluded that only one well designed study using voluntary desegregation demonstrated a positive educational outcome for black children. By contrast, they found seven strong studies involving mandatory desegregation that reflected positive educational outcomes for black children. They carefully considered various

[29] Id. at 36–37.
[30] Id. at 38.
[31] Id. at 38–39.

hypotheses to explain these counterintuitive results and tried to relate them to previous observations about the challenges inherent in social migration for children. They suggested that black children fare better under mandatory desegregation programs because the desegregated school might be making stronger attempts to adjust in order to accommodate them. Further, black children may be more likely to move to a new school with peers from their neighborhood.[32] More recent studies have concluded that "there are stronger achievement gains when desegregation is voluntary."[33]

The Crain and Mahard study was consistent with the findings from an article authored nearly two decades later by Maureen Hallinan.[34] As Crain and Mahard had, Hallinan carefully reviewed the empirical evidence on student performance in various learning environments and examined what factors were most likely to be associated with strong academic performance for minority students in majority-white schools. She found that "the earlier a black student is placed in a majority white school or classroom, the higher the student's academic achievement."[35] She also found that "cooperative learning techniques" that fostered friendships between minority and white children were associated with positive educational outcomes for minority children.[36] From these various findings, she concluded that "peer influence, role modeling, instructional quality, and educational expectations are factors that transmit the effects of desegregation to student achievement."[37] Then, stepping back to consider broad research on how students learn, she concludes: "It is not desegregation per se that improves achievement, but rather the learning advantages some

---

[32] Id. at 47.
[33] See Brief of 553 Social Scientists as Amici Curiae in Support of Respondents in *Seattle* litigation, at *15.
[34] Maureen T. Hallinan, *Diversity Effects on Student Outcomes: Social Science Evidence*, 59 Ohio State L. J. 733 (1998).
[35] Id. at 741.
[36] Id. at 742–43.
[37] Id. at 743.

desegregated schools provide."[38] In other words, desegregation only produces positive educational outcomes for minority children if accompanied by some of the other factors discussed by Hallinan (as well as by Crain and Mahard).

These studies could have been used by the Court to assess whether the Seattle and Louisville desegregation efforts were likely to be successful. Chief Justice Roberts's opinion discusses none of these studies; they only receive mention from other members of the Court. Justice Thomas cites the Crain and Mahard study for the proposition that some scholars "have concluded that black students receive genuine educational benefits" from what he calls "racial balancing."[39] Crain and Mahard, however, disavow an interest in being put in the "positive" or "negative" camp for the effects of desegregation. The purpose of their study was to identify factors that lead to successful programs rather than proclaim that all desegregation efforts are positive or negative.

As for the Hallinan article, Justice Thomas dismisses its usefulness quickly by noting Hallinan's ending observation about the importance of the learning opportunities available at the desegregated school.[40] But he takes that observation completely out of context, not acknowledging the careful previous discussion about what factors are likely to lead to positive educational outcomes. The fact that Hallinan does not simplistically attribute desegregation to positive educational outcome does not mean that she considers desegregation to be an irrelevant factor. As are Crain and Mahard, she is trying to help shape social policy by giving school districts insight into how to achieve effective desegregation.

Justice Thomas's opinion gives significant weight to studies that tried to determine whether desegregation, as a whole, has led to positive educational outcomes for minority children. One of the most

[38] Id. at 744.
[39] *Seattle*, 127 S. Ct. at 2776.
[40] Id. at 2776 n. 11.

thorough literature reviews provided to the Court on this topic was an amicus brief written on behalf of the social scientists David J. Armor, Abigail Thernstrom, and Stephan Thernstrom.[41] While acknowledging that the Crain and Mahard study did find positive results for children who benefited from desegregation in early grades, they concluded that there is "no clear and consistent evidence" that desegregation produces positive educational outcomes for minority children.[42] Not surprisingly, other social scientists submitted amicus briefs disputing Armor and colleagues' overall conclusion, suggesting that their argument rested on "incomplete analyses of the literature, critiques of well-established scientific methodologies, and reliance on studies that are outdated or inconsistent with more recent research."[43] This amicus brief, as the Armor et al. brief, though, does not offer good guidance on what kind of educational program is likely to generate positive results. The fact that desegregation may have produced a range of results is not a very surprising (or helpful) finding. The more important question is what factors tend to lead to successful desegregation attempts.

Justice Kennedy's opinion in *Seattle* is often seen as the pivotal opinion because it provides the important fifth vote to strike down the school districts' race-conscious desegregation efforts. Because his opinion is less sweeping than that of Chief Justice Roberts in dismissing the use of race in school assignments, school officials are likely to read his opinion closely for hints as to how they might fashion a constitutionally permissible race-conscious plan. The Kennedy opinion, however, does not reflect consideration of any of the empirical work on effective desegregation programs. His sole concern seems to be how "narrowly tailored" is the use of race.[44] He suggests ways that school

---

[41] Brief of Armor, Thernstrom & Thernstrom as Amici Curiae in Support of Petitioners in *Seattle* litigation.

[42] Id. at *29.

[43] Brief of the American Educational Research Association as Amicus Curiae in Support of Respondents in *Seattle* litigation, at * 2 fn. 3.

[44] *Seattle*, 127 S. Ct. at 2744.

districts might attain desegregation and use less race-conscious mechanisms such as "strategic site selection of new schools; drawing attendance zones with general recognition of the demographics of neighborhoods; allocating resources for special programs; recruiting students and faculty in a targeted fashion; and tracking enrollments, performance, and other statistics by race."[45] Kennedy is correct that those mechanisms might be more "narrowly tailored," but the more important question should be, are they likely to produce better educational results for African-American children? Justice Kennedy's opinion notes that the famous axiom that "our Constitution is color-blind" cannot be a universal constitutional principle if we are to overcome a legacy of race discrimination in the United States.[46] Nonetheless, he uses the "color-blind" criterion as the primary yardstick in determining the constitutionality of a school's desegregation efforts.

Justice Thomas and Justice Breyer extensively cite empirical literature in their opinions in the *Seattle* case but primarily use those citations to determine whether desegregation has led overall to positive educational outcomes for minority children. Neither opinion spends much, if any, time isolating what factors might lead to positive educational outcomes. Although Justice Kennedy seeks to offer a middle ground position that leaves open the possibility of the narrow use of race-conscious mechanisms to attain integration, he does not rely on empirical research to identify acceptable race-conscious mechanisms.

B. Empirical Literature *Not* in *Seattle* Litigation

One problem for the Supreme Court in these kinds of cases is that they are being presented with empirical evidence for strategic purposes – in support of arguments made by proponents of a particular position. The

---

[45] Id. at 2745.
[46] Id. at 2791.

justices may not have the inclination or the skills to read these studies closely or to look beyond the studies called to their attention by litigants. Undoubtedly, there are many studies that the Court could have examined that were not cited by litigants, possibly because they did not lend themselves to quick "sound bytes" that could be cited in support of one proposition or another. In this section, I would like to examine some data *not* discussed by the Court that might lend insight into how to develop *effective* integration programs that are likely to lead to positive educational outcomes for minority children.[47] Data collected from the Texas public schools, which are not cited by the Court in the *Seattle* litigation, support the argument that minority students are likely to improve their academic performance if they attend integrated schools rather than predominantly black schools. As do the data discussed earlier, their data also support the argument that integration must start in the early grades and must create genuine, rather than token, integration to be effective.

The Texas data are remarkable and provide many opportunities for researchers to consider many important policy issues. The Texas Schools Data Base (TSDB) contains data for more than 2 million students over at least an eight-year period. The data contain more than twenty-six years/grades of standardized test data for three different standardized tests. The students are identified by many factors and the data include millions of records.

The first assessment of these data that is relevant to the present study is the relationship between where African-American children receive their education (suburbs or inner city) and educational levels. John F. Kain and Daniel M. O'Brien studied that question for a working paper series published by the Cecil and Ida Green Carter Center

---

[47] I have examined these data closely because they were the most comprehensive data that I was able to locate while writing this book. I am not an expert in this area and would welcome others to examine other data that might be available. My discussion simply reflects what kinds of questions we might ask of such data, and what conclusions might be plausible.

for the Study of Science and Society. After controlling for many factors, including the prior year's reading or math score, they concluded
that African-American students who would move from an inner-city
school in Texas to a suburban school would be likely to see a "substantial improvement" in educational attainment as measured by
standardized tests.[48] In this 1998 study, they did not discuss the differences between suburban and inner-city school districts as being one of
differences in racial composition. They simply considered the suburban schools to be "better" schools and concluded that African Americans would be likely to show substantial improvement in standardized
test scores if they were able to attend these suburban schools.

Two years later, they offered a refined version of the prior paper.[49]
In this paper, they provide the percentage of black enrollment in inner-
city and suburban school districts. Not surprisingly, the percentage of
all students who are African American was higher in the inner city than
suburban school districts. They described "inner city black exposure
to Anglos" as about 11 percent during the years of the study and
"suburban black exposure to Anglos" as ranging from 42 to 47 percent
during the years of the study. (Anglos are not a majority in the suburban districts because of the presence of Asians and Hispanics.) This
paper made two other observations not found in the prior paper. First,
they investigated whether access to suburban schools has as big an
influence on Asian, Hispanic, and Anglo students as it does on African-American students. While they found that attending a suburban
school had a positive impact on those groups, they found that the effect
was smaller than for African-American students.[50] Further, they tried

---

[48] John F. Kain & Daniel M. O'Brien, *Has Moving to the Suburbs Increased African
American Educational Opportunities* (January 5, 1998) (paper prepared for the meetings of the American Economic Association, Chicago, Illinois) (a working paper
series, the Cecil and Ida Green Carter Center for the Study of Science and Society).

[49] John F. Kain & Daniel M. O'Brien, *Black Suburbanization in Texas Metropolitan
Areas and Its Impact on Student Achievement* (March 9, 2000).

[50] Id. at 25.

to quantify what would be the result if more African-American students attended suburban schools. They concluded that "attending a school of average suburban quality would eliminate nearly 58 percent of the black-white achievement gap for fifth graders, 27 percent of the black-white achievement gap for sixth graders and nearly 38 percent of the black-white achievement gap for seventh graders."[51]

Finally, in 2002, John Kain joined with Eric Hanushek and Steven Rivkin to ask how school racial composition affects student academic achievement.[52] Using the same data set, they were able to control for school quality, differences in student abilities, and family background. After controlling for these factors, they concluded that the academic performance of African Americans was better in integrated settings than in settings with high concentrations of African-American students. This effect was strongest for those in the upper half of the ability distribution; in fact, there was only statistical significance for those in the top two quartiles of achievement.[53] The racial composition of the classroom was not found to have a significant impact on the academic performance of whites or Hispanics, strongly suggesting that the results were not a simple reflection of unmeasured school quality.

Their research suggests that it is very important to begin integration, especially for high-achieving African Americans, in the early grades because the effects of integration are cumulative. Moreover, 10 percent changes in racial composition can have a statistically significant effect on the achievement of African-American children. They reported: "The magnitude of the proportion black coefficient for blacks of -0.25 suggests that a 10 percentage point reduction in

---

[51] Id. at 24.
[52] Eric A. Hanushek, John F. Kain & Steven G. Rivkin, *New Evidence about Brown v. Board of Education: The Complex Effects of School Racial Composition on Achievement*, Working Paper 8741, available at http://www.nber.org/papers/w8741 (National Bureau of Economic Research, 1050 Massachusetts Avenue, Cambridge, MA 02138) (January 2002).
[53] Id. at 25.

percentage black would raise annual achievement growth by 0.025 standard deviations. These estimated effects apply to the growth of annual achievement and thus accumulate over grades."[54] This 10 percent figure is important because, as we will see, school districts have been permitting a large degree of racial imbalance before requiring racial desegregation efforts. Yet, this empirical literature suggests that more than a 10 percent racial imbalance should not be permitted, especially for high-achieving African-American students.

While no empirical research is perfect, other researchers have described the Texas study as effectively controlling "for a variety of potential confounding factors, including student-specific rates of change in achievement test scores and hard-to-measure factors that vary at the level of the school-by-grade or even attendance zone-by-year."[55] Reviewing the available studies, these researchers have also concluded, "A complete elimination in district efforts to integrate public schools could raise test score gaps significantly in some cases."[56] That conclusion was offered before the *Seattle* decision made it more difficult for school districts to engage in desegregation efforts.

III. CONCLUSION

The Supreme Court's decision in the *Seattle* litigation presents school districts with few effective options. Justice Kennedy is considered to be the "swing vote" in this kind of litigation, and he did not embrace the most extreme formal equality language found in Chief Justice Roberts's opinion. But there is no reason to believe that Justice Kennedy would have preferred Seattle or Kentucky to engage in *more*

---

[54] Id. at 23.

[55] Jacob Vigdor & Jens Ludwig, *Segregation and the Black-White Test Score Gap*, National Bureau of Economic Research Working Paper 12988, available at http://www.nber.org/papers/w12988 (March 2007) at 21.

[56] Id. at 24.

use of race to attain substantive equality. Playing into the formal equality model, he embraced the notion that race should be used as little as possible in school assignments. As this chapter has argued, that kind of minimalist approach might appease the parents of white children but is unlikely to attain substantive equality for African-American children.

It would appear that the only hope for progress in the racial area is for a transformation in the membership of the Supreme Court. The good news is that the Texas school data suggest that meaningful integration can help attain dramatic increases in educational attainment for African-American children. The bad news is that neighborhood housing patterns are unlikely to attain such integration "naturally," and the Supreme Court has precluded the kind of race-conscious policies that can attain those results deliberately.

While formal equality notions may have assisted the Court in rejecting segregation in *Brown v. Board of Education*, they has outlived their usefulness as a vehicle to attain substantive equality. An anti-subordination perspective that does not reflexively dismiss race-conscious tools is needed to attain genuine equality in our society. Some school districts are willing to implement such tools, but they can only do so in a more receptive legal environment.

Index

Index